The
BUILDER'S
BOOK *of*
BATHROOMS

The BUILDER'S BOOK of BATHROOMS

ANDREW WORMER

The Taunton Press

Cover photo: © Carolyn Bates

Back cover photos: Charles Miller (top)
and Carolyn Bates (bottom)

Taunton
BOOKS & VIDEOS
for fellow enthusiasts

Text © 1998 by Andrew Wormer
Photos on pp. 9, 53, 61, 75, 76, 106 (right), 109, and
    110 (right) © 1998 by The Taunton Press, Inc.
Illustrations © 1998 by The Taunton Press, Inc.

Printed in the United States of America
10 9 8 7 6 5 4 3

For Pros / By Pros™: The Builder's Book of Bathrooms
was originally published in 1998 by The Taunton Press, Inc.

For Pros / By Pros™ is a trademark of The Taunton Press, Inc.,
registered in the U.S. Patent and Trademark Office.

The Taunton Press, Inc., 63 South Main Street, PO Box 5506,
Newtown, CT 06470-5506
e-mail: tp@taunton.com

Library of Congress Cataloging-in-Publication Data

Wormer, Andrew.
        For Pros / By Pros™: The builder's book of bathrooms /
Andrew Wormer.
            p.   cm.
        Includes bibliographical references and index.
        ISBN 1-56158-334-0
        1. Bathrooms—Design and construction. I. Title.
TH3000.B38W67   1998
643'.52—dc21   97-42881
                                                CIP

To Sam and Anna—so much depends on them

*Also, to Steve Smith, who gave me my first real lessons in carpentry
and in the process inadvertently taught me a lot about life*

ACKNOWLEDGMENTS

A couple of years or so ago Kevin Ireton, the editor of *Fine Homebuilding* magazine, offered me the opportunity to come work as an assistant editor there. As a carpenter and longtime fan of the magazine, this was the equivalent of landing the dream building job; you know, the kind with an unlimited budget, enlightened clients, and all the time in the world to complete it. For various personal reasons, my actual time spent in the editorial offices lasted a little over a year, far too short of a time really. But while I was there I had the chance to work with an amazing group of people who helped me far more than they will ever know. So, to Kevin, Chuck, Chuck, Chuck, Joyce, Chris, Roe, Steve, Andy, Dan, Reese (wherever he may be), Jon, and all the rest of the crew at The Taunton Press, thanks for everything. Without first meeting all of you, I doubt that I would have had the confidence or energy to tackle this book.

I also want to thank Julie Trelstad, who helped to crystallize the ideas for this book in the first place, and Karen Liljedahl, who cheerfully dogged me with the details the whole way, for their faith and encouragement with this project. You two are way too nice for your own good! I also want to thank fellow builder and writer Herrick Kimball for his commiseration on the travails of an author's life.

Carolyn Bates, the photographer on this project, deserves a lot of thanks and credit for the way the book looks. She essentially took some vaguely worded directions and a few "wish lists" and, with her skill and experience with construction photography, was able to come up with some great photographs of bathrooms in all stages of completion. As a wanna-be photographer myself, I'm both extremely thankful for and jealous of her ability.

There are also a number of individuals and manufacturers whose work is featured in this book. There is a resource guide in the back of the book for all of the manufacturers who helped me with information and/or photography; hopefully, they will consider it thanks enough if readers of this book turn to them for further information about their products and services. For the individuals—architects, builders, tradespeople, building suppliers—with whom I've met, spoken to on the phone, or who have generously allowed Carolyn Bates to photograph them: My hat is off to you because you folks are in the trenches doing the work, not writing about it.

Some of these helpful companies and individuals in the Burlington, Vermont, area include (in no particular order): Cathedral Living Log Homes, Blodgett Supply Co., Bard Home Decorating Center, Sondik Supply Company, Vermont Paint Company, MacIntyre Plumbing and Heating, New England Floor Covering, Phinney's, Paul Lafayette Painting Co., East Shore Drywall, A&M Stoneworks, Three Seasons Construction, Sam Scofield, David Jaqua, Todd Aylward, John Campbell, Bird's Eye Building and Design, Bill Burke, Hubbard Construction, Yankee Plumbing and Heating, Classic Kitchens and Baths, Connelly Mechanical, Roundtree Construction, Snyder Group, Sweeney & Belisle, S & J Electrical, J.W. & D.E. Ryan, Inc., Yandow-Dousevicz Construction Co., Herb Clement and Jullee Singo, Sam Scofield, Peter Morris, Tim Seinkiewycz, and Steven Lowther.

I should also thank those whose work has been a resource for this book and without whose written expertise my own work as a carpenter and builder would surely have suffered. Those resources include Michael Byrne's excellent book *Setting Ceramic Tile* and Peter Hemp's two books *Plumbing a House* and *Installing & Repairing Plumbing Fixtures* (all three published by The Taunton Press, Inc.). Besides serving as a guide in my own work as a builder, I turned to their pages often during the writing of this book when I had questions of a technical nature. Finally, the National Kitchen and Bath Association should be mentioned as a resource to designers and builders of bathrooms; they provided me with considerable design and technical information and are (I think) a largely untapped resource for small-scale builders like myself.

CONTENTS

INTRODUCTION

Every summer since I was a young boy I've visited my grandmother's cottage on a lake in upstate New York. While the house has an unassuming bathroom inside, it also has a fully functional outhouse—a two-holer complete with wooden toilet seats, spiders, and a big bag of lime for "flushing." Over the years, I've come to appreciate the alternative ambiance of the outhouse, in part because of its simplicity and focused purpose. There is no confusing this place with a spa, and no one has ever been accused of lingering too long in there. Families with teenagers might want to consider one.

But despite the nostalgic or practical appeal of the outhouse, most visitors to the cottage prefer to use the bathroom instead. For some reason, a warm room with running water, counter space, and plenty of light is more popular than a cramped and dark outbuilding with spiders in the corners and who-knows-what underneath the seats. Even the fact that you can go there with a friend doesn't seem to add much to the outhouse's popularity. Few

would argue that even the most plain bathroom is a marked improvement over an outhouse.

But make no mistake: The cottage bathroom is non-descript, though amazingly it has undergone little change in the decades that I've been going there, despite an extended family that includes veteran builders and professional putterers. Despite an occasional paint job and the new vinyl floor I installed over a decade ago, the bathroom looks nearly the same as it always has. The shower stall is an unattractive but serviceable metal unit, the sink an old freestanding porcelain pedestal with some sort of fabric-covered hamper alongside it serving as a countertop, the toilet a water-consuming antique. I love it, but not because it is beautiful or particularly functional. It just looks unintentionally old-fashioned, like the rest of the house, and this charm is hard to improve upon.

Not that this bathroom couldn't be improved upon functionally. There are plenty of building materials available now that weren't when the house was originally built around the turn of the century—plastic-laminate and solid-surface countertops, fiberglass and acrylic tub/ shower units, washerless faucets and antiscald shower valves, low-flush toilets, GFCI outlets, cement-based substrate panels, waterproofing membranes, even ventilation fans—that make modern bathrooms considerably safer, more environmentally friendly, easier to clean and maintain, and less apt to leak. In short, there are many new ways to make a bathroom work better than my grandmother's does.

In fact, there are so many options in materials and fixtures that designing and building a distinctive bathroom today is a real challenge. Standard-size fixtures and the limited space normally allotted to bathrooms tend to simplify design decisions on one hand, but also tend to discourage variety on the other. Renovating an existing bath to take advantage of new technology can open a real can of worms, exposing inadequate or failing framing, plumbing, and electrical systems, not to mention odd-shaped spaces with doors and

windows in the wrong places. And rules for design and construction, whether mandated by building codes or dictated by common sense, complicate matters even more. Another factor is money: Quality bathroom components are expensive, renovating and moving things around is expensive, and making mistakes is expensive.

Of course, being a real challenge to build well makes bathrooms interesting and keeps even experienced builders on their toes. And it makes a handbook on construction and design an asset for builders of all levels of experience. Hence this book. In it you'll find up-to-date synopses of code requirements, National Kitchen & Bath Association guidelines for design and construction, and considerations for universal accessibility. You'll also find the detailed information necessary for doing specialized framing, plumbing, and electrical work required by modern bathrooms. There is an overview of fixtures, systems, finish materials, vanities, and storage systems, as well as detailed information on how everything goes together. In

short, this book should act as the guide that I wish I had when I remodeled my first bathroom over a decade ago, as well as a distillation of the experience that I've gained building baths and writing about construction since then.

With this information in hand, it should be much easier to design and build bathrooms that meet the needs of everyone, from working couples to families with small children to people with disabilities. And the ideas here should inspire you to confidently try new design approaches using new materials and techniques. While intended for experienced builders with a need for more specific information about bathroom design and construction, relatively inexperienced but capable do-it-yourselfers will find this book useful as well. With it, you should be able to imagine and take on the most challenging bathroom projects, including your own.

Part One

DESIGN

Chapter 1

BATHROOM BASICS

A BRIEF HISTORY
OF THE TOILET

BEYOND THE TOILET

A NEW BATHROOM
TRADITION

You've heard about the finish carpenter, I suppose, who claimed that the room he trimmed out the most carefully was the bathroom. When asked why, he pointed out that no other room in the house presented someone so many opportunities to sit down in such a well-lighted space and scrutinize the finish work.

Of course, it doesn't take a lot of scrutinizing to realize that bathrooms have changed considerably lately. A couple of decades ago, the main difference between a master bath and a regular bath was the presence of an extra sink in a double vanity, a concession to the woman of the household. Master baths now still have that extra sink, but they also often have a whirlpool tub and a walk-in shower, maybe a bidet, and perhaps even a sauna or a steam bath. All of these extras are now reasonably affordable, in-demand options for a residential bathroom.

While master bathrooms are growing larger, even compact bathrooms are expanding in terms of their level of performance. New combination tub/shower units are available that also offer options like steam, multiple showerheads, and whirlpools (see the bottom left photo on the facing page). Features like these can make even a compact bathroom feel luxurious, and some of these units are designed to be retrofitted into the space occupied by a regular 5-ft. tub.

Large or small, today's bathroom is not so basic, and a one-size-fits-all approach to bathroom construction just won't work anymore. I've found that in all sizes and types of bathrooms—from simple powder rooms to luxurious master suites—more features, more performance, and more comfort are expected than ever before. The expectations are high because bathroom spaces are finally being considered in relation to the realities of the changing roles and the special needs of the people who use them. Working couples and the fast-track lifestyle of recent years have helped to redefine the bathroom, but so has the recognition that people come in all sorts of sizes, shapes, and levels of physical ability. Even in relatively basic bathrooms that are built in small spaces with limited budgets, accommodations for universal access by children, the elderly, and the disabled should be a part of the planning process.

A whirlpool tub may be a luxurious convenience in today's master bathrooms, but a walk-in shower is often considered a necessity by working couples. (Photo © Carolyn Bates.)

New designs like Jacuzzi's J-Steam Tower offer features like a whirlpool, an adjustable showerhead, and a steam bath yet still fit in the space of a traditional tub. (Photo courtesy Jacuzzi.)

Making accommodations for universal accessibility, like adding grab bars and handrails, doesn't require major concessions in bathroom planning or style. (Photo courtesy CareMate, Inc.)

From a builder's perspective, bathrooms today deserve special scrutiny because they are one of the most interesting and challenging rooms in the house. There are plenty of new materials, technology, and information resources to assist in the planning and construction of these new bathrooms. But there are also plenty of proven ideas and traditional materials that have provided clean and safe bathing environments for years. Being innovative and up-to-date doesn't mean throwing out the baby with the bathwater. The best bathrooms use the best of both old and new technology and materials, and they respond to the needs of the individuals who use them.

But before digging into the details of bathroom planning and construction, some historical perspective is in order. After all, what better way to see where you are and where you're going than to take a look back at where you've been?

A BRIEF HISTORY OF THE TOILET

The next time you reach over to pull the lever (or push the button) to flush a toilet, take a moment to think about a world without these marvels of human engineering. Okay, the invention of the toilet doesn't carry the same sense of drama that the invention of lightbulbs or airplanes does, but in their own not-so-small way, toilets have transformed the world we live in.

A modern bathroom can provide both a functional and comfortable environment yet still have traditional aspects, like this tile wall and pedestal sink. (Photo © Carolyn Bates.)

The idea of a room in a home dedicated to personal hygiene and grooming is, strictly speaking, a recent one. For the most part, houses built much before the turn of the century didn't have bathrooms. So, in the span of about 100 years, the modern bathroom has evolved from a novelty into an almost-universal residential fixture. But there has always been a need for disposing of human waste, as well as a need for providing facilities for bathing and grooming. How those human needs evolved into the modern bathroom is a story about both technology and culture.

The Englishman with the unfortunate surname, Thomas Crapper, often gets credit for inventing the flushing toilet, and he undoubtedly was a major player in its development. His valve-and-siphon design was patented in 1891, and his company manufactured water closets that found wide acceptance all over England in the decades preceding World War I. His toilets—imprinted with "T. Crapper Brass & Co., Ltd."—inspired a generation of young American soldiers stationed in England during World War I, and they returned to America with a new slang term for the relatively new household fixture. But was Crapper the father of the so-called crapper?

Let's put it this way: Crapper didn't one day sit down in an outdoor privy and decide that what the world really needed was an indoor toilet. His product was simply another refinement of a design problem that the Victorians in particular had been puzzling over: how to build a flushing water closet that would efficiently and sanitarily remove waste without allowing dangerous sewer gases to enter. When Crapper refined his design, flushing water closets weren't exactly a new idea. For example, Queen Elizabeth I's godson Sir John Harrington had designed one for her use in 1596, although it never caught on with the rest of English society, royal or otherwise, and was considered to be more of a novelty than a practical invention, especially in the absence of an extensive sewer system.

An early bathroom. Not many of us would like to return to the world of outhouses and Saturday night soaks in a portable wooden tub. (Photo by Scott Phillips.)

Nonflushing water closets—portable pieces of furniture with removable containers for waste—became the standard in pre-Victorian England, though many households continued to rely on the backyard privy. The problem of waste disposal—whether from a chamber pot or from an overused hole in the ground—remained.

The Victorians made the connection between unsanitary conditions and disease that the Elizabethans hadn't and developed municipal sewer systems to try to keep their cities cleaner. The problem was that they didn't have a good way of connecting individual households to the system. Nonflushing water closets could be dressed up, but their contents couldn't be taken out. In the late 18th and early 19th centuries (about the same time the sewers were built), English patents were granted for several different types of water-closet valves, but their

What's in a Name?

Have you ever had to use a donicker? I'm not sure that I have either, but according to one thesaurus I consulted, a donicker is just one of the many synonyms for a bathroom. I wasn't able to find the word in any of my other dictionaries, and I've never heard it used before, but I sure like the sound of it. It trips off of the tongue much more easily than the more-prosaic bathroom.

The first documented use of the word bathroom as a place to wash was around 1780, but its origins go back much further. Bath is an old Teutonic word that originally referred to the ritual immersion or washing of baptism. Lavatory, another word with roots that go way back to medieval times, is derived from the Latin *lavatorium*, which means a place for washing. Like the word bath, lavatory also originally had a specific religious usage, being an ecclesiastical term for the ritual washing of a celebrant's hands at the offertory and after the cleansing of communion vessels. By 1660, it had come to be used to refer to the place in a residence that was used for washing the face and hands.

The word toilet derives from the French, and it was first used to refer merely to a bag or wrapper for carrying nightclothes. By 1684 or thereabouts, it came to refer variously to a towel thrown over the shoulders while dressing the hair, to the often-elaborate cloth covering for the dressing table, to the dressing table itself, and to the various articles used for furnishing the dressing table. To eliminate confusion (or add to it), it eventually came to mean the actual act of dressing, and during the 18th century it became very popular for women to receive visitors during the final stages of their "toilet." Eventually these toilets, or dressing rooms, were furnished with bathing facilities, and by 1895 "toilet-room" had appeared in an American dictionary with a modern meaning.

It is, of course, tempting to think that the use of the term crapper originated with a misappropriation of the name of Thomas Crapper, a pioneer in the development of the sanitary flushing water closet, but there are instances of the use of the word crap as early as 1846, long before Crapper made a splash. Water closet (1755) didn't originally refer to a mechanism but rather to a place for washing that became a piece of furniture. John? This American slang term has been around in some form or another since 1735, when it appeared in Harvard bylaws prohibiting underclassmen from certain unsavory activities.

Latrine is derived from the much more elegant sounding *lavatrina*, which itself comes from the Latin verb *lavare* (to wash). First used around 1642, latrine once referred specifically to military and institutional toilet facilities. Head also has a military origin, where it referred to the ship's latrine, which was usually located in the bow. The origins of the term loo are a little mistier. Some claim it is a usurpation of the French word for water—*l'eau*—while others think it might have been derived from Waterloo.

What does all of this signify? Not much; after all, to paraphrase the Bard, a rose by any other name still smells as sweet (or not). Just some words to think about next time you are sitting on the throne.

flushing actions were pretty inefficient. The wall-mounted cistern that became popular in the 1870s vastly improved the situation because it provided a large volume of water under more pressure. Water-closet bowls remained a problem, though, because their rudimentary traps didn't do a very good job of either letting waste go down the drain or keeping sewer gases out of the building. At first these bowls were made of earthenware and glazed with sometimes-elaborate designs. In 1885, Thomas Twyford built the first vitreous-china toilet, inspiring competition from other notable English potteries such as Wedgwood and Doulton; it wasn't long before vitreous china became the standard for the fledgling industry.

American inventors were also seeking solutions to the problem of building a sanitary water closet. As early as 1875, James Henry and William Campbell patented a plunger-type water closet; over the next 50 or so years more than 350 applications for patents for various types of water-closet designs were received by the U.S. patent office. In 1907, Eljer Plumbingware Co. introduced the first American vitreous-china water closet, despite popular skepticism about the strength of a ceramic product for such a purpose.

With the invention of the sanitary flushable toilet—the fixture that made the modern bathroom possible—the crowded urban masses no longer needed to rely on chamber pots and open windows and backyards to dispose of their waste. Nor did they have to fear sewer gases like methane seeping back up into their homes and igniting explosively.

The first indoor bathrooms that were made possible by the refinement of the toilet were communal affairs shared by many people. Previously, water closets were portable, so a dedicated space for their use wasn't necessary. More elaborate residences might have had a dedicated dressing room that contained a water closet, a moveable tin or iron bath, and a washstand, but this type of centralized "bathroom" didn't become widespread until indoor plumbing and permanent water closets gained acceptance toward the end of the 19th century. Within a few short decades, the toilet became a permanent fixture as bathrooms proliferated and portable washstands and tubs gave way to dedicated spaces. It didn't take long for indoor plumbing to gain acceptance as a good idea, and by the 1920s, American building codes required indoor bathrooms in all new single-family residential construction.

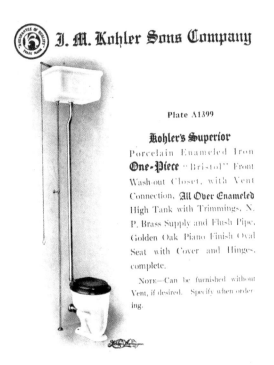

J. M. Kohler Sons Company

Plate A1399

Kohler's Superior

Porcelain Enameled Iron One-Piece "Bristol" Front Wash-out Closet, with Vent Connection. All Over Enameled High Tank with Trimmings, N. P. Brass Supply and Flush Pipe, Golden Oak Piano Finish Oval Seat with Cover and Hinges, complete.

NOTE—Can be furnished without Vent, if desired. Specify when ordering.

While the idea of a water tank high on the wall may seem charming now, early toilets relied on the extra water pressure for their siphon action. (Photo courtesy Kohler Co.)

Interestingly, the modern toilet and its associated plumbing was as much a response to urban industrialization as it was a result of the manufacturing technology that industrialization made possible. In a rural society, an indoor toilet may be a convenience, but it isn't essential. In a crowded urban environment, however, the sanitary elimination of human waste becomes a real problem, and in the absence of sufficient soil to contain and break down human waste, water became the only other medium available to carry it away. The development of municipal sewage systems in London and Paris in the 18th and 19th centuries was a direct response to the threat of disease that came from increasing population densities and inadequate waste disposal. The modern world needed the modern toilet not so much for convenience but for its own survival.

Unfortunately, while 19th-century engineers refined the process of using water to flush away waste, people living in the 20th century found out that it wasn't possible to just flush their problems completely away. Widespread contamination of large parts of the world's freshwater supplies is one of the legacies of the modern flush toilet. So the evolution of the toilet continues, necessitated by the need to use less water and so place less of a demand on water resources. Perhaps the next revolution will occur in the development of waste-treatment systems that minimize our reliance on water. In the meantime, look for technology to become increasingly water-conscious, both in toilets and in other bathroom fixtures. The work begun by Thomas Crapper and the others isn't over yet.

BEYOND THE TOILET

If we think of the bathroom as simply a response to the practical need to manage human waste, then bathrooms have a pretty short 100-year or so history. But bathrooms of some sort existed long before the invention of the modern flushable toilet. Early on, man recognized the personal benefits of a cleansing soak in warm water. And in any society where people live in close proximity, personal hygiene is more than an issue of vanity.

In this regard, bathrooms—in the sense of a room that is devoted to bathing and personal care—are as old as civilization itself. Evidence of sophisticated bathing facilities dating back to 2000 B.C. have been found in the palaces of Knossos and Phaistos on the island of Crete. Hittite houses in Anatolia (c. 1400 B.C.) contained paved washrooms with clay tubs. The Greek cities of Pylos and Tiryns had bathrooms with water supply and drainage systems, and later Greek vase paintings indicate that the Greeks used showers. Bathhouses in India, common in palaces, monasteries, and some wealthy homes as early as 200 B.C., contained steam rooms, sitting areas, and swimming pools.

Of course, the Romans mastered the art of the bath. As early as the 3rd century B.C., elaborate baths were being included in the villas and townhouses of wealthy Romans. With separate rooms for damp and dry heat and warm and cold tubs, the buildings were heated with hypocausts, furnaces with flues extending through the floors and walls of the building. The furnaces also heated boilers that supplied hot water. The public baths, or *thermae*, of imperial Rome expanded on the facilities of the smaller private baths and necessitated the construction of reservoirs and aqueducts to supply the enormous quantities of water needed. These baths were also heated by hypocausts and had dressing rooms, warm rooms, hot baths, steam rooms, recreation rooms, and cold baths. Hot-spring spas in far-flung locations of the Roman Empire, such as Bath in England and Aix-les-Bains in France, are still in use today.

Some might argue that the bathing rituals of the Romans went too far, and in part the asceticism of the early Middle Ages was a reaction to the hedonism of imperial Rome that found such expression in their public bathhouses. Many of the early Christians took an entirely different viewpoint than the Romans about the body, regarding it as a place of sin to be conquered by the spirit. Dirt and disregard for excessive personal hygiene were regarded as appropriate responses to a sinful world, while bathing and personal luxury were regarded as excessively (or sinfully) indulgent—attitudes that to this day still find occasional expression in our culture. But as the plagues that periodically ravaged Europe during the Middle Ages demonstrated, personal hygiene plays a practical as well as a spiritual role.

In fact, despite the ascetic attitude toward bathing, centralized bathing facilities continued to exist in Europe. Many monasteries had fairly sophisticated systems to supply, distribute, and carry away water. Medieval castles and palaces generally incorporated a system of water supply and drainage, even if the sewage reservoir did happen to be the castle's moat. Henry III's (1217–1272) palace at Westminster had a bathhouse with hot and cold running water. And other cultures outside the western European tradition continued to regard bathing and personal hygiene as acceptable and culturally significant activities. *Hammams*, or public baths, have long been a fixture in Islamic society. And the Japanese have always regarded a long soak in a hot tub as both ritual and cleansing activity.

Early American settlers brought European attitudes toward bathing with them to the New World, continuing to view excessive bathing as an unnecessary indulgence. In part, this was because of the religious beliefs in some of the early colonies, but it was also a practical response to life on the frontier. However, by the middle of the 19th century there was a permanent tub in the White House, and bathing had evolved for many into a Saturday night ritual, whether they felt they needed it or not.

Originally, bathtubs were unwieldy metal-lined wooden affairs that were brought into the kitchen for the weekly event and filled with hot water from the stove to be shared by everyone that needed a bath. But early enameled cast-iron tubs began to appear in the second half of the 19th century, although demand for them was limited by their weight and the scarcity of dedicated bathroom spaces. These tubs were—and still are—heavy. John M. Kohler, founder of the Kohler Co., got his start manufacturing cast-iron farm implements, but he saw an opportunity to sell to a new market. He modified a combination horse trough/hog scalder by enameling it and adding legs, then sold it as a bathtub to meet the growing demand for bathroom fixtures around the turn of the century (see the photo below).

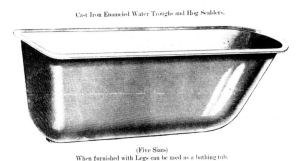

Cast Iron Enameled Water Troughs and Hog Scalders.

(Five Sizes)
When furnished with Legs can be used as a bathing tub.

Kohler's early tubs were adaptations of hog scalders and water troughs. (Photo courtesy Kohler Co.)

So bathrooms evolved as a response to fundamental needs for personal hygiene, as well as an expression of available technology and cultural standards. And in the short half-century between 1875 and 1925—the period of time between when indoor plumbing began to be widely available and when it became almost universal—our attitudes toward privacy and modesty changed significantly. What were once communal and family activities have become very personal and private activities. Whereas once single bathrooms served several families in urban apartment houses, now it is not unusual, nor even considered particularly extravagant, for households to have a bathroom for every bedroom.

A NEW BATHROOM TRADITION

I've noticed that early versions of the modern bathroom—that is, those built during the 1920s—are much more interesting than their successors. If they are fortunate enough to have escaped remodeling, these bathrooms tend to be larger and have better tile and finish work and better quality fixtures than those built later (see the photos below).

Early bathrooms and bathroom fixtures—this tub is c. 1914—celebrated style and craftsmanship. (Photo courtesy Kohler Co.)

In the 1920s, before the Depression and the post-World War II housing boom made economy and efficiency paramount, bathrooms such as this were relatively common. (Photo courtesy Kohler Co.)

During the Depression and the later post-World War II housing boom, construction shifted its orientation away from traditional labor-intensive methods and toward more efficient assembly-line type production. This resulted in a lot more houses being built a lot more quickly and economically, but it also required a standardization of components, room sizes, and even house styles to keep pace with demand—just think of split-levels, ranches, and Levitown. In the same way that kitchens both benefited and suffered from this component-type approach, so too did bathrooms. The primary goal of architects and builders seemed to be to squeeze as much utility as possible out of the least amount of space. These pared-down bathrooms were quick to install and didn't require a lot of room or a squadron of specialty tradespeople, but they all began to look alike (see the photo at right).

Only recently have bathrooms begun to break out of their conformist rut. Recent research into how bathrooms are really used by people (for example, Alexander Kira's groundbreaking 1976 book *The Bathroom*) and a maturing of the bathroom industry itself (in particular, the leadership of the National Kitchen and Bath Association, or NKBA) have resulted in a re-examination of the conventional wisdom about what had become a somewhat neglected room. While economy and efficient construction are still important considerations, so too are the needs of the people who use the bathroom.

The new bathroom tradition goes beyond the utilitarian bathrooms of the recent past and takes advantage of both technology and tradition. It recognizes that people of all ages and abilities need to be able to safely, comfortably, and efficiently perform the basic tasks of body cleansing and elimination. But in addition, it recognizes that bathrooms have traditionally been a place to attend to the less tangible—but no less important—needs of

Though functional and efficient, the bathrooms that evolved during the baby-boomer era lacked the style of their earlier counterparts.

personal well-being: a place for solitude and relaxation, for sensuous pleasure, and for ritual personal care and grooming. So, on one hand, bathrooms should perform like machines for living—the more efficient and functional they are, the better. They need to be easily maintained, easily cleaned, and well-thought-out ergonomically. But on the other hand, bathrooms that are unpleasant environments—that are too cold or too hot, too bright or too dark, awkward or uncomfortable—fail to provide to their users the equally important qualities of comfort and pleasure. Finding the right balance is the key.

Chapter 2

PLANNING

Everyone has been in bathrooms that don't seem very comfortable or that just don't seem to function very well. Maybe the mirrors steam up because there's no ventilation fan and no window to open. Maybe the shower door bangs against the vanity, making it hard to get in and out of the shower, or maybe the water suddenly gets way too hot or too cold when a toilet is flushed in another part of the house. Maybe there isn't enough storage space for cleaning supplies, towels, or linens. Maybe the bathtub area is too dark (or too bright). More than any other room in the house, a bathroom is a sum of its parts, or systems. They should function efficiently, and a major part of bathroom planning is making sure the right systems are in place and working well.

In addition to effective plumbing, electrical, heating, and ventilation systems, bathrooms need to have enough room for fixtures and the people using them. There is a big difference between simply fitting and fitting correctly. Think, for example, of how many times it has seemed that you had to be a contortionist simply to retrieve some toilet paper while sitting on a toilet seat. We could reinvent the wheel every time we set out to build a bathroom—that is, measure fixtures and people to see if everything will fit into an allotted space—but fortunately all of the necessary ergonomic engineering has already been done. The trick, of course, is to incorporate these clearances in the bathrooms that we build.

The third component of planning is making bathrooms accessible to the young, the old, and those with physical limitations. It isn't all that hard to plan for the future needs of changing families, and a good bathroom design can incorporate ideas that will make it easier to respond to those changing needs, making homes a more hospitable environment for everyone throughout their lifetime.

BATHROOM SYSTEM PLANNING

So when planning any bathroom, a good place to start is with its individual mechanical systems. This means understanding and planning for the room's major plumbing, electrical, and heating/cooling/ventilation requirements. In renovation work, existing deficiencies—a system that doesn't meet code or an inadequate dimension—often have to be corrected, a potentially costly and unforeseen addition to the project. Knowing how the various systems go together, as well as the requirements of applicable building codes, is an essential part of the planning process.

Plumbing

I've often heard it said that stacking bathrooms one above the other or arranging baths and/or kitchens so that they can take advantage of a "wet wall" is desirable because it minimizes plumbing runs and the number of drains and vents required in the system. In theory this makes sense, and in commercial multifloor construction that is often exactly what designers and architects do. But in the real world of residential construction, sometimes this happens and sometimes it doesn't. Sure, putting a second-floor bathroom directly above the first-floor bath and configuring them identically is more economical than a more random placement, but it's not that much more economical and generally not worth the sacrifice in planning flexibility. Since plastic ABS (acrylonitrile butadiene styrene) and PVC (polyvinyl chloride) pipe (the materials most commonly used in most residential DWV

The plumbing, electrical, and ventilation systems that make the modern bathroom function are hidden behind its floors, walls, and ceilings.

systems) are cheap and install quickly, positioning the bathrooms advantageously to one another is less important in the long run than making sure that they are properly situated in the house.

Bringing water into the house, delivering it where it is needed, and then removing it is the responsibility of the plumbing system. While plumbing a whole house is outside the scope of this book, knowing enough about plumbing systems to know when you need help and when you can go it alone can save a lot of aggravation and installation time. And new fixtures and features in today's bathrooms, like multiple showerheads and jetted tubs, make planning an adequate system essential for proper fixture performance. A tub that takes forever to fill or an anemic shower system that dribbles when more than one showerhead is turned on won't win many repeat customers.

Essentially, residential plumbing consists of two basic subsystems: the water supply system and the drain/waste/vent (DWV) system (see the drawing on the facing page). The water supply system must have adequate pressure to deliver proper water flow to each fixture, particularly when more than one fixture is used simultaneously. The DWV system doesn't rely on pressure to remove fluids, so pipe diameters must be large in order to allow gravity and atmospheric pressure to work.

Water supply system Municipal systems typically supply between 45 lbs. and 75 lbs. per square inch (psi), while well systems often have lower pressures. A useful working range for a domestic system is 30 psi to 80 psi; lower pressures require increased pipe sizes to supply adequate volumes of water to the fixtures.

The main service line supplies water to a building from the water source and is usually 1 in. in diameter (see the chart below). Branch lines distribute the water from the main and are typically ¾ in. in diameter. The closer lines get to their destination, the smaller the diameter, so ½-in.- or ⅜-in.-diameter pipe usually supplies individual fixtures. But some fixtures, like multiple showerheads and large tubs, require a higher volume of water that can only be supplied by a ¾-in. supply line—sometimes called a home run—that is supplied directly from the main and water heater.

The age and material of the supply pipes and the chemical composition of the water supply can also affect the performance of the water-distribution system. Scale and corrosion are typical in old galvanized-steel pipe and can reduce the effective inside diameter of the pipe, resulting in a reduction in the pressure and volume of water available. I've seen more than one ¾-in. galvanized-steel supply pipe that actually had an inside diameter about the size of a pencil. This problem is particularly prevalent with water supplies containing high amounts of minerals such as calcium and magnesium—hard water. Water softeners remove these minerals but unfortunately replace them with sodium. The resulting bland taste and health hazards associated with sodium are the reasons why most softening systems should only treat hot water and not drinking water.

Copper is a common material for supply piping, though there are other options as well, such as galvanized steel and chlorinated polyvinyl chloride (CPVC). Polybutylene pipe (PB) was once widely used, but some problems with leaking joints have prompted most building

Recommended Supply Pipe Sizes

House main	1 in.
House service	¾ in.
Supply riser	¾ in.
Toilet (close coupled)	⅜ in.
Toilet (one piece)	½ in.
Bathtub	½ in.
Bathtub (high volume)	¾ in.
Shower	½ in.
Shower (high volume)	¾ in.
Sink	⅜ in.
Bidet	⅜ in.
Washing machine	½ in.

Residential Plumbing System

A residential plumbing system actually consists of two separate subsystems. The water supply system brings water into the house from an outside source, such as a well or municipal water supply. The drain/waste/vent (DWV) system removes waste water from the house either into a self-contained septic system or into a municipal sewer.

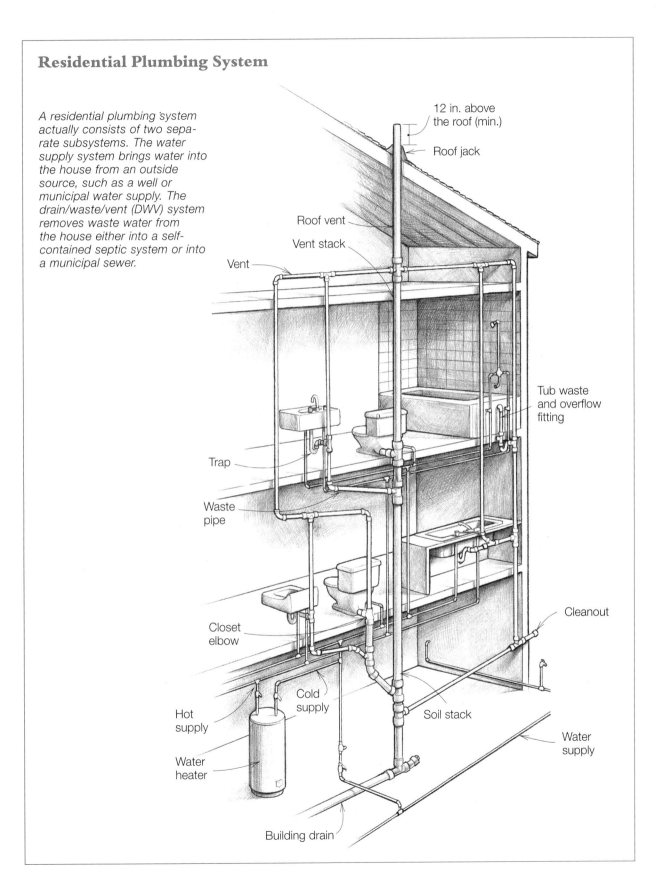

12 in. above the roof (min.)

Roof jack

Roof vent

Vent stack

Vent

Tub waste and overflow fitting

Trap

Waste pipe

Cleanout

Closet elbow

Hot supply

Cold supply

Soil stack

Water heater

Water supply

Building drain

codes to prohibit its use. A relatively new option (at least in the United States) is cross-linked polyethylene (PEX). PEX is quickly replacing PB as an option to copper in areas with high nitrate levels in the water supply, which can corrode copper. Each type of pipe has specific advantages and disadvantages, and cost can be a factor as well (see the chart on the facing page).

And keep in mind that pipe materials aren't always easily mixed and matched. For example, copper and galvanized steel will chemically react to each other through a process known as galvanic corrosion. To make a connection between the two pipe materials, a dielectric union should be used, which will prevent the buildup of corrosion on the inside of the pipes.

Drain/waste/vent system The DWV system empties into the house's septic system or into a municipal sewer and relies on gravity rather than water pressure to move fluids through the system. In addition to drain and waste pipes that carry liquid and solid waste away, a DWV system consists of vent lines that provide an exit route for sewer gases and that equalize atmospheric pressure within the DWV system, allowing liquids to flow freely down and out. Vents are required at each trap location and eventually link back up with the soil stack, which is then vented through the roof. Traps—curved sections of pipe that retain water—block sewer gases from entering the house through the fixture (see the drawing on p. 22).

Because DWV systems rely on gravity, they must always be sloped a minimum of $\frac{1}{8}$ in. per ft., though the optimal slope is $\frac{1}{4}$ in. per ft. Any slope greater than $\frac{1}{2}$ in. per ft. tends to make liquid and solid waste separate, leaving the solid waste behind and eventually possibly clogging up the system. In addition, DWV pipes are typically large in diameter, which can sometimes make it difficult to route them through framing.

Cast iron and plastic are the two most common DWV pipe materials. Copper is also sometimes used, though the materials are more expensive and sweating joints is more time-consuming. Sometimes threaded galvanized steel is still used, but it is more often seen in older installations and renovation work. Again, local building codes usually specify which type of pipe is acceptable and which is not, as well as whether or not pipe materials can be mixed.

In general, plastic is the easiest and least-expensive pipe to work with. It's lightweight, and different sizes of pipe and fittings are readily available. Cemented joints are very resistant to leaks, particularly when there is movement or vibration, so plastic is particularly suited for use with jetted tubs. ABS and PVC are the two common types of plastic pipe used; local building codes typically specify the use of one or the other, but usually not both. It's easy to tell the two pipes apart: ABS is black or charcoal-gray, while PVC is white or cream.

DWV Waste-Line Sizes

Fixture	Minimum Drain Size	Maximum Trap-to-Vent Distance
Bathtub	1½ in.	3 ft. 6 in.
Bidet	1½ in.	3 ft. 6 in.
Toilet	3 in.	6 ft.
Wall urinal	1½ in.	3 ft. 6 in.
Single sink	1¼ in.	2 ft. 6 in.
Double sink	1½ in.	2 ft. 6 in.
Shower stall	2 in.	5 ft.
Laundry tub	1½ in.	3 ft. 6 in.
Washing machine	2 in.	5 ft.
Floor drain	2 in.	5 ft.

DWV and Supply Pipe Materials

Material	Usage	Attributes	
Copper pipe	WS, DWV	• Lightweight • Easy to assemble • Resists corrosion • Widely available	• Can be damaged if frozen • Expensive
Copper tubing (flexible)	WS	• Appropriate for cramped spaces • Can be bent around corners • Resists damage from freezing	• Joints can be damaged by water hammer
Galvanized pipe	WS	• Strong and resistant to water hammer • Heavy • Time-consuming to install	• Scale can reduce inside pipe diameter
CPVC (chlorinated polyvinyl chloride)	WS	• Lightweight • Can be used for hot or cold supply • Resists damage from freezing	• Requires structural support • Easy to cut and assemble
Cast iron (hubless)	DWV	• Durable and quiet • Resists chemicals • Easier to assemble than bell & spigot cast iron	• Heavy • Expensive • Must be supported at joints
Cast iron (bell & spigot)	DWV	• Durable and quiet • Resists chemicals • Lead vapor used in assembly • Expensive	• Labor intensive • Difficult to cut and assemble
ABS (acrylonitrile butadiene styrene) and PVC (polyvinyl chloride)	DWV	• Lightweight • Inexpensive • Easy to cut and assemble	• May not be approved by some codes • Not resistant to some industrial chemicals
PE (Polyethylene)	WS	• Used for supply main from well to house • Resists corrosion	• Cannot be used for hot-water lines
PEX (cross-linked polyethylene)	WS	• Resists corrosion • Easy to assemble • Flexible	• May not be approved by some codes • Requires specialized fittings

Key: WS = Water supply   DWV = Drain/waste/vent

Types of Traps

P-trap

This is the type of trap you should use. Water that remains in the trap provides an airtight seal against sewer gases in the drain lines.

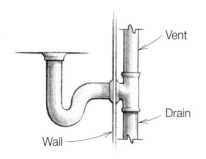

Vent

Drain

Wall

S-trap

The S-trap is no longer permitted by building codes but is still found in existing structures. Suction from a draining sink can evacuate water from the trap and allow sewer gases to enter.

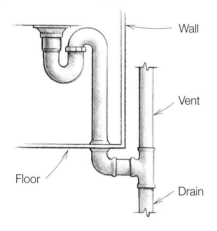

Wall

Vent

Floor

Drain

Drum trap

Sometimes found in old construction, the top of the drum trap doubles as a cleanout, but the seal is unreliable.

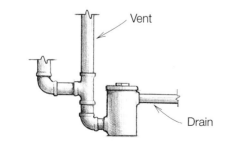

Vent

Drain

Give serious consideration to using no-hub cast iron for second-floor drains. Even though it's more expensive and harder to work with than plastic, iron pipe is considerably less noisy, a real consideration when an upstairs bathroom is over a living space. Plastic or copper pipe can be insulated to reduce noise but will still probably be noisier than cast iron. There is nothing quite so disruptive to a dinner party as the sound of Niagara Falls rushing overhead when the upstairs toilet is flushed.

Code requirements The Uniform Plumbing Code (UPC), published by the International Association of Plumbing and Mechanical Officials, and the International Plumbing Code (IPC), published by the Building Officials and Code Administrators International, Inc. (BOCA), the International Conference of Building Officials (ICBO), and the Southern Building Code Congress International, Inc. (SBCCI), are the two major plumbing codes upon which most local codes are based (see p. 209 for the publishers' information). The details of your local plumbing codes should be known by your plumbing contractor, but there are a few code highlights that can have an impact on bathroom planning.

For example, particularly in bathrooms with operable skylights, place the roof vent at least 10 ft. horizontally from or at least 3 ft. above any opening (UPC 906.2) (see the drawing on the facing page). This minimizes the possibility of sewer gases being drawn back into the bathroom through the open skylight. In addition, in new construction most local codes require the use of low-flow (1.6 gal per flush) toilets, as well as antiscald valves in showers and combination tubs/showers (IPC 425.4).

Another code requirement that can have an impact on bathroom planning is the necessity of an antisiphon valve when a handheld shower is installed near a tub, a pretty typical scenario these days. If the showerhead is on a long-enough hose that it can dangle below the level of the overflow valve of the tub or be immersed in dirty bath water, it can allow the bathwater to backflow into the water supply. A code inspector won't allow that and will require the addition of an antisiphon valve and access panel for maintenance in the lines. Some handheld showers have this valve already.

Remember to leave an access panel for the motor of a jetted tub. This is not only a good idea but also required by code (UPC 413.1). Providing this access is not always easy, but if you've ever tried to work on a tub motor when there is a problem after it's installed, you know that you want the access as large as possible. Sometimes the panel can be hidden in a room that adjoins the tub area or inside a vanity.

Plumbing codes also include guidelines about sizing and placing fixtures (see the drawing on p. 27), approved pipe materials and sizing, and other details that impact the planning of the bathroom. In some cases, codes might also limit your choice of fixtures and fittings, since they also specify the different ANSI (American National Standards Institute), ASSE (American Society of Sanitary Engineering), or ASTM (American Society of Testing and Materials) standards that bathroom components must meet. This means that some imported or custom valves and fixtures may not be allowable under your local code. Knowing your applicable code can help avoid some headaches and save you from making some expensive mistakes.

Typical Vent/Roof-Jack Installation

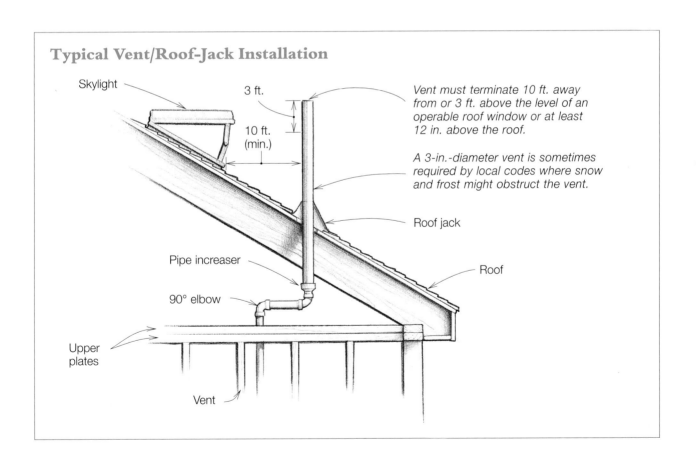

Skylight

3 ft.

Vent must terminate 10 ft. away from or 3 ft. above the level of an operable roof window or at least 12 in. above the roof.

10 ft. (min.)

A 3-in.-diameter vent is sometimes required by local codes where snow and frost might obstruct the vent.

Roof jack

Pipe increaser

Roof

90° elbow

Upper plates

Vent

Electrical system

Residential electrical systems aren't particularly complicated, but working with them requires an understanding of basic electricity and knowledge of the requirements of applicable building codes. Electricity is also dangerous, and mistakes can be fatal. So when planning the bathroom's electrical system or actually installing wiring and electrical components, be sure to work safely. This means knowing when you're in over your head and you need the help of a qualified electrician, who in most cases will need to sign off on work done by unlicensed personnel anyway. If you do decide to do much of the work on your own, be sure to turn the electricity off at the panel and to double-check supposedly dead circuits with a tester. My $3.99 tester has kept me from being unpleasantly surprised more than once by improvised wiring that was still live even after the circuit had supposedly been turned off.

The service panel is the central distribution point for electricity after it enters the house. In new construction or in houses that have been built fairly recently, the service entrance will in all likelihood be a circuit-breaker-protected 150-amp to 200-amp 240-volt service. But older houses often still have fuse boxes with either round or cartridge-type fuses protecting the circuits. There are plenty of houses with 60-amp 120-volt services, knob and tube wiring, and only four 15-amp circuits. This type of system isn't inherently unsafe—in fact, fuses are more reliable than circuit breakers—but it is inadequate for most modern households and can mean that a bathroom upgrade will require that the electrical system be upgraded as well, a potentially costly and likely unanticipated add-on. A 100-amp 240-volt service will likely have little room for additional circuits, though piggy-back breakers (two breakers that fit in a single

slot) may provide the additional circuitry needed for a bathroom upgrade. Panels with 150 amps or 200 amps usually have enough room for additional breakers.

Branch circuits, protected by either circuit breakers or fuses, distribute electricity to different parts of the house. Circuits are sized according to the electrical demand of the particular branch. For example, a lighting and general purpose household circuit might have a 20-amp circuit breaker and be wired with #12 type NM (or Romex nonmetallic sheathed) cable. Individual appliances—a jetted tub, for example—usually require an individual circuit. Sizing circuit breakers and wiring is governed by local building codes, which in turn are based on the National Electric Code (NEC), published by the National Fire Protection Association (see Resources on p. 209). Local codes may also allow only certain types of wiring.

All fixtures and appliances that use electricity are rated for the amount of current they use. This figure is measured in amps (the rate of flow of electricity) and should be available with the appliance's technical literature, as well as right on the appliance itself. This information is essential for planning bathroom wiring because it determines how many circuits will be needed and their size. So it's important to know exactly what is going into the bathroom and to either have the fixture's technical literature or the fixture(s) itself in hand before planning the electrical layout. For example, there are a few low-flow toilets that require an electrical outlet, and any sauna, steam unit, or whirlpool tub is going to require additional electrical capacity and usually its own circuit.

Another code requirement is that light switches be no closer than 5 ft. from any type of tub or shower. This is to keep switches out of the reach of someone standing in a pool of water. Outlets of course also aren't allowed in tub or shower spaces (NEC 410-57), but bathrooms are required to have at least one GFCI (ground-fault circuit interrupter)-protected 20-amp wall receptacle outlet adjacent to each sink (NEC 210-8). A GFCI continually compares the flow of electricity through the hot and neutral sides of a circuit and will shut off almost instantly (in less than $5/1000$ of a second) if the difference becomes greater than 5 milliamps. All bathroom outlets and jetted tubs need to be protected by GFCIs (NEC 680-70), which can be installed in the service panel as a GFCI circuit breaker or in the bathroom itself as a GFCI outlet. GFCI circuit breakers are typically more expensive and less convenient to reset than outlet GFCIs if they trip, but they are less affected by the sometimes excessive humidity in a bathroom, which can cause false tripping of the circuit.

The code also requires that appropriately rated fixtures be used in damp or wet parts of the bathroom. Most codes prohibit track lighting above a tub. And any cord-connected fixtures—this includes hanging fixtures or ceiling fans—should not be located either directly above a tub or 3 ft. horizontally or 8 ft. vertically above the rim of a tub (NEC-410-4).

Heating, cooling, and ventilation

Like other rooms in the house, bathrooms need to be adequately heated and, in hot climates, cooled. While in new construction this generally is dependent on the type of heating and/or cooling system the rest of the house has, there are some considerations specific to bathrooms that can affect design. The first, of course, is that bathrooms should be warmer than other rooms in the house since bare wet skin is more sensitive to cool air and drafts than fully clothed skin. A separate zone or thermostatic control for the bathroom's heat is a good idea so the bathroom can easily be kept warmer—as much as 5°F—than adjacent rooms. The other consideration is space: There just isn't a lot of room for baseboards or registers. Often, bathroom renovations require an upgrade in the heating system simply because the original bathroom is too cold. (Specific options for supplementing the bathroom heating system are discussed in Chapter 5.)

Bathrooms also have a problem that other rooms in the house don't have to the same degree: moisture. Uncontrolled moisture is a building's biggest enemy. Showers can bring the relative humidity of a bathroom up to 99% in just a few minutes, while an energetic child can turn an entire bathroom floor into a wading pool in even less time. A ventilation system won't do much for standing water, but it is essential for controlling the water vapor that a shower generates.

The easiest and most economical way to ventilate a bathroom is by opening a window. But this isn't always the most practical or reliable way to let fresh air into the room, particularly when it is cold outside. Most local building codes don't require bathrooms with large-enough operable windows to have mechanical ventilation, but I think it's a good idea for all bathrooms to have fans. I've seen too many baths—even those with sufficient windows—with lifting and peeling wallpaper and mildewed corners.

But even in bathrooms with fans, excess moisture is still a problem. Unfortunately, many bath fans are just too noisy, and if they're operated independently of the main bathroom light, they often don't get turned on. Choosing a quiet fan with a low sone rating—below 2.5 sones—is the best solution to this problem. (For more on bathroom ventilation, see Chapter 5.) Bathroom ventilation systems should be sized to properly handle the volume of air in the bathroom and be ducted directly to the outside (see Chapter 9 for installation details).

BATHROOM LAYOUT: FINDING ROOM FOR EVERYTHING

Knowing the type of bath that is going to be built and the physical properties of the space that it's going to be built in are the first steps in the process of sorting out fixtures. A half-bath in a converted walk-out basement might need an up-flush toilet; an elaborate master bath might call for a designer one-piece toilet, a bidet, a whirlpool tub, and a steam shower. But whatever the type of bath, usually the biggest design hurdle is space—simply finding enough room for everything can be tricky. Seldom have I seen a bathroom that is too big, but I've seen plenty that have been shoehorned into some pretty small spaces. Everything seems to fit until someone tries to use it.

Full bath

Certainly the most common plan, the full bath—with one sink, one toilet, and a combination tub/shower—provides all of the essential services and can be fit into a 5-ft. by 7-ft. space. There is some room for varying door and sink placement within the basic 5-ft. by 7-ft. footprint, but there isn't much. Window placement is also a bit of a problem with this plan. Windows can be placed above tubs, but this isn't an ideal location because water splashing on the window trim and sash will quickly penetrate into the wood, causing rot.

Half-bath

Often called powder rooms, half-baths are an economical and space-saving alternative to full baths in public areas of the house. Oftentimes they can be combined with laundry rooms, and they can be squeezed into spaces as small as 4 ft. by 4½ ft. yet still maintain recommended minimum clearances for the toilet and sink.

Because half-baths are often intended for use by guests, they are usually placed near the living room or dining room. This placement can be a problem if the door to the bathroom is strategically located. For example, I once built a half-bath that was part of a remodeled kitchen/dining area. Though I carefully soundproofed the walls, the bathroom door opened directly into the dining area; there just was no other place to put it, though a future addition was planned that would later provide better access. Except for the noise transmission through the doorway, the bath functioned well and served its purpose, but the homeowners were relieved when the new addition (and new doorway to the bath) was finally built.

Three-quarter bath

While a bathroom with just a shower stall instead of a tub doesn't really save a lot of space over a bathroom with a full tub, it does provide extra room within the same footprint for shelving or a linen closet. A three-quarter bath may be just the thing for certain families. While families with small children still need a tub for bathing, most adults and older children use the shower because it is faster. There is still nothing quite like a nice hot soak in the tub, but how many of us have time for that?

Master bath

Once a bathroom has more than minimal room and can accommodate more than the basic three fixtures, then I think it falls into the category of master bath, whether or not it is attached to a master bedroom (though it usually is). The luxury of having plenty of room to work with makes a wide range of fixture configurations possible, but high on the wish list of most people now is a whirlpool tub and a

Standard or Minimum Sizes of Bathroom Fixtures

Toilet

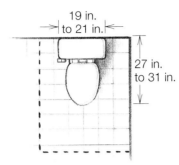

19 in. to 21 in.

27 in. to 31 in.

Bidet

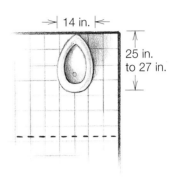

14 in.

25 in. to 27 in.

Sink

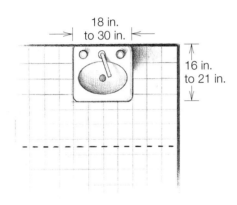

18 in. to 30 in.

16 in. to 21 in.

Shower

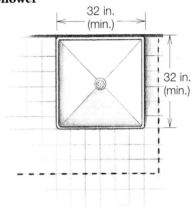

32 in. (min.)

32 in. (min.)

Tub (rectangular)

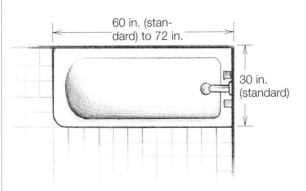

60 in. (standard) to 72 in.

30 in. (standard)

Tub (square)

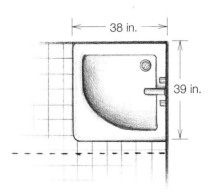

38 in.

39 in.

Bathroom fixtures need to be located carefully relative to walls and each other so that there is enough room for them to be used comfortably. The drawing above provides nominal fixture dimensions.

separate walk-in shower. Working couples, seeking the amenities of the good life that two incomes should provide, want the indulgence of a whirlpool tub, but the reality of working long hours makes a shower a practical necessity for the morning rush hour.

Master baths have long had multiple sinks to accommodate more than one person in the room at a time. But sometimes it seems that having side-by-side bowls just means having one extra sink to keep clean, while having an extra sink in a separate area may make more sense. If there is room for a partitioned area for the toilet and a separate sink, you can give a master bath the ability to offer both multiple functions and different levels of privacy for more than one user.

A master bath is both a practical place for the body and a refuge for the spirit. (Photo © Carolyn Bates.)

Other bath options

Outdoor showers aren't very practical in New England, where I live, but I know that if I lived in a warm climate, I would have one. Showering outdoors in warm weather is the next best thing to a swim and a real practical way to keep humidity out of the house in the summer. An outdoor shower would never supplant a primary bathroom, but you might consider one for a home in a warm climate (see the photos below).

One type of bath that would work as well in New England as anyplace else is the wet-floor bath. Instead of a separate and curbed shower stall, this type of bath has a waterproofed (generally tiled) floor slightly sloped toward a central or offset drain (see the photo on p. 30). The shower valve and showerhead generally are mounted on the wall farthest from the toilet and lavatory, and usually (but not always) a track-mounted shower curtain separates the

An outdoor shower can be tucked away in a private space and is a good way to clean up when the weather is warm. (Top photo © Carolyn Bates.)

Wet-floor bathrooms offer a clean look and eliminate curbs, making them more accessible to wheelchair users. (Photo courtesy HEWI, Inc.)

shower from the rest of the bath. A wet-floor bath has the advantage of being readily adaptable for accessibility because there is no curb, and the lack of enclosing shower walls allows the entire room to fit in a relatively compact space without violating fixture-clearance guidelines.

Not quite so exotic as the previous examples, combination bath/laundry rooms serve a dual role and are a good way to bring the washer and dryer up out of the cellar. There are a number of different configurations possible that make room for both appliances and, in some cases, a separate laundry sink as well. If there is enough space, another option is to make room for an exercise area adjoining the bath.

PLANNING FOR AN ACCESSIBLE BATH

Recently, my grandmother moved out of her home of more than 50 years. She loved her home and didn't want to leave, and she was fully capable of living there alone, as she had for many years already. But there was only a tiny half-bath on the first floor, no room for a larger one, and a forbiddingly steep staircase separating her from the full bath on the second floor. Active, healthy, and still a lot sharper than I'll ever be, she just was unable to coax her 90-year-old legs up those stairs any more.

Accessibility is a real issue. In my grandmother's case, simply having room for a full bath instead of a half-bath on the first floor would have allowed her to remain in her house. In other cases, bathrooms need to be adaptable to people with walkers, or people who use wheelchairs, or people with other physical limitations. Because bathrooms serve such a specialized and necessary function, they should be planned for a lifetime of use by people with a wide range of abilities. It is simply unrealistic to expect that a household will never need a bathroom facility to accommodate people who get old or who have physical limitations. This doesn't necessarily mean that specialized—and therefore expensive—equipment is required. Space planning can go a long way toward making a bathroom accessible. So can the judicious use of grab bars and handholds. In some instances, specialized fixtures might become necessary, but usually adapting conventional fixtures by providing plenty of room, sufficient handholds, and supplemental access is enough.

In many cases, neglecting the issue of accessibility is prohibited by law. Federally funded housing projects and commercial construction typically fall within the jurisdiction of standards published in such guidelines as the American National Standards Institute's A117.1 (updated in 1981 to include standards for private dwellings), the Uniform Federal Accessibility Standard (UFAS) of 1985 (for dwellings in federal projects), the 1988 Fair Housing Amendments Act, and the Americans with Disabilities Act (ADA) of 1990. While these laws don't all have the same specific provisions and don't generally apply to private residential construction, their common goal—to provide equal access to bath facilities for people with a wide range of abilities—can and should be incorporated into residential design.

Sometimes, simply making the bathroom adaptable—that is, capable of being altered by adding or removing certain elements—for persons with varying degrees of disabilities is enough. This can mean providing blocking in the framing to accommodate the installation of grab bars or installing a base cabinet under a sink that can be removed later to provide knee space for someone in a wheelchair.

Sometimes, though, accessibility considerations challenge conventional construction wisdom and economics. The fact that first-floor half-baths can be inserted into such small spaces at relatively small expense is one of the reasons why they are so popular. A full-size bath

An accessible bathroom doesn't have to look institutional; from the wall-mounted sink to the soap dispenser to the waste receptacle, this sink area is designed for universal access. (Photo courtesy HEWI, Inc.)

Typical ADA-Compliant Bathrooms

While ADA compliance isn't required in most residential bathroom construction, many of its guidelines can be incorporated to make bathrooms more universally accessible.

Sink and toilet

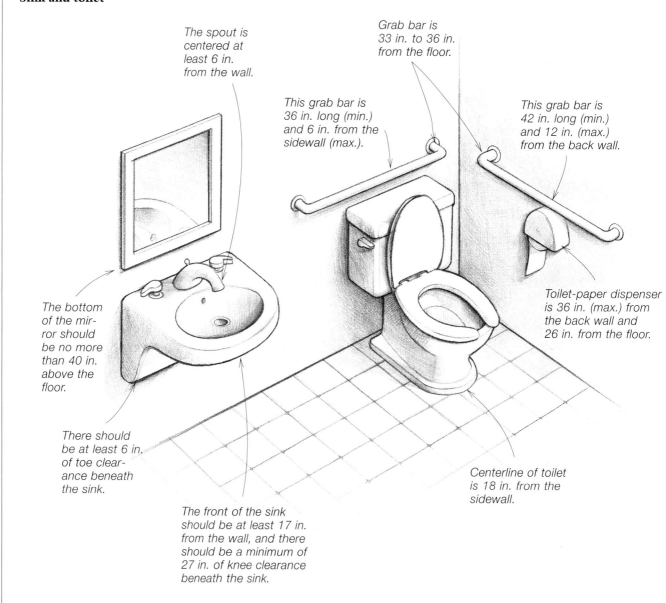

The spout is centered at least 6 in. from the wall.

Grab bar is 33 in. to 36 in. from the floor.

This grab bar is 36 in. long (min.) and 6 in. from the sidewall (max.).

This grab bar is 42 in. long (min.) and 12 in. (max.) from the back wall.

The bottom of the mirror should be no more than 40 in. above the floor.

Toilet-paper dispenser is 36 in. (max.) from the back wall and 26 in. from the floor.

There should be at least 6 in. of toe clearance beneath the sink.

The front of the sink should be at least 17 in. from the wall, and there should be a minimum of 27 in. of knee clearance beneath the sink.

Centerline of toilet is 18 in. from the sidewall.

Tub

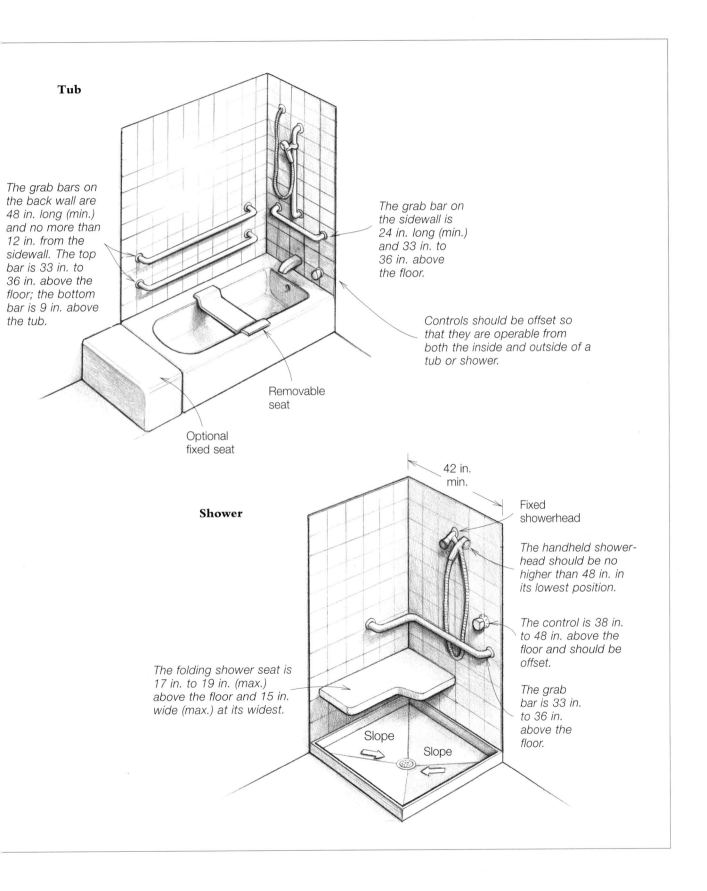

The grab bars on the back wall are 48 in. long (min.) and no more than 12 in. from the sidewall. The top bar is 33 in. to 36 in. above the floor; the bottom bar is 9 in. above the tub.

The grab bar on the sidewall is 24 in. long (min.) and 33 in. to 36 in. above the floor.

Controls should be offset so that they are operable from both the inside and outside of a tub or shower.

Removable seat

Optional fixed seat

Shower

42 in. min.

Fixed showerhead

The handheld shower-head should be no higher than 48 in. in its lowest position.

The control is 38 in. to 48 in. above the floor and should be offset.

The grab bar is 33 in. to 36 in. above the floor.

The folding shower seat is 17 in. to 19 in. (max.) above the floor and 15 in. wide (max.) at its widest.

Slope

Slope

undoubtedly requires more floor space. But an accessible or adaptable bathroom need not be prohibitively large and can fit in a relatively compact 5-ft. by 7½-ft. space.

If at all possible, each level of living space in a house should have at least one full-size bath or the capability to accommodate a full-size bath with minimal renovation. One economical approach is to frame and rough-plumb the bath to accommodate a full-size tub but hold off on installing the fixture itself. This 3-ft. by 5-ft. area can be converted to closet space with access either from inside or outside the bathroom. If doorway locations and framing headers are planned in advance, it's relatively easy to patch in or remove screwed-in studs and drywall when the time comes to remove the closet and install a tub, and few people will argue against the extra—though temporary—storage space.

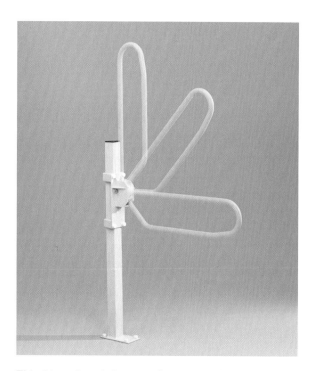

This hinged grab bar can be mounted near a toilet, swings out of the way for easier access by wheelchair users, and offers rigid support in either the up or down position. (Photo courtesy Otto Bock Reha.)

Grab bars and handholds

Grab bars and handholds are an important component of accessible design. They should be capable of supporting loads of 300 lbs. and be placed to facilitate the use of the different bathroom fixtures (NKBA #26). This sounds straightforward, but in fact the different building codes and accessibility guidelines have different design requirements for placement that actually impact the overall design requirements of the bath itself. For example, the Fair Housing Amendments Act requirements are less strict than those of ANSI, UFAS, or ADA and permit swing-down bars adjacent to a toilet, eliminating the need for a wall next to the toilet (see the photo below). In most cases, adhering to NKBA guidelines regarding grab-bar placement and using common sense should meet the requirements of most people with disabilities. And remember that grab bars aren't just for the disabled. A bathroom can be a slippery place full of hard surfaces and edges. All of us would appreciate something to grab onto when we find ourselves in an awkward and off-balance position.

Unfortunately, grab bars aren't particularly attractive, at least the institutional-looking stainless-steel variety aren't. But there are some options that can help a residential bath avoid that institutional look. Shelves, countertops, and ledges that are strategically placed and structurally sound can serve as handholds. Some towel racks can double as grab bars, provided that they are designed for that use and are sufficiently strong. New grab-bar designs are more colorful and better looking than the institutional variety; if chosen with the same care as fixtures and lighting, these accessories can actually enhance the look of the bath. (See Resources on p. 209 for manufacturers and suppliers of accessibility products.)

There are a couple of approaches to providing a strong backing for grab-bar installation. The conventional method is to install 2x blocking in

ADA Guidelines for Clear Floor Spaces

Clear floor space guidelines, which vary slightly according to the agency or organization issuing them, are intended to provide adequate access to bathroom fixtures for people with disabilities. Clear floor spaces for individual fixtures may overlap in an actual bathroom.

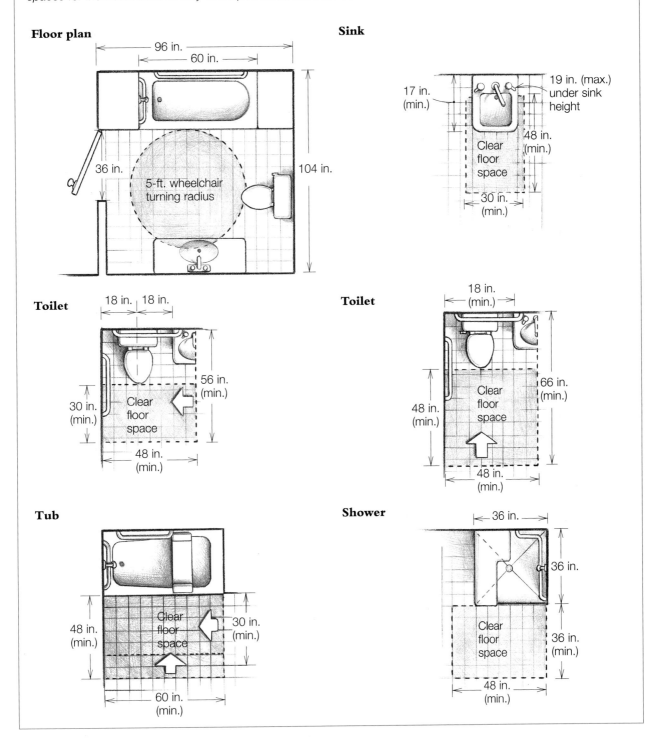

Floor plan

96 in.

60 in.

36 in.

104 in.

5-ft. wheelchair turning radius

Sink

17 in. (min.)

19 in. (max.) under sink height

48 in. (min.)

Clear floor space

30 in. (min.)

Toilet

18 in. | 18 in.

30 in. (min.)

56 in. (min.)

Clear floor space

48 in. (min.)

Toilet

18 in. (min.)

48 in. (min.)

66 in. (min.)

Clear floor space

48 in. (min.)

Tub

48 in. (min.)

Clear floor space

30 in. (min.)

60 in. (min.)

Shower

36 in.

36 in.

Clear floor space

36 in. (min.)

48 in. (min.)

locations where grab bars might be necessary. This is relatively inexpensive because framing cut-offs generated during construction can typically be used, but it does limit future grab-bar locations to areas where the blocking is installed. Another approach is to sheath all of the interior walls with ¾-in. plywood, then install drywall over the plywood. This method is more expensive, but it allows the grab bars to be mounted anywhere on the wall.

Clearances

While NKBA recommendations for grab-bar locations are generally sound, in many cases their recommendations for clear floor space conflict to some degree with federal accessibility guidelines. For example, NKBA Guideline 23 recommends 16-in. clearance (15-in. minimum) from the centerline of a toilet to a sidewall or other fixture. People who use a wheelchair or a walker would probably find that dimension extremely cramped, if not impossible, and would consider the wider 18-in. clearance required by most federal agencies the minimum.

Bathroom fixtures should have at least a 30-in. by 48-in. clear floor space in front of each fixture (NKBA #3), and there should also be room for the 5-ft. turning radius generally recommended for wheelchairs. If possible, toilets should be located so that they are easily accessible from either side (although toilets located in a separate compartment can only be approached from the front, which limits their use by some people).

Entries and doors

Entryways need to be at least 32 in. wide to accommodate wheelchairs (NKBA #1). If possible, try to make the door swing out into the hallway rather than inward. That way, if someone has fallen or needs assistance in the bathroom, the door can be opened easily. One way to eliminate the problem of door swing is to use pocket doors. Though more costly to install, pocket doors slide completely out of the way and make entry and exit for someone in a wheelchair much easier. (See the NKBA guidelines on p. 206 for other pertinent doorway and entry specifications.)

It's also a good idea to eliminate thresholds and height transitions in the entryway. They can be stumbling blocks for people using walkers or wheelchairs. Either bring one floor up to the level of the other, or gradually shim up the low side so that the transition isn't abrupt. And make the finish flooring a nonslip material, or install nonslip strips. For example, ceramic tile with a matte finish is less slippery than glossy tile.

Accessible fixtures

A typical sink sits on a 30-in.-high by 22-in.-deep cabinet topped by a countertop. Unfortunately, this arrangement is very difficult for people in wheelchairs to use. They need to get in closer than the cabinet will allow, which is why most federal standards require an open area underneath the sink. Sinks are also usually too low at 30 in.; most people except children and very short people prefer a sink somewhere near 32 in. off the floor, though I've installed sinks up to 36 in. high. In general, a 32-in.-high sink is a good compromise for most people.

Wheelchair users need an open 27-in. clearance between the floor and the front rim of the sink (NKBA #12), so a vanity base is going to get in the way. Wall-hung and pedestal sinks most easily meet this requirement, but they don't provide any undersink storage. If you are planning with future accessibility in mind, one solution is to provide removable cabinetry under a wall-hung sink or a sink mounted in a built-in countertop. That way, knee space can be created without removing the entire sink. If plumbing is exposed under the sink, you'll need to cover or insulate the supply pipes and drain and make sure there are no sharp surfaces.

The problem with most standard toilets is that they are too low, which makes them difficult to use for people of limited strength. Toilets should be 17 in. to 19 in. high, the height of standard seating, but most toilets are about 15½ in. high. Wall-hung toilets are available that are the right height, provide more clear floor space, and make it easier to clean under and around the toilet. Another option is a power-elevating toilet seat that mounts on a conventional toilet (see the left photo below). Or a seat mounted on an aluminum frame that fits around a conventional toilet can also raise the seat height, while providing a graspable handhold.

If you've ever tried to give a young child a bath, you know that the traditional tub has a few flaws. For one thing, it's too low, not only for a parent bending over to scrub a tiny body, but also for many people who have difficulty getting up from a seated position, much less from floor level. Also, tubs can get pretty slippery, and many of them don't have much to grab onto if someone starts to fall.

Strategically located grab bars and handholds are an important first step in making a tub area accessible. There should also be an 18-in.-wide seat capable of supporting 250 lb. per sq. ft. either added to one end of the tub or securely mounted in the tub area itself (see the right photo below). Raising the tub on a platform that brings the rim up to conventional seat height will make it easier for small children to get in and out of the bath. And while track-mounted sliding-glass shower-door enclosures are popular, they make access difficult, and ADA 4.20.7 specifically prohibits rim-mounted tracks on tubs. Rod-mounted shower curtains are a better choice.

The elderly and the disabled will appreciate this power-elevating toilet seat. It raises, lowers, tilts, provides arm support, and fits on a conventional toilet. (Photo courtesy Med/West.)

Adding a seat and grab bars easily upgrades a conventional tub so it meets ADA accessibility requirements. (Photo courtesy Kohler Co.)

The door in the side of this tub is designed for easy entry and exit, making it user-friendly for people with disabilities. (Photo courtesy Kohler Co.)

A number of manufacturers are addressing the shortcomings of the traditional tub with designs that incorporate recent research and new technology. While these tubs clearly offer more accessibility to a wider range of people, they are not inexpensive, ranging in price from $3,000 in a basic tub configuration to over $5,000 for whirlpool versions (see the photo above). On the other hand, showers designed to accommodate persons with a wide range of physical abilities are not significantly more expensive than "normal" showers. The addition of appropriate handholds, seating, and a bit more space can easily upgrade a conventional shower to an accessible one.

A 36-in. by 36-in. shower stall is large enough to fit most users, but it's compact enough that grab bars can be used for support on all sides. This size will fit the required seat yet still leave plenty of room for standing. An alternative shower plan fits in the 32-in. by 60-in. space of a conventional tub, and if there's no curb, a wheelchair can roll right into it. Curbless designs are best because they don't present an obstacle for wheelchairs or other walking aids.

Showerheads, controls, and valves

A handheld showerhead mounted on an adjustable track is a great addition to a shower system and is a necessity for any accessible unit (see the photo on the facing page). There are a number of different styles available, and the addition of a long hose and a volume control makes these units perfect for washing kids, pets, and the shower itself afterward. Usually, the mounting track is 2 ft. long, so the showerhead is adaptable to a wide range of heights.

Shower controls should be mounted between 38 in. and 48 in. above the floor of the shower and should also be accessible from outside of it (NKBA #22). Lever-handled controls are simpler to operate than knobs and require less agility and hand strength. And now required by most building codes are valves that automatically regulate the water temperature of the shower should the hot/cold balance be disrupted (NKBA #21).

Bathroom accessories

Most bathrooms have a mirror mounted over the sink, but in many cases this mirror is too high to be of any use to someone in a wheelchair. Extending the mirror down to the backsplash is one way of correcting this; another is to tilt the mirror down or to mount the mirror so that it is tiltable. It's also a good idea to provide another full-height mirror elsewhere in the bathroom.

Planning for accessibility can also extend to such areas as light-switch selection. Rocker-style switches for bathroom lighting are easier to control for people with limited hand mobility than conventional single-pole switches. Another option might be a passive infrared occupancy sensor switch, which turns lights on in the presence of motion. This switch also saves energy because lights can't inadvertently be left on.

A handheld showerhead offers more flexibility than a fixed showerhead, even in a conventional tub/shower unit. (Photo © Carolyn Bates.)

Chapter 3

CHOOSING FIXTURES AND COMPONENTS

TOILETS

BIDETS

SINKS

COUNTERTOPS

FAUCETS

There was a time not so long ago when bathroom fixtures came in any color that you wanted...as long as that color was white, pink, or light blue. Times have changed, though. Basic white—and its many variants—is still the most popular color, but fixtures are now available in colors with names like merlot, seafoam green, and cobalt blue. All of these colors look great in the catalogs, and there is nothing wrong with being daring once in a while, but remember the fate of once-popular avocado-colored kitchen appliances. If an unusual color becomes outdated, a toilet or sink is usually not that difficult or expensive to replace, but a tiled-in tub is another matter altogether. Besides, white fixtures are consistently less expensive than the same fixture in a designer color (see the photo on the facing page).

Color and style may be the factors that sell a fixture, but true satisfaction in a long-term relationship will only come about if the fixture performs well. Toilets that are noisy and don't clear waste after a single flush won't be popular for long. Sinks and countertops that quickly show signs of wear and that are hard to keep clean will also lose support. And nobody likes a leaky faucet.

Bathroom fixtures are available today in a rainbow of styles and colors, although basic white is still the most popular choice. (Photo courtesy Porcher, Ltd.)

Evaluating how well a fixture will perform over the long run requires an understanding of its construction, including the way it is designed and built and the material that it is made from. It helps to know that brass is durable but can tarnish, that fiberglass can scratch and fade, and that some kinds of tile are more appropriate than others for bathroom countertops. It also helps to know why some toilet designs flush better than others, as well as the practical differences between cartridge and compression faucets. Choosing a fixture without knowing how it is built and the advantages and disadvantages of the particular material it is made from is just like buying a book based on its cover.

TOILETS

The toilet industry has been in a bit of an upheaval of late, primarily because of the federal 1.6 gallon per flush (gpf) mandate, which took effect for residential construction in January 1994. Manufacturers had to refine toilet designs to reduce water consumption to meet the mandate, but now there's talk in Congress of easing up on the 1.6-gpf benchmark. The problem? Consumer complaints that low-flow toilets just don't work very well. But low-flow toilets have gotten a bum rap. Yes, early models were prone to skid marks left by waste and often needed a second flush to clear waste. In fact, I have one of these toilets in my house right now, and it can be annoying to have to flush it and then clean it as well. But it is even more annoying to smell the local sewage treatment plant, which is failing because of my hometown's growth and the increased wastewater coming from all of those 3.5-gpf and higher water-consuming toilets.

The newer 1.6-gpf designs work just as well as the old water guzzlers, with refined hydraulics that maximize the flushing effects of lower water volumes. Some new technology—particularly the addition of air pressure to the flush—helps too. Manufacturers are finding ways of engineering larger water spots (the area of standing water in the bowl) and increasing the vacuum effect of the flush. Happily, gone are the days when pure water volume—up to 7 gpf in some cases—made up for deficiencies in design and manufacture. The bottom line is that low-flow toilets are here to stay. And for good reason: They save a lot of water, putting less stress on water supplies, private septic systems, and municipal treatment plants.

Toilet materials and construction

Vitreous china—commonly called porcelain—has been the material of choice for toilets since the Eljer Plumbingware Co. introduced its first ones back in 1907. Other materials like plastic or enameled steel just aren't as adaptable to the complex shapes required by the toilet. Like any fired-clay product, porcelain can be brittle, which makes it prone to cracking, particularly when a closet bolt, tank bolt, or seat bolt is overtightened. But porcelain provides a hard and smooth glazed surface that is easy to clean on both the inside and outside and that won't be scratched by abrasive cleaners. This smooth surface also reduces hydraulic friction between the internal passageway walls and the fluids and waste passing through them, making the toilet work more efficiently.

The common rough-in dimension for most toilets now is 12 in. from the center of the outlet to the finished wall. However, it isn't uncommon in renovation work to run across old toilets with 10-in. or 14-in. rough-in dimensions, and while toilets are still available from manufacturers to fit these older rough-in dimensions, style and color choices are more limited. Another option is to use an offset flange, which allows a standard 12-in. rough-in toilet to be used on a nonstandard drain outlet. Offset flanges can vary the position of the toilet up to 2 in. from the center of the existing closet flange and in many cases can save the plumbing expense of moving it.

I haven't found much difference in quality or performance among the basic models of toilets from the major manufacturers. While local availability and the presence of a major chain like The Home Depot may make one brand more price appealing than another, the basic models of the major manufacturers are all reasonably priced and are of top quality. But with some of the less familiar brands, a little more caution is in order; buying one because it's a bargain may cost money in the long run. As with any vitreous-china fixture, the finish of the porcelain is a clue to the quality of the manufacturing process, with the best porcelain finishes being smooth and pinhole free all over, both inside and out. Fixtures with marginal finishes often have other problems as well, such as plated-steel parts (that will rust) instead of brass and warped surfaces or hairline cracking, that aren't apparent until the fixture is installed.

Different Toilet Designs

Siphon-vortex
- low-profile one-piece construction
- quiet flush
- efficient
- expensive

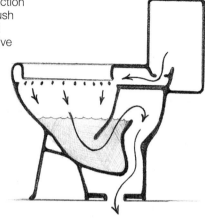

Reverse-trap
- moderate performance
- moderate noise
- moderate cost

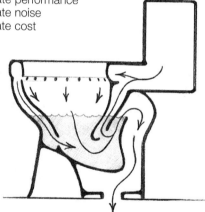

Pressure assisted/tankless
- noisy
- expensive
- commercial use
- requires flushometer valve

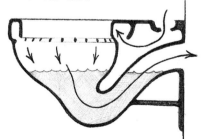

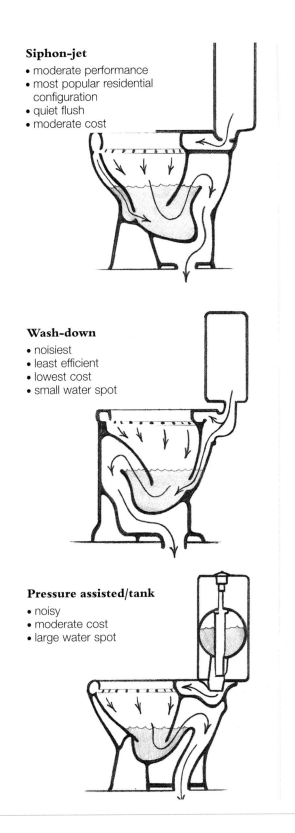

Siphon-jet
- moderate performance
- most popular residential configuration
- quiet flush
- moderate cost

Wash-down
- noisiest
- least efficient
- lowest cost
- small water spot

Pressure assisted/tank
- noisy
- moderate cost
- large water spot

Toilets are now available in a number of both gravity-fed and pressure-assisted models, and both systems have their advocates. Toilets are also available with either round bowls, which are more compact in tight quarters, or elongated bowls, which are generally more comfortable for most people to use.

Gravity-fed toilets

These toilets are essentially redesigned versions of traditional siphon-jet-type toilets. Compared to the larger-capacity toilets of a few years ago, they have smaller-capacity water tanks, steeper-sided bowls, and smaller water spots. Gravity-fed toilets can come either in two-piece—or close-coupled—configurations, where the tank is bolted to the back of the toilet, or as a one-piece

A low profile one-piece toilet seems appropriate in this elegant setting. (Photo © Carolyn Bates.)

unit. One-piece toilets have a lower profile and are typically considerably more expensive than close-coupled toilets (see the photo on p. 43). Some one-piece toilets are much easier to clean because they have simpler lines and fewer nooks and crannies that dirt can accumulate in, a potential consideration when choosing a toilet.

Pressure-assisted toilets

If you can visualize a turbocharger for your toilet, you essentially have the idea behind pressure-assisted toilets, which were developed with the theory that air pressure could compensate for the lower volume of water available in 1.6-gpf low-flow toilets. The most common method of supplying this air pressure is to capture supply-line pressure in a small tank within the toilet. As new water comes into the toilet tank after flushing, the tank is repressurized. When the toilet is flushed, the compressed air expands and forces the tank water into the bowl at a higher velocity.

Both close-coupled and one-piece toilets are available with pressure-assisted flushing actions. These toilets have the advantage of having a larger water spot than gravity-fed toilets, which

A wall-mounted toilet is easier to clean underneath and can be more accessible for wheelchair users. These toilets are typically found in commercial applications. (Photo courtesy Kohler Co.)

may make them less prone to skid marks. But their turbulent air-and-water flush makes these toilets noisier than their gravity-fed counterparts, which could make nocturnal use less than desirable, and the additional engineering required by the pressurizing mechanism makes these toilets more expensive.

Another way to supply more pressure to a low-flow toilet is with an electric pump. Kohler's Trocadero Power Lite has a small electrically powered 0.2-hp pump to push water through the flush. This toilet, which plugs into a conventional wall outlet, draws a minimal amount of current and is quieter than conventional pressure-assisted toilets.

Wall-hung toilets

Wall-hung toilets have the advantage of being easy to clean underneath and more accessible to disabled users (see the photo below). Typically found in commercial installations, wall-hung toilets are relatively unusual in residential bathrooms, in part because they are fussier to install than their floor-mounted counterparts. Wall framing has to be fairly beefy for these units. While manufacturers consider 2x6 framing to be a minimum, consider using at least 2x8 framing and plywood interior sheathing to reinforce the wall. Wall-hung toilets also require a heavy metal bracket, or carrier, bolted to the framing. Most wall-mounted toilets also are tankless and are fitted with a special "flushometer" valve that meters the volume of incoming water for each flush.

The Kimera wall-mounted toilet by American Standard features a concealed tank and bowl carrier that mount inside the wall. The tank is insulated to eliminate condensation, which could be a problem inside a wall, and locating it within the wall makes the flush quieter. The toilet-bowl height is also adjustable from 15 in. to 19 in. (see the top photo on the facing page).

This wall-mounted toilet's tank is concealed in the wall, and its height is adjustable. (Photo courtesy American Standard, Inc.)

Specialty toilets

It's possible to install toilets in some unusual locations, including corners and basements that are below the level of the main drain pipe. Toilets configured to fit into a corner make the most of limited space without sacrificing necessary clearances for comfortable use (see the photo at right), while toilets installed in basements often must fight gravity. If a full bath is planned for below grade, then a sewage ejector system will often be needed. This is a labor- and cash-intensive prospect because it requires a 30-gallon or so holding tank and pumping unit buried beneath the floor of the bathroom. These systems retail at around $500 and are available from a variety of manufacturers.

A corner-mounted toilet can optimize limited floor space in a small bathroom. (Photo courtesy Eljer.)

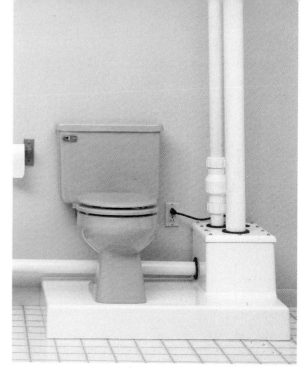

The Quik Jon compact ejector unit can simplify a basement bathroom installation because it can pump waste up. The pump compartment, which is able to handle the waste from a 1.6-gpf toilet, tub, and sink, can be concealed in a wall (left) or be kept freestanding (right). (Photos courtesy Zoeller Pump Co.)

Custom toilet seats, like Jammin' Johns' guitar-body toilet lid, offer a novel way to jazz up a bathroom. (Photo courtesy Jammin' Johns.)

Another option, when only a toilet is needed, is to install an up-flushing toilet. These units have self-contained pumps, and in some cases a macerator, a small tank that holds waste for a short time and begins to break it down before pumping it. There is also an above-floor ejector unit, which can either mount in a wall or underneath the toilet, that is easier to install than a buried system (see the photos above). With all of these units, you should check local building codes for compliance.

Toilet seats

Choosing a toilet seat is simply a matter of picking out the right color, right? Wrong. Besides the plain-Jane toilet seats that everyone is used to, there are also padded soft seats, seats with sculpted designs in the lid, seats that accept a fabric or wallpaper insert in the lid, and even seats with guitar-body lids (see the photo at left).

Toilet seats are generally made of either pressed wood, solid wood, or plastic. Pressed-wood toilet-lid seats are potentially the most susceptible to moisture damage, particularly from water splashing up from the bowl. But these seats usually feel heavier and more solid than either plastic or laminated-wood seats, and better-quality pressed-wood seats typically have a multicoat enamel finish to protect against the chipping and cracking that allow moisture to penetrate. Molded seat lids can also readily accept different patterns, giving the seat a sculptural look.

Lower-quality seats usually have less expensive hardware to mount the seat to the bowl. Rather than using more costly brass, these seats sometimes have hinges and screws of plated steel that corrode fairly quickly when they come in contact with water and urine. Plastic seats usually have plastic mounting hardware that is immune from corrosion, but sometimes it can be difficult to keep tightened. Better-quality plastic seats are very durable, and some seats have a plastic core padded with foam and enclosed with a vinyl cover. These seats are pretty comfortable to sit on, but they don't seem to have a particularly long life span because the vinyl cover tends to split.

BIDETS

In Europe, bidets are quite commonplace because they offer a convenient way of cleaning the pelvic area for a general population that isn't as shower-obsessed as Americans. Bidets originally evolved out of Napoleon's cavalrymen's necessity to keep their pelvic area clean after a long day in the saddle; hence the name, which loosely translated means "little horse." Their European origins give bidets a certain cachet, and they are certainly more accepted as a bathroom fixture in the United States than ever before; you would be hard-pressed to find a water-closet catalog without a matching line of bidets. And in a bathroom with plenty of room and a substantial fixture budget,

a bidet makes what many feel is an attractive, if not exactly necessary, companion to the conventional toilet (see the photo below).

Bidets are usually installed side-by-side with toilets, so in most cases the bidet will be chosen at the same time and from the same manufacturer. Drain locations for bidets aren't standardized, and they also need both a hot and a cold water supply, so the manufacturer's literature will need to be consulted before roughing-in the plumbing. Valves are problematic, too; fittings from one manufacturer may not be compatible with the hole configurations on the fixtures of another manufacturer.

There are two basic types of bidets. The less expensive type is basically a low-mounted sink with a valve that sprays horizontally rather than vertically. The other type of bidet has a rim-filled flush like a toilet, a vertical spray fitting in the center of the bowl, a diverter to direct water to either the vertical spray or the rim flush, and

Ambivalent about bidets? While bidets have found a place in catalogs and showrooms, the American public has been slow to accept them as a necessary fixture.

Two Types of Bidets

Because bidets aren't standardized like toilets, their installation is more complicated. The manufacturer's technical literature will need to be consulted before planning hot- and cold-water supply and DWV connections.

Over-rim bidet with horizontal spray

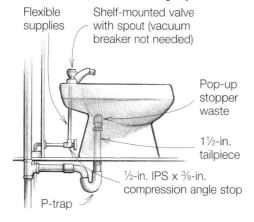

Flexible supplies

Shelf-mounted valve with spout (vacuum breaker not needed)

Pop-up stopper waste

1½-in. tailpiece

½-in. IPS x ⅜-in. compression angle stop

P-trap

- less expensive than rim-filled bidet
- easier to install than rim-filled bidet

Rim-filled bidet with vertical ascending spray

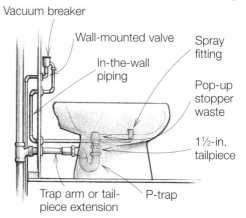

Vacuum breaker

Wall-mounted valve

Spray fitting

In-the-wall piping

Pop-up stopper waste

1½-in. tailpiece

Trap arm or tail-piece extension

P-trap

- requires vacuum breaker to prevent possible potable water-supply contamination
- more expensive than over-rim bidet
- more difficult to install than over-rim bidet

The IntiMist personal-hygiene system combines the functions of a bidet and a toilet. (Photo courtesy Panasonic.)

a vacuum breaker to prevent siphoning of contaminated water back into the fresh-water supply (see the drawing above).

Sometimes the perineal cleansing function of a bidet is desired, but there isn't enough room in the bathroom or in the budget for an additional fixture. In that case, you might consider a unit like the IntiMist. For less than $1000, this personal-hygiene system mounts onto a toilet like a toilet seat but also offers electronically controlled self-cleaning bidet nozzles and a warm-air dryer (see the photo at left). Personal-hygiene systems like the IntiMist are more common in Japan, but they are becoming increasingly available in the United States from manufacturers like Panasonic and Toto.

Enameled cast-iron sinks are heavy, but their extremely durable surface will stay beautiful for years. (Photo courtesy Kohler Co.)

Vitreous-china pedestal sinks have remained popular because of their durability and classic looks. (Photo © Carolyn Bates.)

SINKS

Like toilets, sinks are an essential component of any bathroom. But there is a lot more design leeway with bathroom sinks, partly because of their relatively simple function and partly because they can be constructed out of so many different materials. The range of styles, shapes, colors, and materials available today can actually be a little bewildering, and it is essential to know the specific sink type before doing the rough plumbing.

Sink materials

Most pedestal and wall-hung sinks are made from vitreous china, and the same qualities that make this material a good choice for toilets work well for sinks too: a durable, abrasion-resistant, easy-to-clean surface that maintains its luster year after year (see the photo at left). Choose vitreous-china sinks—particularly pedestal sinks—with care, especially if you're unfamiliar with the brand, because any ceramic manufacturing process produces a high number of seconds that may have defects ranging from minor blemishes or depressions in the surface to hairline cracking and out-of-plumb or warped mating surfaces. This can mean drop-in self-rimming sinks that don't sit flat (particularly larger ones) and two-piece pedestals that just don't quite go together correctly.

Enameled cast iron has most of vitreous china's good qualities, and it is much less prone to cracking (see the right photo above). Cast iron is strong, rigid, and quiet when water is running into it, although it can chip if mishandled during shipping or if a hammer gets dropped on it during installation. Cast-iron sinks are very heavy, which may not make that much of a difference with smaller vanity bowls, but can make handling larger sinks hard on the back.

Enameled steel is similar to enameled cast iron but considerably lighter and less expensive. It is much more likely to chip than enameled cast iron because its porcelain coating is thinner and the steel is more flexible. Water running into it makes more noise, too, and cools down more rapidly because the thin steel walls tend to dissipate heat pretty quickly. Formerly a low-budget alternative to porcelain and cast iron, enameled steel seems to be rapidly losing ground to synthetic materials that are competitively priced and that perform just as well, if not better. I've removed a few of these sinks in remodels, but I haven't put any new ones back in lately.

Cultured marble is one of those synthetic materials, and it's been around for a long time. Cultured marble, like cultured onyx and cultured granite, is technically a cast polymer, created by mixing crushed minerals like marble, onyx, or limestone with a polyester resin. This mixture is then poured into a mold and cured at room temperature. Like fiberglass, the surface is usually then gel-coated with the actual sink color and pattern, so some cast-polymer sinks are prone to scratching and damage. One

problem often associated with cast-polymer sinks is "crazing," or cracks and blisters in the gel coat. This typically occurs around the drain opening and is caused by the thermal shock of alternating hot and cold water, by abrasion from cleaning, and/or by a gel coat that is too thin or thick. Much of the do-it-yourself and lower-end sink market has been dominated by these sinks, in part because they're relatively inexpensive and look good on the shelf. Some of the newer and more expensive cast polymers have a higher percentage of materials like quartz, which is very hard, and aren't gel-coated. These cast polymers are much more heat and impact resistant and are sandable, making damage easier to repair (see the photo below).

Solid-surface materials like Corian and Surell are similar to cultured marble in that they too can be cast into easily cleaned one-piece sink/countertops. They have the advantage of having colors and patterns that are an integral part of the material, so repairs can be made simply by sanding away dents and scratches, and the nonporous synthetics are stain resistant (though not stain proof). Individual sink bowls are also available, though they are generally laminated into larger countertops of the same material. Expect to pay a lot more for solid-surface sinks than for cultured marble. (For more information on solid-surface materials, see p. 120.)

Cast-polymer sinks range from less expensive gel-coated cultured marble to more expensive solid-color sinks made out of durable materials like Swanstone. (Photo courtesy Swan Corp.)

Ceramic earthenware bowls offer a colorful and organic alternative to mass-produced sinks. Because they are handmade, these sinks have irregularities that sometimes make getting them to fit correctly a real challenge, particularly those made outside the United States. Often these sinks don't have an overflow—a secondary outlet to the drain to keep a stoppered sink from flooding—which is sometimes required by local building codes. And because they are somewhat fragile, they require careful installation to make everything fit together well—tight enough not to leak but not so tight as to fracture the bowl.

But they add a custom touch to a bathroom, particularly when matched with tilework from the same pottery (see the photo at right).

Stainless-steel sinks have long been popular in the kitchen, and their somewhat industrial look sometimes lends itself well to bathrooms, too (see the photo below). They are certainly durable and easy to clean. There is a wide range of quality in stainless-steel sinks, with a corresponding range of prices. The best ones have a higher percentage of chromium and nickel, making them more stain and corrosion resistant, and are typically made of 18-gauge stainless steel, making them stronger and giving them a higher luster. Less expensive sinks feel flimsier because they are made of lighter 22-gauge (or less) steel; they have a duller finish, tend to be noisy, and tend to warp.

A hand-thrown ceramic sink can provide a colorful custom touch in a powder room or bathroom.

While more typically seen in the kitchen, stainless-steel sinks are at home in the bathroom, too, in both contemporary and traditional styles. (Photo © Carolyn Bates.)

Metal sinks are also available in brass, copper, aluminum, and bronze. Sometimes these sinks are mass-produced, but more often than not the more esoteric ones are handmade, and the same reservations that apply to ceramic sinks apply here. Like handmade ceramic sinks, metal sinks can be fussy to install and sometimes require some modification to adapt them to plumbing and fittings. Tempered-glass sinks are also available in a number of distinctive styles, including a sink basin mounted above the countertop (see the photo below).

Wall-hung sinks

These sinks are usually hung on brackets fastened to the framing and are often the sinks of choice in an accessible bathroom because of

Above-the-countertop sink basins are available in a number of different materials, including ceramic, metal, and spun glass. (Photo courtesy Kohler Co.)

the open area underneath them. In addition, some manufacturers have wall-mounting systems that allow the height of the sink to be adjusted, a real plus in accessible installations, though not always allowed by local codes. Styles range from pedestrian to stunningly architectural, and there are also wall-hung sinks designed to fit into a tight corner. If you choose this type of sink, keep in mind that only a metal mounting bracket and the strength of the vitreous china can keep an overly energetic child from pulling everything to the floor.

Freestanding sinks

Pedestal sinks were once very common, then experienced a decline in popularity in the middle of the century, and now are quite popular again. They can have a certain retro charm that many manufacturers emphasize by their traditional styling, or they can also have a sleek postmodern look. The pedestal stand makes them sturdier than wall-hung sinks and helps to hide the plumbing connections that are otherwise quite visible. Sometimes pedestal sinks are chosen because of their relatively compact profile, but they look better if there is ample wall space on either side of the fixture (see the photo on the facing page).

Leg-mounted wash basins, like wall-hung sinks, are open underneath, but they also enjoy the extra support of a pair of front legs (and in some cases, rear legs too). While a traditional arrangement might feature a marble countertop supported by brass or chrome legs, new designs that emphasize the structure and material of the countertop can be made of stainless steel, glass, or other materials.

Cabinet-mounted sinks

The vanity—a base cabinet mounted with a sink—evolved when bathrooms shrank and fixture sizes were standardized during the post-World War II housing boom. Premanufactured vanity cabinets are quick to install, are compact and economical, and provide needed storage while offering a standard-size platform for mounting a countertop and sink.

The most economical, leak-proof, and easy-to-clean option for cabinet-mounted sinks is the integral one-piece sink/countertop. These come in a wide range of materials, styles, and price ranges, and they are a staple of the bath home-improvement market. They don't require particular skill or special tools to install and can range from economical to elegant, depending on the style and material.

Vanity sinks can also be installed in a separate countertop, which gives you a wider variety of choices in countertop materials, sink styles, and bathroom layout. Oftentimes, if the vanity cabinet is anything other than a standard size and shape, this is the only choice. These kinds of sinks are either self-rimming, rimless, or undermount (see the drawing on p. 54).

Self-rimming sinks have the disadvantage of blocking the drain-back of splashed water from the countertop into the sink, but the rim also has the advantage of adding an attractive profile to the countertop while hiding the sink cutout. Also, this cutout doesn't have to be perfect, and templates supplied with most drop-in sinks make laying out the cut easy. If you choose a self-rimming sink, keep in mind that the countertop material needs to be relatively smooth so that water can't seep underneath the rim and into the cabinetry.

Rimless sinks mount flush with the countertop with a stainless-steel or aluminum trim ring, which allows the top of the sink to remain flush with the top of the countertop so water splashed on the countertop is more easily pushed back into the sink. Some find the metal trim ring's appearance objectionable, and it does tend to be hard to keep all of the junctions between the countertop, trim ring, and sink clean. This is

The simple and classic looks of this pedestal sink contrast nicely with the more rustic-looking beaded hemlock wainscoting. (Photo by Charles Miller.)

also a spot where water seepage can be a problem, particularly with surfaces that aren't as smooth as plastic laminate. Sinks that require this special trim ring are still available, but they aren't nearly as popular as they once were.

If a countertop is a particularly attractive design or material and you want to de-emphasize the look of the sink, then an undermount sink might be a good choice. These sinks can be attached with bolts or special cast-in connections from underneath. Undermount synthetic-marble sinks (like Corian) can be laminated to the matching countertop material

Sink Styles

Self-rimming cast-iron sink

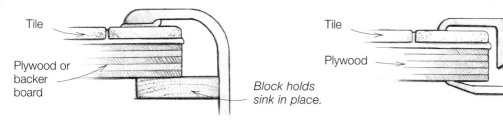

Tile

Plywood or backer board

Block holds sink in place.

Relatively smooth countertop surfaces, such as tile or cut stone, work best with self-rimming sinks.

Self-rimming metal sink

Tile

Plywood

Rim clip

Rimless sink

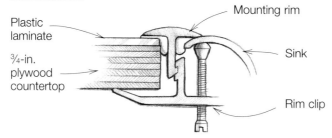

Plastic laminate

¾-in. plywood countertop

Mounting rim

Sink

Rim clip

Rimless sinks require a flat surface such as plastic laminate to avoid water leakage around the trim ring.

Undermount sink

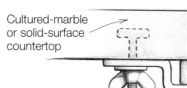

Cast-iron, porcelain, stainless-steel, solid-surface sink

Cultured-marble or solid-surface countertop

Underhung bowl clip

Undermount sinks present no barrier to water drainage.

Mudded-in sink

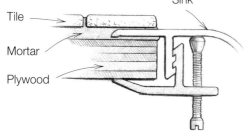

Sink

Tile

Mortar

Plywood

Mudded-in sinks are self-rimming metal sinks that have tile set over them, making them similar in appearance to an undermount sink.

to make an almost seamless connection between countertop and bowl. Because the inside of the cutout is exposed, this cut has to be done very carefully. Also, countertop materials like plastic laminate or wood just won't work very well with undermount sinks because water tends to work its way into the area around the cutout.

COUNTERTOPS

Choosing a sink and choosing a countertop material go hand in hand because the style of the sink often depends on the type of countertop. While specific information about choosing countertop materials can be found in Chapter 6, a quick overview of some of the countertop options will help in selecting a sink.

Plastic laminate is far and away the most popular countertop material, and for good reason. It is versatile, durable, moisture resistant, and relatively inexpensive. It comes in hundreds of colors and patterns, in different textures, and in glossy and matte finishes. Self-rimming sinks work well with plastic laminate, as do rimless sinks, because the smooth laminate surface works well with the trim ring to seal against leakage. Undermount sinks are a bit more problematic because of the seam at the rim of the cutout that can allow moisture into the substrate.

The same features that make solid-surface materials like Corian or Surell a good choice for sink bowls also hold true for countertops: durability, resistance to stains, and the ability to be fabricated in the field. A big advantage of solid-surface countertops is the way they can be almost seamlessly joined with premanufactured undermount sink bowls of the same material. This makes it possible to build a custom-fabricated countertop to fit almost any configuration and to perform virtually like a one-piece monolithic countertop.

Tile is a traditional choice for all types of bathroom surfaces, including countertops, because it sheds water like a duck. Tile installation is labor intensive, which makes it potentially expensive, and tile prices can vary widely depending on the type. But the range of patterns and colors that can be achieved with tile is endless, from cool and classical to organic and funky...and anywhere in between. Self-rimming sinks work best with tiled countertops, although another option is to mud-in the sink. This configuration puts the lip of the sink below the surface of the countertop, making it easier for splashed water to find its way back into the bowl. But this type of installation is quite permanent because the sink can't be removed without destroying the tile immediately surrounding it.

Many of the synthetic countertop materials available today attempt to create the look of natural stones like granite or marble. But you also might consider using the real thing instead. Because the bathroom countertop is typically relatively small compared to those in the kitchen, opting for stone in the bath might not be prohibitively expensive, even for bathrooms on a budget. However, you can easily spend five times the amount of a plastic-laminate countertop for a natural stone one. So if the budget prohibits a solid-stone countertop, consider using thin stone tiles on a substrate.

Natural stone is a beautiful material, but it's not totally impervious to the everyday wear and tear that happens in a bathroom. Both marble (to a greater extent) and granite (to a lesser extent) are susceptible to staining, and marble is soft enough that it can scratch, too, although this is less of a factor on a countertop than on a floor. Marble can be cleaned, repolished, and sealed, but I've seen some surprised homeowners unhappy with the maintenance requirements of their new marble bathrooms.

Soapstone is another natural countertop material that has a long tradition of use in the bathroom. Another option with a more recent heritage of use in the home is cast concrete. Though concrete sounds cold and industrial, it is pretty forgiving to work with and can actually be stained and polished to very pleasing colors and textures, and the raw materials are almost literally dirt cheap. If you make a mistake or don't like the results, just break up the concrete with a sledgehammer and try again.

Wood isn't exactly most people's first choice in countertop material, in part because it can be vulnerable to moisture damage. But I don't think that it should be entirely ruled out, particularly for bathrooms that see light or occasional use, like a guest bath or half-bath. One configuration that I particularly like is an antique commode or dresser retrofitted with a self-rimming sink. If care is taken to seal the edges of the cutout, to treat the top with a marine-type varnish, and to caulk the rim of the sink carefully, then this type of countertop can lend an elegant touch. I've also tried using undermount sinks in this situation, but I wouldn't recommend it: The edge of the cutout is just too vulnerable to moisture, and the countertop tends to shrink and swell so much around it that cracks in the wood top inevitably start to appear.

FAUCETS

Manufacturers' catalogs are filled with an astonishing variety of sink faucets, with designs ranging from neo-Victorian to sleek postmodern. Some of these faucets have handles, while others have a single lever; some of them don't have any handles at all and turn on and off electronically. They can range in price from the $29.95 "do-it-yourselfer's special" to the $700 (and more) designer faucets. How do you sort everything out?

Materials

The best place to start is to consider the material that the faucet is made of. The best faucets are of solid brass, an alloy basically composed of zinc and copper but also containing small percentages of other materials like lead. Brass is durable, corrosion resistant, and can be precisely machined so that parts fit together well. Forged and machined brass components typically have smoother surfaces and a lower lead content than cast brass, which is more porous and prone to pinhole leaks. Less expensive faucets are made from metals like zinc, which casts easily with a very smooth surface but quickly corrodes in contact with water if unprotected by a plated surface like chrome. Plastics like ABS and Delrin are often used in faucets because they are easily molded, have a smooth surface, and aren't prone to scale buildup. But they aren't as durable as metals, and moving parts made of plastic will quickly wear out, while plastic-bodied faucets just aren't destined to last very long.

Polished chrome finishes are extremely hard and durable. Electrochemically deposited over a nickel plating, chrome doesn't oxidize when it comes into contact with air, won't corrode, and won't easily scratch when rubbed with abrasives. No wonder chrome is the most popular finish for bathroom faucets and hardware. But chrome can be deposited on plastic as well as on brass or zinc, and chrome-plated brass and chrome-plated plastic or zinc faucets look a lot alike, so much so that it can be impossible to tell what a faucet body is actually made of when holding it in your hand. Chrome plating will protect the outside of inexpensive faucets for a time, but the internal workings will still corrode or wear out sooner rather than later, making more expensive brass actually more economical in the long run. Chrome-plated zinc faucets won't be as durable as solid brass, but they will last longer than plastic-bodied faucets, which will eventually start to lose their chrome plating.

New Life for Brass Finishes

Chrome is a proven durable finish for bathroom faucets, but new technology makes a durable, nontarnishing, polished brass finish possible too. Different manufacturers have different names and different proprietary processes for this type of finish. For example, Moen calls their brass finish Lifeshine and the process used to create it a Moenite hardening process. Delta's brass finish is called Brilliance (it is also used in some Weiser Lock and Alsons products, two other divisions of Delta's parent Masco Company). What these new brass finishes all have in common is a lifetime guarantee against tarnishing, corroding, or discoloration. For anyone who has ever installed a beautiful $700 polished brass faucet that has tarnished in a few short years, this is great news.

Specific information about the exact technical process that these companies use is hard to come by. The Brilliance finish isn't sprayed on, but uses what Delta calls Physical Vapor Deposition (PVD), or low-voltage ionization that electrochemically bonds the finish to the product. Moen is even more obscure about the details of its process, simply saying that it is the same precision engineering used to make silicon chips and fighter jets.

The result of these processes is a finish that the manufacturers claim will stand up as well as chrome to chemical cleaners, salt air, and abrasive powders. And I have to admit that a recent live demonstration of this type of finish's durability had me convinced about the product claims. I had the chance to take some steel wool and try to scratch one of these faucets—to no avail. These finishes seem to perform as claimed, and if they don't, there seem to be pretty solid lifetime guarantees that provide recourse.

Admittedly, the finishes look a little too bright and too polished for my tastes; after all, it isn't really brass that you are looking at. And I'm a lot less bothered by tarnish than other folks; in fact, I like the look of age that an old brass faucet has. But if you or a client is looking for a new faucet with a shiny brass finish that will last and last, it looks like a good solution is at hand.

Delta Select's Contemporary series faucet is an updated version of a traditional two-handled style with an increasingly popular white finish. (Photo courtesy Delta.)

Even though brass is durable and won't corrode, it will oxidize in contact with air. So those beautiful polished brass faucets need to be protected by some finish. Steer clear of sprayed-on lacquer finishes, especially for faucets in high-volume locations, because lacquer doesn't stand up very well to bathroom cleaners or water. A better choice is a clear epoxy coating, which is much more durable and resistant to scratches. But epoxy coatings are also somewhat susceptible to the solvents and abrasives sometimes used in bathroom cleansers, so in heavy-use and high-maintenance locations a chrome finish might be a better choice. A relatively new look for bathroom faucets are

white epoxy finishes, which are baked on and quite durable and easy to keep clean (see the photo at left).

Types

In general, faucets fall into either one of two broad categories: faucets that are operated with separate controls for hot and cold water and faucets that regulate water volume and temperature with a single control. Originally, faucets were simply valves (or taps) at the end of the hot- and cold-water supply lines, and any mixing of hot and cold water was done in the sink itself. Some people prefer the antique look of these simple taps, and there are still many old and functional bathrooms with this arrangement around. But modern mixing valves with a single spout are certainly more convenient, as anyone who has tried to temper the scalding hot water from the hot side with cold water from the cold side can attest.

Stem faucets Faucets with individual controls for hot and cold water are known as stem faucets. Standard stem faucets consist of two valve seats (one for hot water, one for cold) with hard-rubber seat washers mounted on valve stems to control the amount of water flowing toward the spout (see the drawing on the facing page). This type of faucet relies on compression between the washer and valve seat to seal out water, so it can start to leak when the rubber washer starts to wear out or when the valve seat becomes pitted or scratched. Replacing the washer is cheap and easy to do, and worn valve seats can be reground or replaced, if necessary. I've found that sometimes all it takes is a bit of polishing with 400-grit sandpaper to clean up the valve seat. This type of faucet is relatively inexpensive to manufacture and is quite reliable, though some consider it a nuisance to replace the washers periodically.

Most manufacturers are now producing stem faucets that utilize cartridges rather than threaded valve stems with screw-on washers. Some cartridges have spring-mounted rubber washers to control water volume. Other types of cartridges utilize washerless ceramic disks, which are unaffected by temperature, sediment, or minerals in the water supply. Though ceramic valving is initially more expensive than other types of valving, ceramic disks are extremely hard and offer reliable, smooth, consistent performance. In some types of cartridges, the plastic or rubber washers are replaceable, while in other types the entire cartridge will need replacing if leaks develop, which is considerably more expensive than a little rubber washer.

The standard distance between the valves of a stem faucet is 4 in., though many widespread faucets with widths of 8 in. or more are also available. Widespread faucets have individual valves and a separate spout connected by flexible tubing, rather than a one-piece body like the smaller 4-in. center-set faucets. In addition to looking better, these widespread valves are easier for most people to use and to

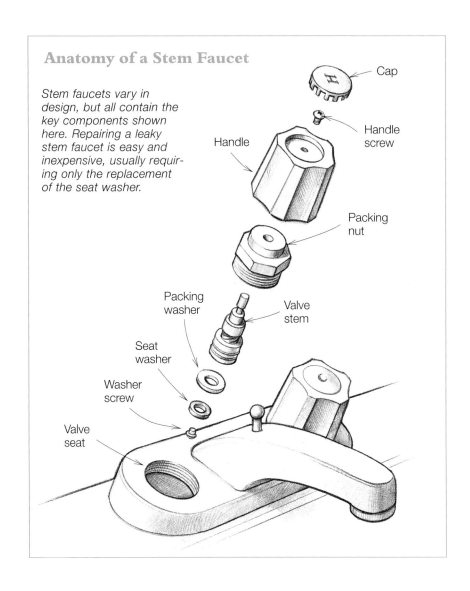

Anatomy of a Stem Faucet

Stem faucets vary in design, but all contain the key components shown here. Repairing a leaky stem faucet is easy and inexpensive, usually requiring only the replacement of the seat washer.

Cap

Handle screw

Handle

Packing nut

Packing washer

Valve stem

Seat washer

Washer screw

Valve seat

Single-Control Faucet Designs

Single-lever ceramic disk faucet

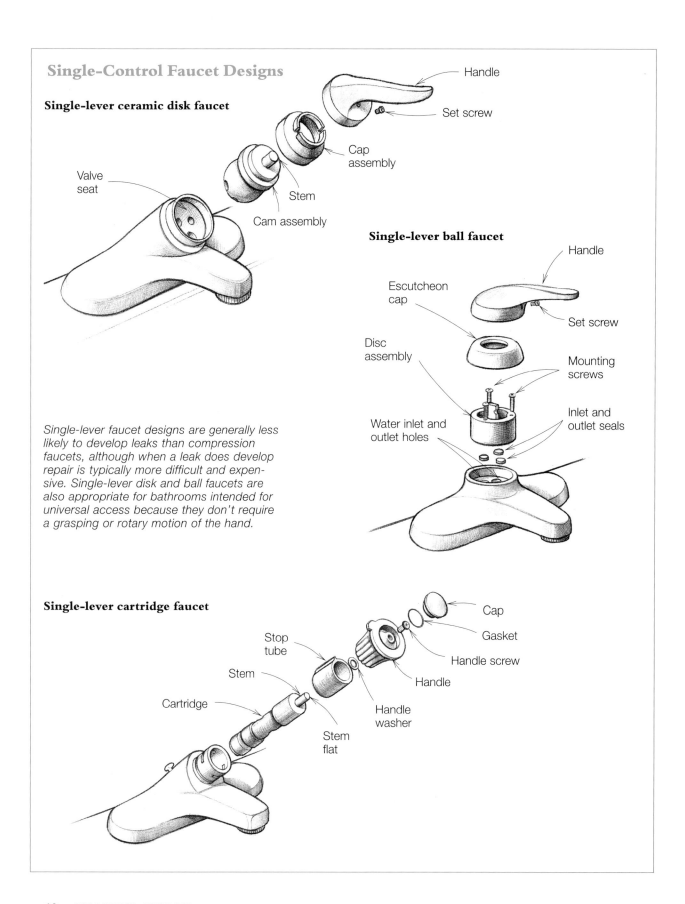

Handle

Set screw

Cap
assembly

Valve
seat

Stem

Cam assembly

Single-lever ball faucet

Handle

Escutcheon
cap

Set screw

Disc
assembly

Mounting
screws

Water inlet and
outlet holes

Inlet and
outlet seals

*Single-lever faucet designs are generally less
likely to develop leaks than compression
faucets, although when a leak does develop
repair is typically more difficult and expensive. Single-lever disk and ball faucets are
also appropriate for bathrooms intended for
universal access because they don't require
a grasping or rotary motion of the hand.*

Single-lever cartridge faucet

Cap

Gasket

Handle screw

Stop
tube

Handle

Stem

Cartridge

Handle
washer

Stem
flat

keep clean because there is a lot more room between the handles. Because many sinks are often predrilled with mounting holes for the faucet, you'll have to know the faucet type when you choose your sink, and vice versa.

Single-control faucets Single-control faucets usually incorporate the valves and spout in a single deck-mounted unit, and a knob or lever is used to control both water volume and temperature (see the drawing on the facing page). Ceramic-disk valving is the most reliable (and most expensive initially) approach to single-control design, and the control action is typically quite smooth and leak free.

Lever-operated ball faucets are a little more variable in performance. While the better ones have balls that are machined to close tolerances, balls that are out of round will have high and low spots that make leaks more likely, and the normal grinding action of the ball against the softer valve seats will eventually wear them down, again causing leakage. Balls in this type of faucet can be either plastic, brass, or stainless steel.

Single-lever cartridge faucets that are pulled to turn on and pushed to turn off are relatively inexpensive and provide good performance initially. But the cartridge sleeve is continually exposed to air, water, and soap residues that wash the cartridge lubricants away and leave a residue behind. The cartridge becomes stiffer to use, making volume control difficult, particularly for kids.

One last point about selecting bathroom faucets. Think about the faucet spout and how the sink will be used. Most bathroom faucet spouts are really too low for anything other than rinsing off a toothbrush or filling a glass of water. For comfortably washing hands, face, or hair, a spout should really be almost 8 in. to 10 in.

While more often seen in the kitchen, faucets with detachable spray heads offer more versatility for washing face, hands, or hair at the bathroom sink. (Photo by Scott Phillips.)

above the rim of the sink and the flow of water should be directed toward the center and away from the back of the bowl, a configuration that you don't often see. Gooseneck-style faucet spouts come close to allowing these clearances, but an alternative is to include a separate deck-mounted spray head (like the one found at a kitchen sink). Another option is the faucet spout with an integral and detachable spray head that is often used in kitchens (see the photo above). And remember that spouts that are higher above the rim of the sink will tend to splash if the sink basin isn't very deep.

Chapter 4

CHOOSING TUBS, SHOWERS, AND SPECIALTY UNITS

If you haven't flipped through a bathtub manufacturers' catalog lately, you're in for a bit of a surprise because there are a lot of bathing options available now that weren't just a few years ago. Besides standard tubs, there are whirlpool tubs, tubs with massaging pillows, tubs with built-in electronically controlled multihead showers, showers with steam and scent generators, showers with foot bubblers…the list goes on and on.

Does a bathroom really need all of these bells and whistles? That's like asking if a car really needs air-conditioning and a CD player. Remember, a bathroom is a place of refuge, a place to feel good, as well as a place to get clean. A basic tub or shower will do the job of cleaning the body, but the new bathing systems offer a chance to indulge the need for pampering. But before trying to sort out all of these options for customizing the bathing environment, it helps to know a little bit about the basic materials that are being used to build these bathing beauties.

Like a full-service station for the body and soul, the new shower-bathing systems offer both efficient cleaning and leisurely relaxation. (Photo courtesy Kohler Co.)

BATHTUBS

Bathtubs are available in all shapes, sizes, and materials. I've seen some stunningly beautiful custom bathtubs built out of stainless steel, nickel silver, or even wood, and I've seen square tubs, round tubs, heart-shaped tubs, and even coffin-shaped tubs, some of them big enough for the whole family. But for the most part residential bathtubs are either made out of plastic or out of a base metal (typically cast iron or steel) coated with porcelain enamel.

The standard bathtub measures 60 in. long, between 30 in. to 34 in. wide, and 14 in. to 20 in. deep. Tubs generally can be either freestanding, have one or more aprons so that they can be recessed into corners or alcoves, or be designed to be dropped in (like an overgrown sink) into a site-built platform.

Enameled cast iron and steel

To my mind, enameled cast-iron is the material of choice for bathtubs. But that doesn't mean that I like moving those things around. Weighing 350 lbs. or more, cast-iron tubs aren't easy to haul up a stairway or maneuver through doorways and into tight spaces. When it comes to performance, though, cast-iron tubs are hard

Keeping the Old

Old tubs can be a real bear to remove from a bathroom. So if they're in good condition, the right color, and in the right place, why not leave them as is? I think an old cast-iron tub in good condition with a new tile or solid-surface surround is a much better (and less expensive) solution than a new plastic combination tub/shower unit once you factor in the labor of removing the old unit and installing a new one. Some chips and stains in fiberglass or porcelain enamel can be economically repaired—at least compared to the cost of replacement—by specialists who are experienced in this type of work (you can find them in the Yellow Pages under "Bathtubs and Sinks-Repairing and Refinishing").

If both the tub and surround are in unsalvageable condition, calling in a specialist to reline the tub with an acrylic liner may be a cost-effective alternative to tearing everything out and starting from scratch. These liners install directly over the existing tub and surround in about a day, saving on the expense and mess of renovation.

If you do decide to keep the existing tub, you'll probably want to replace old shower valves with new pressure-balancing valves. However, if the existing valve is in good condition and replacing it would mean digging through a sound shower surround to get to it, you might want to consider installing an in-line pressure-balancing valve instead. If the old shower valve is a two-handle valve and will be replaced with a single-handle pressure-balancing valve, many manufacturers offer a retrofit escutcheon to cover the old handle openings.

The surround is usually what gives most people who are disgusted with their bathrooms enough motivation to call in somebody to disrupt their bathrooms (and their lives) for a couple of weeks or so. Loose tiles, missing or mildewed grout, deteriorating wall panels, and just plain old leakage through seams are the most common complaints. Loose tiles can be reattached, but generally they come loose for a reason, and that reason is usually moisture in the wrong place. More caulk, grout, and adhesive aren't going to fix this problem, but throwing out the tub just because the wall is leaking doesn't make sense either.

While the customer is always right, exploring all of the options when considering whether to gut or rehabilitate the bathtub can save the client a lot of money and the builder a lot of aggravation.

to beat. The same mass that draws curses when trying to move the thing makes it perfect for holding the heat of a hot-water soak once the tub is in place. Cast iron is quiet when water is running into it, and the smooth, hard porcelain surface is extremely durable and easy to clean. I like it because it feels solid under foot, without that flexing and sponginess you sometimes feel when standing or sitting in a plastic tub. I also like cast iron because it can take a scrubbing and scouring with abrasive cleansers without scratching.

Because of the limitations of the manufacturing process and the weight of cast iron, you won't find it being used for tubs with complex shapes or for those that are much bigger than the standard 5-ft. or 6-ft. tub. A traditional cast-iron tub design is the freestanding claw-foot tub, a style that has been popular ever since Kohler introduced the first modern tubs before the turn of the century. For a time, these tubs were like white elephants, and after being pulled out of a remodeled bath in favor of combination tub/shower units, they were almost impossible

Cast-iron tubs are available in both conventional and traditional claw-foot designs and come in a number of different sizes. Small tubs are perfect for pets or kids. (Photo © Carolyn Bates.)

American Standard's Americast tubs are durable and perform like cast iron but weigh about 50% less, are less prone to installation damage, and are warmer and quieter. (Photo courtesy American Standard, Inc.)

to give away. Now, though, antique claw-foot tubs that are in good condition are increasingly hard to find, and they fetch top dollar at any of the numerous architectural salvage shops that have sprung up around the country. Of course, manufacturers have now reintroduced these tubs in their lines, in both traditional and modern interpretations (see the left photo above).

Enameled cast iron does have some drawbacks besides weight, however. On the one hand, the extremely hard porcelain surface is very durable, but if it does get chipped or scratched, it can be almost impossible to repair (although there are proprietary methods of resurfacing porcelain tubs that can apply a simulated porcelain-like surface). And for the same reasons that cast iron is good at retaining the heat from hot water, it is also good at remaining cold, especially if the tub is located on a poorly insulated outside wall or in a cold and drafty bathroom. There is nothing quite like the feeling of leaning back while

taking a nice hot soak, only to feel the almost-electric shock of a cold tub on your back.

Enameled-steel tubs have the look of cast iron but with a considerable weight savings. Once a less expensive and widely used alternative to cast iron, steel tubs have been replaced for the most part by fiberglass and acrylic units, although they are still available and often used in hotels and motels. You can also find plenty of them at salvage yards and junkyards. In most cases, you'll find that their thinner enamel coating has worn or chipped away in places, making them not worth salvaging. A recent innovation that combines the durability of cast iron with the lighter weight of steel is American Standard's Americast, which uses an injection-molded structural foam and metal alloy base for the porcelain-enamel finish that results in considerable weight savings without sacrificing durability or performance (see the right photo above).

Plastic

Most people are familiar with gel-coated fiberglass, a material that revolutionized the boating industry. The same qualities that serve it so well in the boat-building industry—strength, light weight, design and construction versatility, and economy—are the reasons that fiberglass has captured such a large part of the tub market. But gel-coated fiberglass also has some problems. The relatively thin and soft gel-coat finish is prone to scratches and abrasive damage. In fact, most abrasive cleaners can't be used with this type of tub without fear of damage to the finish. And the gel-coat finish will tend to oxidize and eventually fade, which is particularly noticeable with some of the brighter colors.

Cast cross-linked thermal-formed acrylic tubs have found a niche as a more expensive but more durable alternative to gel-coated fiberglass. The manufacturing processes for both types of tubs are similar, and, in fact, both acrylic and gel-coated fiberglass tubs use fiberglass as a backing material. The difference is in the first layer, the one that you can see.

Gel coat is a pigmented polyester resin that is sprayed onto a mold in a thin 1/64-in.-thick layer. Subsequent layers of fiberglass are then added, building up to a thickness of about 1/8 in. or so. Various "inclusions"—foam, wood or wood composites, or corrugated paper—are added to provide structural rigidity before the unit is popped off of the mold. Acrylic, on the other hand, begins as about a 1/8-in. sheet that is heated and vacuum-molded to the form in a process essentially the same as that used by the toy Vacu-forms that were so popular some years back. The fiberglass backing is then applied in the same way, before the tub is popped off the mold. ABS is sometimes used as a less expensive substitute for acrylic.

Compared to cast-iron tubs, acrylic and ABS tubs are also relatively soft but less prone to scratching than fiberglass. Unlike fiberglass, however, acrylic color is solid, and scratches can be repaired by sanding them out and rebuffing. But significant damage to acrylic or ABS—for example a rupture of the skin—is more difficult to repair than damage to fiberglass. Acrylic is more expensive than fiberglass but less expensive than cast iron, and it is resistant to ultraviolet rays and harsh chemicals.

Another method that is sometimes used in tub manufacture is injection molding. Hot liquid plastic is injected into a hollow mold, then removed when it cools. There are no reinforcing laminations, though there are sometimes sound-deadening undercoatings sprayed on, so the tub's strength is dependent on the strength of the plastic. ABS and acrylic-fortified PVC can be used in this process, resulting in inexpensive and relatively durable tubs. My experience with these tubs is that their finish tends to dull quickly, and they feel very flexible due to the lack of structural reinforcement.

American Standard's Idealcast combines the performance of acrylic with a rigid and sound-insulated composite underbody. (Photo courtesy American Standard, Inc.)

Flexibility is a problem that is shared by all plastic tubs, whether they are laminated or injection molded. While reinforcing and additional layers of fiberglass add strength and rigidity, they also add to the manufacturing cost of the unit. So better-quality—and more expensive—plastic tubs will have thicker walls, be heavier, and feel more rigid. Still, I find the give of a plastic tub more than a little disconcerting. It can be more than an aesthetic problem, too: If a plastic tub isn't adequately reinforced under foot and near the drain, the continued flexing is apt to cause the drain connection to loosen, creating a potential point of leakage. Look for adequate reinforcement in this area; also, a field application of mortar between the floor and the underside of the tub can help to stiffen things up (see Chapter 10 for more on installation). American Standard developed Idealcast, which incorporates an acrylic shell with an injection-molded structural composite underbody, to offer greater structural rigidity than what is normally available in acrylic tubs (see the photo on the facing page).

A relatively new tub material, sheet-molded composites (SMCs) combine polyester resins, chopped glass fibers, and fillers into a strong product that can be molded into one-piece tubs. SMCs are more rigid than conventional fiberglass-reinforced tubs, but my experience is that they are a bit more susceptible to staining than acrylic. Vikrell (from the Sterling Plumbing Group) is probably the most successful of the SMCs (see the photo above).

WHIRLPOOL TUBS

A whirlpool tub is a logical upgrade from a standard bathtub if a quality unit is chosen and the installation is done well. Whirlpools can fit in the space allotted an ordinary bathtub, can provide the same dual bath/shower function, and won't necessarily add megabucks to the bathroom budget. Avoid the temptation to

Kohler's Overture tubs are made with Vikrell, an advanced composite with performance characteristics similar to acrylic and a high-gloss finish. (Photo courtesy Kohler Co.)

stretch a fixture budget by substituting a bargain-basement whirlpool for a quality standard bathtub, though, because installing an inappropriate inexpensive whirlpool is an invitation to disaster. Cost cutting in construction will necessarily compromise quality—not a good idea in a fixture intended for long-term use.

Acrylic seems to be the consensus choice as the best whirlpool material. Some whirlpools can get to be quite large, making cast iron an impractically heavy choice. There are cast-iron units on the market, but they are typically standard-size tubs and are more expensive than comparable acrylic units. Less expensive gel-coated fiberglass tubs are also available, but they stain and scratch too easily and fade too quickly to justify adding expensive pumps and jets to them.

A whirlpool-tub installation involves quite a few different tradespeople working in and around the tub, which creates considerable potential for damage. Because scratches in acrylic are so easily repaired and because acrylic is so resistant to staining and chipping, it is easier to ensure a perfect installation with this material.

Whirlpools come in a range of shapes and sizes, starting with standard and ranging up to spa size. (Don't confuse a whirlpool with a spa, though; whirlpools drain after every use, while spas and hot tubs don't and rely on chemicals to keep the water clean.) Some whirlpools have molded-in seats, armrests, headrests, even lighting systems. Some are built for one; some are built for two. Choosing a whirlpool is a highly individualized choice, much more so than a basic tub or shower, and features that make it attractive to one person may make it less attractive to another. For example, two-person whirlpools hold a lot of water, so it takes a long time to fill them up. There are quite a few people out there who can't conceive of bathing with another and for whom having room for two is uneconomical and unnecessary.

At the heart of every whirlpool are the pump, jet, and control system. Again, jet configuration is a matter of both taste and the style of the tub. One nice feature that you might consider is recessed jets in the backrest of the tub. These bring massage action to bear on the back while reclining, but they don't poke out from the surface of the tub. In general, smaller whirlpool tubs typically have four jets, while larger models have between six and eight jets. Tubs with fewer and larger-diameter jets located higher on the tub walls tend to produce a gentle swirling action, while tubs with more small-diameter jets are intended to introduce more intense massage action on specific points of the body.

The pump is what pushes water to the jets, and its power can range from less than 1 hp to 2 hp

or more; smaller (less than 1 hp) pumps operate on a standard 120-volt circuit, but larger pumps usually require a 220-volt circuit. Some pumps have two or more speeds, or even a variable speed control. Some are operated by a nonelectric air switch located right on the tub, while others are operated by a timer, which can't be located closer than 5 ft. from the tub according to code. That means that if the timer shuts off the pump before you are ready to get out, you'll have to get out to reactivate it. Make sure to provide for pump access when planning tub installation because this too is required by code.

Whirlpools can hold between 50 gallons and 140 gallons of water. The NKBA recommends sizing the water heater for two-thirds the capacity of the tub, so in many cases an extra water heater may be required, either to boost total domestic hot-water capacity or as a dedicated water heater for the tub only. In-line heaters are also available that can extend the soak time in the tub because they continually reheat the water circulating through the pumps. These heaters require a separate 240-volt circuit.

One last note about whirlpool tubs. When filled to capacity with water and people, these things are heavy. How heavy? Well, a tub with 125 gallons of water weighs nearly a half-ton, and that is before you add people to it. While floor systems are usually designed for loads of about 40 lbs. per square foot, bathroom floors might well require a 65-lb.-per-square-foot load-bearing capacity. Depending on the size of the tub and the condition of the existing framing, the floor system may need to be reinforced.

SHOWERS

Soaking in a nice hot tub, with or without whirlpool/massage action, is certainly a luxury. But when time is a luxury that few can afford, a shower is a more efficient means of getting clean. You would be hard-pressed to find a modern bathroom that didn't have a shower,

Acrylic tub/shower units are available in a number of different configurations, ranging from the standard combination tub/shower to this whirlpool with detached shower module. (Photo courtesy Lasco.)

either as a self-contained unit or in combination with a tub (see the photo above). Simply put, showers are a necessity of modern American life.

Unfortunately, the most common type of shower in American bathrooms leaves something to be desired. While the ubiquitous combination tub/shower has the advantage of packaging a bathing and showering area into a meager 15 sq. ft.—no mean feat when space is at a premium—there are trade-offs, perhaps the most important being safety. The curved sides of a conventional bathtub and the oftentimes slippery porcelain or plastic surface contribute to the fact that the bathtub is one of the most dangerous spots in the home. The actual standing area is often less than 20 in. wide, and the water controls are usually inoperable unless standing directly in the shower stream, an

uncomfortable place to be when there is a surge of hot or cold water.

Nevertheless, the combination tub/shower continues to be a popular choice in both new construction and renovation. Builders like these units because they are quick to install and relatively foolproof, while homeowners like them because they don't leak and they're easy to keep clean. One-piece tub/shower units in acrylic (at the higher end of the price scale) or gel-coat fiberglass (at the lower end) are common in new construction, while two- or three-piece units are suitable for renovation and remodeling work because they can be broken down into smaller components that fit through interior doorways, then be reassembled on-site. One-piece units are virtually leak free, but two-

and three-piece units don't present much of a leakage problem either if they are well designed and manufactured and assembled correctly.

Prefabricated showers

If space isn't at a premium and there is room for both a shower and a tub, or if a shower is all that is desired for a particular bathroom, then there are a number of different styles and sizes of prefabricated shower stalls. These range from simple fiberglass or acrylic stalls to self-contained shower modules with options like built-in seats, electronically controlled multiple showerheads, and steam generators. In addition to the regular square and rectangular shapes, prefabricated showers are also available in angled shapes—commonly called neo-angle—to fit into corners

and in multipiece configurations, which may be the only way to fit them into a bath renovation (see the left photo below).

Bigger shower stalls offer more room for features like shelves and molded-in seats. Many units have integral grab bars for safety, although they might not necessarily be rated at the required strength or located properly for ASTM certification (or ANSI Z124.1 or Z124.2). Bigger units also offer more room for bending over to

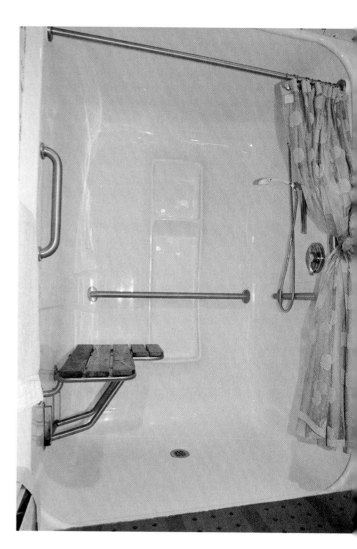

Some shower stalls are manufactured to be assembled on-site, which makes them suitable for renovation work.

A wheelchair-accessible shower stall can fit in the space of a standard tub. Note the folding shower seat and the absence of a curb.

wash legs or for standing out of the shower stream, as well as room for two people to use the shower comfortably at one time. And in addition to the features mentioned previously, some shower stalls have a deeper base, allowing the inclusion of a foot massage. Expect to pay over $1,000 for one of these units.

Prefabricated shower units that are designed for universal access are also available. Typically, these units feature low curbs to make it easier for wheelchair entry and exit and extensive grab bars, as well as options like fold-down transfer seats (see the right photo on the facing page).

Custom site-built showers

Though a totally custom-built shower is technically demanding, I find these showers to be the most satisfying from a builder's standpoint because of the personal satisfaction that comes from creating something from scratch, rather than simply installing components like a technician. Waterproofing such an enclosure is a challenge, however, and in many cases using a premanufactured shower receptor—a waterproof base with a drain already installed—is a cost-effective middle-of-the-road approach. These one-piece receptors are manufactured out of a variety of materials, including fiberglass, acrylic, and cast polymers, and are available in a number of colors, shapes, and sizes. Waterproof sidewalls will still need to be built on-site, but the labor and worry of installing a waterproof shower pan while still retaining a considerable degree of design flexibility are eliminated.

In addition to the personal satisfaction of building a custom shower, there is the flexibility in materials and design that these showers allow. And while materials like fiberglass and acrylic have found wide acceptance in bathroom construction, I still think that natural materials like tile, glass block, and stone have a solid feel under foot that makes them compelling

alternatives to plastic, with a real feeling of quality (see the photo below).

Wall-less showers I've seen a number of appealing ideas recently in custom shower design. One approach is to eliminate the shower walls altogether, waterproof the entire bathroom floor with the use of a waterproofing membrane, and simply situate the shower valve, showerhead, and drain in one corner of the bathroom. A curtain can help to control the splash if the bathroom is quite small, while a larger room might not need any curtain at all if the other fixtures aren't affected by an occasional splashing. This type of shower is particularly appealing for wheelchair users, as it eliminates many of the maneuvering problems

A custom-built shower in ceramic tile or stone is durable, easy to maintain, and has a solid and substantial feel. (Photo © Carolyn Bates.)

associated with bathroom stalls and curbs. Of course, the bathroom will often have a wet floor, which might be a problem, and the entire floor will have to be sloped ¼ in. per ft. toward the drain, but if the floor is a radiantly heated slab (a commonly used approach in this type of bathroom), then the floor will dry out quickly, at least during the heating season.

If a wall-less shower isn't an option, you might consider a doorless one. Again, the shower area has to be sufficiently large, and the controls and showerhead need to be situated so that oversplash doesn't cause any problem with adjoining fixtures (nobody likes to sit on a soaking wet toilet seat, and most cabinets and countertops suffer from constant exposure to water). While oftentimes a shower stall might be deep enough so that a door is simply unnecessary, sometimes simply angling the entrance to the shower will keep water where it belongs. Again, building this type of shower without curbs will make it easier for wheelchair users to use it.

Multiple showerheads There's no rule that states that showers may have only one showerhead, though in most combination tub/showers this is the only alternative. But if a shower has room for two people, then installing two showerheads is a good idea. A configuration that I like is a standard fixed showerhead as the main unit, with a track-mounted handheld shower located on an adjacent or opposing wall. At minimum, each showerhead should have its own volume control, but adding a second valve will provide the option of independently controlling temperature as well. Mounting the handheld shower on a track makes its height adjustable, an especially useful feature for households with children who have outgrown the tub. Showerheads should be mounted so that a person can stand with his head and neck out of the spray, not usually possible with conventional showerheads roughed in at 66 in. high. Besides being convenient for body and

hair washing, a handheld shower mounted on a long-enough hose is also great for rinsing out a shower stall after cleaning.

In addition to showerheads for overall use, consider installing body-spray units too. These offer horizontal spray hydromassage to specific areas of the body. Some have adjustable spray patterns, some are designed to be mounted individually, and some are mounted as complete units (see the photo below).

One point to remember when installing multiple showerheads is that they require a lot

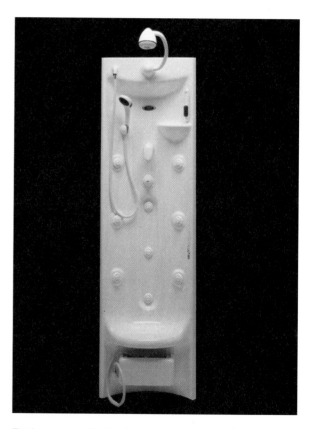

Body-spray units for hydromassage can be mounted individually, but they are also available as preplumbed units for easier installation. (Photo courtesy Lasco.)

of water; simply using ½-in. supply lines won't provide sufficient volume or pressure. In most cases, ¾-in. supply lines and mixing valve will be necessary, as will a manifold loop to equalize pressure and temperature at all of the spray heads (see the drawing below). Also, keep in mind that the flow rate for individual showerheads shouldn't exceed 2.5 gpm (gallons per minute), but that in a multihead system the cumulative demand on the hot water supply will be much greater.

Steam showers It isn't that difficult to add a steam shower to a regular shower enclosure. Compact and self-contained steam generators for residential use are now available that will easily fit in an adjacent vanity cabinet or closet. These generators typically require their own 220-volt circuit and are sized according to the volume of the shower stall. Hookup is relatively simple, with usually a ⅜-in supply line off the hot-water line and a ½-in. copper line supplying the steam to the enclosure. In order for the steam generator to work effectively, the stall

A Shower with Multiple Showerheads

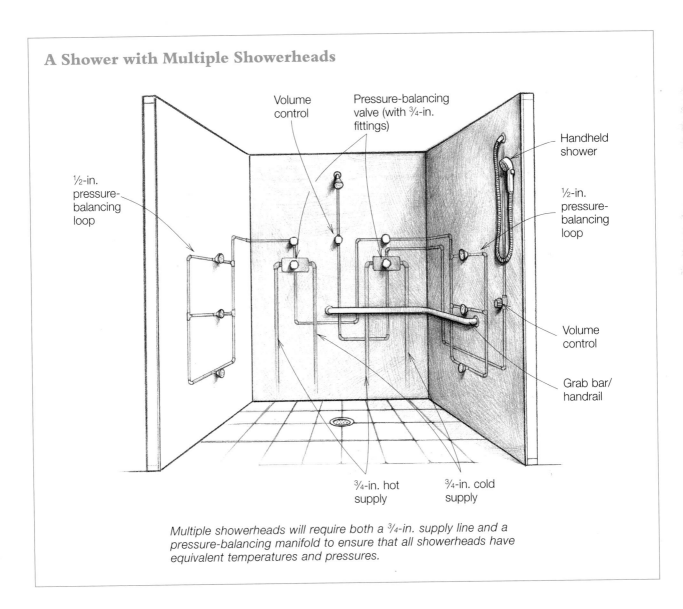

Volume control

Pressure-balancing valve (with ¾-in. fittings)

Handheld shower

Handheld shower

½-in. pressure-balancing loop

½-in. pressure-balancing loop

Volume control

Grab bar/handrail

¾-in. hot supply

¾-in. cold supply

Multiple showerheads will require both a ¾-in. supply line and a pressure-balancing manifold to ensure that all showerheads have equivalent temperatures and pressures.

Compact steam generators and full-height doors transform a regular shower enclosure into a spa. (Photo courtesy Lasco.)

Full-size panels of custom-cut marble (shown here) or Corian eliminate the grout lines of a traditional tile shower surround.

needs to be vapor-proof, which might mean that curb-to-ceiling doors, additional glass panels, or a vapor-proof ceiling needs to be added (see the left photo above).

TUB/SHOWER SURROUNDS

Any discussion about tubs and showers would be incomplete without mentioning the option of adding a shower surround to a conventional or whirlpool tub mounted against the wall. This surround can be either prefabricated or custom-built, depending on the project budget, and allows a builder to add a custom element to this space relatively economically.

Prefabricated surrounds are available in different materials, including ABS, fiberglass, acrylic, and decorative laminates. Typically, these surrounds are in three, four, or five pieces to accommodate variations in tub length. Some surrounds have built-in shelves and grab bars, while others are just flat panels. These surrounds are quick and easy to install, generally requiring only a bit of cutting around the valve openings and adhesive to attach them to the walls. Besides the individual drawbacks related to the specific type of material that surrounds are made of, plastic surrounds also feel flimsy to me, and their seams are prone to leakage, particularly around the base where the edge of the surround butts against the tub. This is a difficult joint because it is here that water tends to collect, and relying on caulk to make a long-term waterproof seal is a sure-fire recipe for problems later on. I think this is potentially the ugliest spot in the bathroom, especially when mold starts to grow—a common condition with silicone caulk.

Surrounds can also be constructed out of sheet goods like high-pressure (HP) decorative laminates and low-pressure (LP) melamine laminated boards. More expensive surround options include natural stones, like marble or granite (see the right photo on the facing page), and solid-surface materials, like Corian, which help to solve the flimsiness problem but are still prone to the caulking problems mentioned previously. Solid-surface materials are more adaptable to customizing because they can be routed, cut, and laminated on-site. Ceramic tile is a traditional choice for shower surrounds; its hard surface feels solid and is easy to keep clean (see the photo at right). (For more on shower surround materials, see Chapter 6.)

The simplest way to prevent water from splashing out of a tub or shower is with a shower curtain mounted on a curtain rod. These don't necessarily have to look tacky, although they certainly often do. Brightly colored curtains on combination tub/shower units in a child's bathroom somehow seem appropriate and have the advantage of being easily pushed aside for full access to the tub; shower curtains also work well on shower stalls in cramped quarters. Plastic and nylon effectively shed water and work well as liners, but they aren't very pleasing to the touch. Better curtains in treated cotton and cotton/nylon blends are sometimes treated with water repellents and mildewcides.

Glass doors are usually considered to be an upgrade from shower curtains, but they aren't without their problems. In a confined area, pivoting glass doors or hinged doors can swing out into floor area needed for maneuvering or

Ceramic tile is a functional surround material that can transform a simple space into an elegant design. Lit by its own skylight, this tiled surround was designed by Sarah Susanka. (Photo by Kevin Ireton.)

Swinging glass doors offer easy access to a shower in a large bathroom, but they tend to drip water on the floor when they're opened after a shower. (Designer Paul Egee. Builder Stephen Tobin. Photo by Kevin Ireton.)

into an adjacent fixture. I've also noticed that they tend to drip a lot of water on the floor when they're open. Sliding doors don't have this problem, but they cut in half the available entry space into a tub. While this might not sound like a problem, try giving a child a bath in a tub with sliding glass doors to find out how limited this access can actually be. Accordion folding

doors are also available, with multiple panels that fold flat against each other when open, providing more access through the opening and less interference with the free space in front of the tub or shower. These doors aren't generally as waterproof, however, and there is a lot of hardware to keep clean and free of mildew. Showers designed to fit into corners can have

TUB AND SHOWER VALVES

Until recently, I was one of those who believed that a hot-water supply meant a *very* hot water supply. I guess I believed that dirty dishes didn't come clean unless the water was painfully hot, and that the same held true with bodies (or at least there had to be the capability of boosting the temperature of the shower way up). And after all, didn't automatic dishwashers need extremely hot water? But a recent experience has helped to change my way of thinking regarding water temperature.

My recently toilet-trained three-year-old daughter had just finished going to the bathroom and was in the process of washing her hands. I'm usually there to help her, but this particular time the phone had just rung and I was in the process of answering it. The bathroom faucet is the push/pull type with a twist-control temperature setting that is easy to adjust but difficult for a small child to turn on and off. This faucet seems to be either fully on or fully off, and in my daughter's case she had turned it fully on while the faucet was at its maximum hot setting. Usually hot water takes a little while to reach the faucet, so there isn't a problem because the faucet gets turned off again quickly. But my daughter sometimes dawdles, and the water temperature had worked its way up to maximum before she finally stuck her little hands in.

Fortunately, our domestic hot-water supply is temperature-controlled to 120°F, which was hot enough to hurt and scare her but not hot enough to cause any burns. But had the same sequence of events happened elsewhere, the burns might have been severe.

Temperature control of the domestic hot-water supply is just one part of a plan to minimize the chance of hot-water burns in the bath or shower. The other is the use of antiscald valves, now required by the four national plumbing codes. That means that most building codes will

Glass shower doors come in a number of configurations, including this neo-angle unit, which is popular for corner showers. (Photo courtesy Kohler Co.)

either a curved front and a corresponding curved shower door or a faceted front (often called neo-angle) and a regular swinging flat-panel door (see the photo above).

Glass doors are usually constructed of ⅜-in. or ½-in. tempered glass, which can be clear, frosted, mirrored, or custom patterned. Frameless enclosures maximize visibility for a shower space with a more open feel, while framed enclosures have a more self-contained and traditional feel. Frames are usually of aluminum or of brass, and they can also be powder-coated in white or colored finishes.

Pressure-Balancing Valves

Piston-type valve

When the water pressure drops on the cold side (a toilet flushing, for example), the increased pressure on the hot side pushes the piston over, which closes off the inlet on the hot side and balances the pressure. This system is slightly noisier than the diaphragm style (right) and more expensive.

Diaphragm-type valve

A flexible rubber diaphragm between the cold and hot water supplies in the valve continually adjusts to pressure fluctuations, maintaining an equalized flow of water. This type of valve may reduce the flow rate as it reacts to pressure fluctuations, but will recover pressure as the supply pressures normalize.

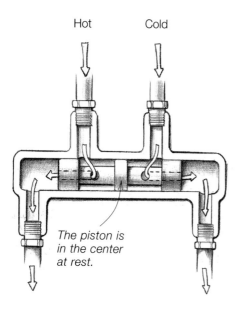

Hot   Cold

The piston is in the center at rest.

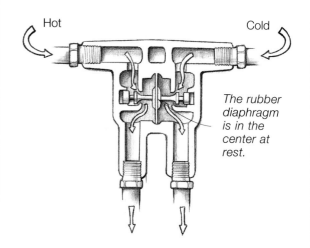

Hot   Cold

The rubber diaphragm is in the center at rest.

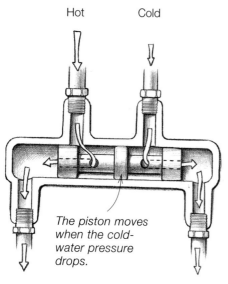

Hot   Cold

The piston moves when the cold-water pressure drops.

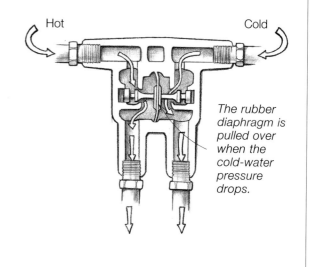

Hot   Cold

The rubber diaphragm is pulled over when the cold-water pressure drops.

require them for new construction and oftentimes for remodels as well. Anyone who has experienced the wild temperature swings of a shower when a toilet is flushed nearby can vouch for the necessity of these valves.

Most antiscald valves for residential use are pressure-balancing units operating either with a piston or with a rubber diaphragm (see the drawing on the facing page). The Symmons Temptrol 2000 valve is a popular type of piston valve extensively used in my region of the country (see the right photo below). Moen's Moentrol is another popular valve of this type (see the left photo below). Grohe's Temprasafe valve is an example of a rubber-diaphragm valve, as is Kohler's Rite-Temp unit. (See Resources on p. 209.)

Symmons Temptrol 2000 pressure-balancing valve. (Photo courtesy Symmons.)

Moen Monticello Moentrol single-lever pressure-balancing valve. (Photo courtesy Moen.)

Pressure-balancing control valves are typically single-handle units and come in two types. Units like the Moentrol and Symmons can adjust both water temperature and volume. Other units, like Grohe's Taila (see the left photo below) are cycling-type valves and are either all the way on or all the way off; the lever controls the water temperature only. Two-handle pressure-balancing valves are also available. Delta Select's Scald-Guard valve controls water volume with the left handle and water temperature with the right (see the right photo below).

Pressure-balancing valves can also be added in-line with a conventional faucet set. This is particularly appropriate in a traditional bath with a two- or three-handle control and in retrofits. Precision Plumbing Products makes the Tempera Automatic Compensating Valve, which is an in-line pressure-balancing valve designed to be used in conjunction with an existing tub/shower valve without antiscald capability (see Resources on p. 209). This unit costs around $70 (plus the labor to install it).

Another antiscald valve is the thermostatic valve, which isn't widely used in the United States. These valves are generally two to four times more expensive than pressure-balancing valves. Combination valves respond both to temperature and pressure-balance changes.

All antiscald valves are not created equal. The recent almost-universal acceptance of these valves in new construction and remodeling has created a surge in demand and a corresponding surge in production by manufacturers to meet product demand. There are less expensive, do-it-

Grohsafe Taila single-handle pressure-balancing valve. (Photo courtesy Grohe.)

Delta Select Scald-Guard two-handle pressure-balancing valve. (Photo courtesy Delta.)

Showerhead Options

I'm a big fan of handheld showerheads mounted on an adjustable track. An important component of an adjustable showerhead system is the hose, particularly if there is a volume-adjustment valve on the showerhead. I've seen hoses blow out because of the water pressure or wear out because the quality just wasn't good enough and the hose kept on twisting and kinking. It's worth the extra money to buy a hose that can take the added water pressure and physical abuse.

Both handheld and fixed showerheads can suffer from lime buildup, which can clog jets and reduce the volume of water flowing through the system (or deflect it all over the place). Grohe's SpeedClean system is an attempt to minimize this problem, with a flexible conical-shaped silimer spray-nozzle design. Any lime that does accumulate does so at the tip of the nozzle, and wiping the nozzle clean bends the resilient surface and flakes the lime away.

Showerheads with different types of (and sometimes adjustable) spray patterns are available for fixed showerheads, for handheld showerheads, and for wall-mounted body sprays. Again, quality counts: There are a number of inexpensive hardware-store massage showerheads available with a lot of plastic parts, but the more expensive solid-brass units will perform better for a longer time. Different manufacturers call the spray patterns by different names, such as a soft or hard jet spray, an air-mixed "champagne" spray, or a pulsator spray.

yourself valves out there that simply don't perform as well as the proven models. Any plumber who has installed these valves can give a good personal recommendation on what to buy and what to avoid based on his experience.

SPECIALTY UNITS

For those who take their showering and bathing seriously there are totally integrated units that combine all of the features and functions mentioned previously into a preplumbed, prewired spa. Like one-piece acrylic combination tub/showers on steroids, these bathing systems offer add-on options like steam heat, foot massage, fragrance injection, bubbler systems, full multijet whirlpool functions, mood lighting, and a heated blower. Some of these systems offer plenty of room for two and built-in reclining seating, while others are more compact. The appeal of these units is that they function for both those in a hurry and for those who want a more leisurely bathing experience, but they don't take up the space required by a separate custom shower and whirlpool tub.

Dedicated saunas offer a drier heat than steam baths, though steam can be introduced by splashing water on the heated rocks. Sauna kits designed for residential use are available in a number of different configurations. While panelized, insulated, and fully plumbed enclosures are available, it is also possible to buy just the heating and control units. A panelized, insulated enclosure can make an extravagant addition to a large bathroom. Amenities like this or an exercise area require lots of room, which rules out their use in most bathrooms. However, these functions can often be accommodated in separate but adjacent areas to the bathroom.

Chapter 5

CHOOSING SYSTEMS

HEATING

VENTILATION

LIGHTING

While there may be some who enjoy the bracing feeling of taking off all of their clothes in a cold, drafty, poorly lit room, I'm not one of them. So I like to see particular attention paid to controlling the climate in the bathroom. Maintaining the right temperature—called the comfort zone by industry professionals—controlling humidity, and providing appropriate task and general lighting is probably more challenging in the bathroom than in any other room in the house.

HEATING

Central heating systems aren't typically designed around the specific needs of a bathroom, but sometimes I think that they should be. Designing a whole-house system is outside the scope of this book, but it's important to know a bit about them. Working with the heating contractor, it's possible to optimize the performance of the system, both in new construction and in a remodel or a renovation.

The goal of the heating system should be to maintain a comfortable temperature that is within the occupant's comfort zone. Plan on maintaining a temperature about 5° higher than other parts of the house because bare wet skin is sensitive to cool temperatures and drafts that might not be a problem in the rest of the house. Providing a separate heating zone controlled by a thermostat is the most effective way to do this without overheating adjacent areas.

Assessing Existing Bathroom Systems

If you are remodeling a bathroom instead of starting from scratch, you'll need to determine which bathroom systems need to be upgraded to meet codes and to ensure that the bathroom is safe and functional.

To determine if the plumbing system is adequate, you should check water-supply pipes to make sure they are sized to provide an adequate volume of water to each bathroom fixture, and look for unvented or undersized drains as well, a real problem that is quite common in older homes. Venting a fixture properly can become a real thorny issue in a renovation because it is often unantici-pated and can involve opening up walls. Other things to look for include the presence (or absence) of shut-off valves, leaky pipes, and an adequate hot water supply.

The big wild card is changing fixture locations. Practically speaking, there isn't a lot of difference between changing the location of a toilet 1 ft. or 10 ft.; in both cases a large drain pipe will have to be cut and moved. Moving any plumbing fixture involves substantially more work than simply replacing it, particularly if access to the floor system is limited.

Don't ignore the bathroom's heating system, which often isn't up to the task of keeping its occupants comfortable. If the heating system has insufficient capacity, it will need to either be upgraded or supplemented with another heat source.

Usually a bathroom isn't a very large space, and a ceiling-mounted fan/light/heater will sometimes provide adequate supplemental heat. I think that tying into the existing system is a better option when feasible, either to provide more capacity or to upgrade the heat-delivery system (for example, with new adjustable diffusers or new baseboard convectors). Remember, too, that heat is more effective when delivered at or near floor level, something that a ceiling-mounted heat source has trouble with. Upgrading a bathroom's heating system can involve considerable expense, however, particu-larly if the existing system is marginally adequate itself.

Almost inevitably, the electrical system in an old bathroom will be subpar, usually because there will be no GFCI protection. It isn't unusual to find a bathroom without any outlets, except perhaps an ungrounded one in the medicine cabinet.

Unswitched light fixtures and non-GFCI-protected outlets will need to be disconnected and replaced with a code-compliant system, which usually means bringing another electrical circuit to the bathroom. An additional circuit might be required, too, for a supplemental electric heat source if the primary heat system is inadequate.

A ventilation system may also need to be installed or upgraded. Many bathrooms don't have a ventilation fan, and many that do have noisy ones. It's also important to make sure that the fan is ducted correctly with either metal or PVC duct directly to the outdoors. I've seen some fans ducted into an attic, apparently in the hope that the humid exhaust air would eventually escape through gable vents. It will, but not before its moisture condenses on cold sheathing and framing, eventually causing them to rot. I'm not much impressed with flexible plastic duct either because it deteriorates rapidly and develops holes and leaks. It's easy to install and that fact alone often makes it an attractive choice, but it just won't hold up well in the long run.

Hydronic heating systems—where water is heated by a boiler and distributed through pipes to radiators or convectors—are common where I live in New England. Forced-air systems are the other main type of central heating system, with a furnace heating air that is then distributed throughout the house via ducts. Electric heat is a third option, though whole-house systems in colder climates aren't very practical due to the high cost of electricity. Each of these systems has their advantages and disadvantages relative to heating a bathroom.

Hydronic systems

The first centralized heating systems were hydronic—large boilers generating hot steam that circulated out to cast-iron radiators. While the original boilers for these systems are, for the most part, long gone, there are still a fair number of heavy, hissing steam radiators around. These radiators have a certain charm, but they're also bulky, heavy, and hard to keep clean. That is why most hydronic systems use hot water instead of steam, and baseboard fin-tube convectors have replaced those big radiators for the most part (see the drawing on the facing page).

This is a popular type of heating system for many good reasons. Less drafty and generally quieter than forced-air systems, hydronic baseboard heat also has less of a tendency to dry out the air, and it is easily divided into separate thermostatically controlled zones. But there are a couple of problems with baseboard heating in the bathroom. The first is the problem of wall space for the convectors. Usually space is at a premium in a bathroom, and adequate lengths of baseboard convectors have to compete with the fixtures for room on the walls. Sometimes you'll find runs of baseboard convectors extending behind the toilet, which in my general experience is a mistake. That is a pretty moist environment, with splashover and condensation from the toilet, and it doesn't take long for the steel housings on the baseboards to start to corrode and rust.

Runtal's Omnipanel wall-mounted radiator is ideal where space is limited. It is adaptable to either hydronic or electric heat and doubles as a towel bar. (Photo courtesy Runtal North America, Inc.)

Also, many fin-tube convectors are—to be brutally honest—pretty clunky looking. In a larger room they aren't as obtrusive, but in a small bathroom they are very noticeable. An alternative is to use a thin-profile baseboard like Runtal's (see Resources on p. 209), which is only 2 in. deep and which varies in height from 3 in. to 12 in. off the floor, depending on the heat output of the unit. With a heat output of about 900 BTU/hour per running foot for the 12-in.-high 4-tube unit, this baseboard is well suited for the limited free wall space of a bathroom. Another solution is to use a wall-mounted panel radiator; some of them can double as a towel warmer (see the photo at left).

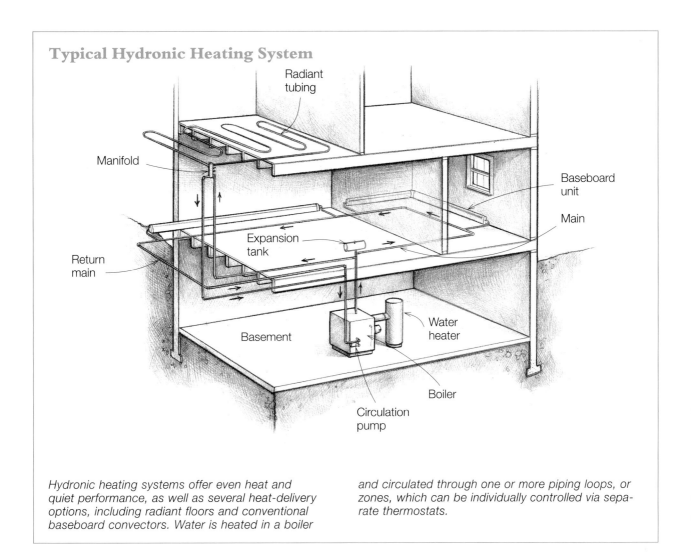

Typical Hydronic Heating System

Radiant tubing

Manifold

Baseboard unit

Main

Expansion tank

Return main

Water heater

Basement

Boiler

Circulation pump

Hydronic heating systems offer even heat and quiet performance, as well as several heat-delivery options, including radiant floors and conventional baseboard convectors. Water is heated in a boiler and circulated through one or more piping loops, or zones, which can be individually controlled via separate thermostats.

If there is a vanity in the bathroom, another option is to mount a compact fan-coil convector underneath, in the toekick space. These units tie into the existing hydronic system; they have a small electrically driven fan, which circulates air around a heating coil before blowing it out into the room. They put out plenty of heat, typically have an adjustable blower, and the warm air they exude feels good on the feet without being so hot that it might burn them.

In my experience, these fans can be pretty noisy, and they also require a working water temperature of about 140°F to put out adequate heat, so they don't work very well with lower-temperature systems (like heat pumps). Another problem is their lack of a filtration system. The fans pull in air along the toekick, generally a very dusty place, and it doesn't take long for the fins on the blower to get clogged up with dust, cutting into the performance of the blower. And I haven't been very impressed with their longevity; replacing or servicing a unit mounted underneath a cabinet is not fun, even with an access panel cut into the bottom of the cabinet.

Hydronic systems are also well suited to providing radiant heat, an increasingly popular way to warm a home. Instead of being routed through convectors, radiant hydronic systems

Radiant Heat in the Bathroom

If you can imagine an invisible and silent heating system that puts warmth exactly where you need it—at floor level—then you can imagine radiant heat. Radiant heat is surprisingly adaptable to both new bathroom construction and bathroom renovation work, depending on the type of central heating system the house has. Hydronic radiant heating is the most energy-efficient type of radiant heat, but new materials and techniques for installing electric radiant heat make this an appealing alternative as well.

Hydronic radiant tubing has typically been installed in concrete slabs, but it can also be installed both above the subfloor in a 1½-in.-thick concrete or gypsum-based thin slab or stapled beneath the subfloor utilizing aluminum heat-transfer plates. Hydronic tubing can also be installed in the ceiling, beneath a walk-in shower, or even in a wall, turning any of these surfaces into a large low-level heat radiator.

Where a hydronic heat source isn't available, electric radiant heat can be a cost-effective alternative. Hydronic radiant-heat systems have a long cycling time: They heat up and cool down slowly, so usually the thermostat controlling them remains relatively constant. Electric radiant heat, on the other hand, has a quick response time. The heat can be turned on only when needed, like a light, and the room quickly warmed. After use, the system can be turned off again to conserve energy.

There are several different electrical radiant-heating methods. Perhaps the most versatile is a thin mat that is applied to the subfloor with thinset just before the tile is set. This system's main advantage is that it only raises the finish floor elevation about ⅛ in., making it a good choice for retrofits. Some types of hardwood flooring and carpeting can also be used with this product. Another system relies on cables that are set into either a ½-in.-thick mortar bed on top of a conventionally framed subfloor or into a regular concrete slab floor. A third type of system is a foil consisting of an electric heating element sandwiched between two layers of mylar. Sheets of this foil can be installed beneath the subfloor between the floor joists or between the ceiling joists and the finished ceiling.

A final type of radiant panel is comprised of a gypsum sheet embedded with electrical wiring. These ½-in. panels can be installed and finished just like regular drywall and turn the wall or ceiling into a radiant surface. This type of system has a slower cycling time than other types of electric radiant heat.

Slab-on-grade radiant-floor heating system

Slab-on-grade systems are economical when a concrete floor is already planned.

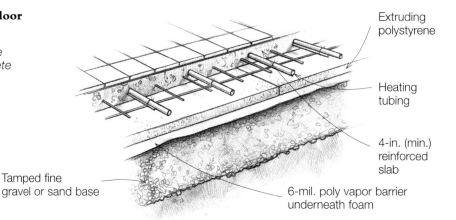

Extruding polystyrene

Heating tubing

4-in. (min.) reinforced slab

6-mil. poly vapor barrier underneath foam

Tamped fine gravel or sand base

Plate-type radiant floor system

Plate systems are a good choice for above-grade bathrooms and for renovations.

Heat-transfer plates installed above the subfloor

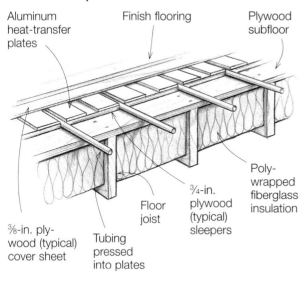

Aluminum heat-transfer plates

Finish flooring

Plywood subfloor

Poly-wrapped fiberglass insulation

¾-in. plywood (typical) sleepers

Floor joist

Tubing pressed into plates

⅜-in. plywood (typical) cover sheet

Heat-transfer plates installed below the subfloor

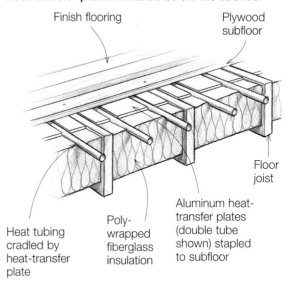

Finish flooring

Plywood subfloor

Floor joist

Aluminum heat-transfer plates (double tube shown) stapled to subfloor

Poly-wrapped fiberglass insulation

Heat tubing cradled by heat-transfer plate

Thin-slab radiant-floor heating system

1½-in. thin-slab systems offer the heating efficiency of a slab-on-grade system but can be used with conventionally framed floor systems.

Portland-cement-based thin slab

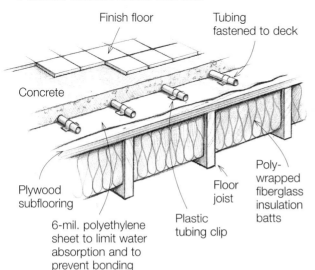

Finish floor

Tubing fastened to deck

Concrete

Poly-wrapped fiberglass insulation batts

Floor joist

Plastic tubing clip

Plywood subflooring

6-mil. polyethylene sheet to limit water absorption and to prevent bonding

Gypsum-based thin slab

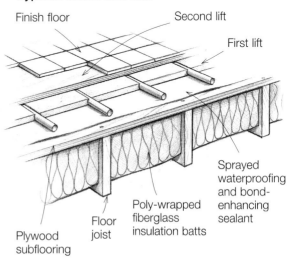

Finish floor

Second lift

First lift

Sprayed waterproofing and bond-enhancing sealant

Poly-wrapped fiberglass insulation batts

Floor joist

Plywood subflooring

send heated water through flexible plastic pipes buried in the floors, walls, or ceilings, turning these surfaces into heating elements. Though more expensive than regular convection hydronic heat, radiant systems offer invisible mechanical presence, quiet operation, and even and predictable heat (see the sidebar on pp. 86-87).

Forced-air systems

Forced air, the other main type of central heating system, distributes warm air that is heated by a furnace through a system of supply and return ducts (see the drawing below). This type of system is more economical to install than a hydronic system, and it is generally easier and more economical to extend this type of system in a remodel or renovation, particularly with the new insulated flexible ducts that are now available. The same ductwork can also be used to add central air-conditioning to a house, a decided advantage in warmer climates.

While forced-air systems can heat a space rapidly, some people find the air motion and noise associated with this type of system objectionable. More important, in the bathroom moving air—warm or not—will feel like a draft

A Forced-Air System

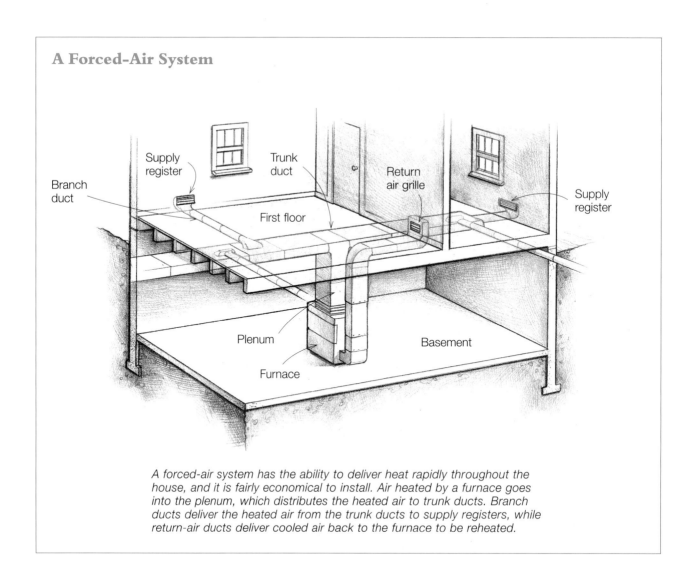

A forced-air system has the ability to deliver heat rapidly throughout the house, and it is fairly economical to install. Air heated by a furnace goes into the plenum, which distributes the heated air to trunk ducts. Branch ducts deliver the heated air from the trunk ducts to supply registers, while return-air ducts deliver cooled air back to the furnace to be reheated.

on bare wet skin, though registers with diffusers that direct air away from vulnerable bare skin will help, particularly if they have adjustable vanes. If there is a vanity, the supply register can sometimes be mounted in the kickspace. Air stratification—layers of air of different temperatures—is less of a problem if supply registers are mounted close to the floor because hot air rises, mixing in with and warming existing air.

Like many other smaller rooms that have a typical forced-air system, bathrooms often don't have return-air intakes. Usually there is enough air circulation underneath the door and into the adjoining room, although larger bathrooms would probably benefit from having both a supply and a return.

Electric heat systems

There was a time not so long ago when utility companies throughout the country encouraged the installation of electric heat systems. Power was plentiful, and electric resistance heat was cheap to install because there was no plumbing, ductwork, furnaces, or boilers. Energy policies changed dramatically during the 1970s, though, when oil prices shot up and nuclear power began to lose its luster. Skyrocketing electric bills forced many to augment their simple electric baseboards with more esoteric heating solutions, such as off-peak thermostats and massive electric thermal storage units.

Electric resistance heat is still around, but in anything other than a mild climate these systems are economical only during installation. I've pulled more than a few electric baseboards out during renovation projects, as well as their more energy-efficient and technologically advanced electric upgrades. But in moderate climates and within the relatively small space of the bathroom, electricity is still a viable option for supplying heat.

Besides conventional baseboards, electric resistance heat—where heating elements convert electricity directly into heat—can be provided by drywall-like radiant panels that install just like regular drywall on walls and ceilings. Also, several different systems are available for heating radiant floors electrically. Electricity's greatest advantages are its minimal infrastructure requirements and low installation costs, making it perhaps the best choice for supplemental heating systems (see below).

I should also mention electric heat pumps, which have become increasingly popular in moderate climates because of their capacity to both heat and cool a house. Heat pumps operate a bit like a giant refrigerator, using electricity to transfer heat from one source to another. The transfer medium is a special refrigerant fluid that is contained in a continuous tubing loop. Air-source heat pumps have given way recently to ground-source heat pumps in which the tubing loop runs vertically or horizontally underground because ground-source heat pumps are effective year-round and are quieter.

Supplemental heat sources

A properly planned bathroom in new construction should not require a supplemental heat source. Often, though, the cost of extending an existing hydronic or forced-air system in a remodel or an addition is prohibitive. In some cases, the new bathroom may be too far away from the furnace, or perhaps there is no additional capacity in the existing system to supply more heat. In this situation, where upgrading the entire heating system isn't a practical choice, a supplemental heat source might be more appropriate.

I don't much like recommending electric heat because it's expensive to operate, but in this case it makes sense. Adding an additional electrical circuit is inexpensive, and because these heaters don't see continuous use, their power demand

Understanding Heat Loss

While heating and cooling systems are intended to mechanically offset the effects of heat loss and gain, oftentimes not enough attention is paid to the factors that cause it in the first place. These include the size and type of windows relative to the room size, the functional amount of insulation (as opposed to the nominal amount—more on this later), and the degree of air infiltration through windows and doors and through air leaks in the floor, walls, and ceiling.

A heat-loss analysis, done by an independent energy consultant or an HVAC contractor, will take into account these and other factors in order to establish how much heat should be made available to heat a particular space. But before figuring out how to supplement heat, a conscientious builder should first figure out how to avoid losing it.

Windows—skylights in particular—can be a major factor contributing to heat loss (and gain). Some building codes specify the allowable amount of window area relative to the total square footage of a room; most bathrooms, which have relatively little available outside wall area anyway, have little difficulty meeting these energy-efficiency

requirements. Besides, windows also contribute natural light and (if they are operable) ventilation; except in unusual circumstances, the challenge is usually in figuring out how to gain more window area in a bathroom, not reduce it.

Skylights can sometimes provide this additional fenestration, but they can cause some special problems in a bathroom. In a cold climate, warm and humid air will come in contact with the cool glass of the skylight, causing water vapor to condense and quickly cooling the air. This cooler air will then sink, reinforcing an air-circulation pattern that can feel like a draft to someone sitting in a tub (see the drawing on the facing page).

Effective insulation will make a big difference in reducing the amount of supplemental heat that a bathroom will need. While local building codes establish minimum standards for insulation in new construction, pay special attention to installing it correctly, making sure that there are no voids or places where some of the other trades have pushed aside insulation. Take the time in a renovation to ensure that there is adequate insulation in a wall or ceiling, which might mean digging into the wall cavities

or blowing in insulation. And no matter what its nominal R-value is, fiberglass batts—by far the most common residential insulation—won't stop air flowing through it. In order for it to work effectively and provide its rated R-value, wall and ceiling cavities need to be completely filled, and routes for air infiltration through the insulation need to be blocked off.

Air infiltration is an often-overlooked part of a heat-loss analysis. Old and rattling windows are an obvious culprit that most analyses take into account. Less obvious are air bypasses in the building shell and, more important, in the ceiling. Heated air will pressurize the bathroom, and any leak—around a ceiling-mounted ventilation fan, a recessed light fixture, a crack in old plaster—will allow the warm and often very humid air to escape into building cavities. Not only will this draw in cooler outside replacement air and cause drafts, but the warm, moist air will also condense when it hits the cooler surfaces in the building cavities, causing moisture damage. Sealing up these leaks is not difficult and will result in both a healthier building and a less-drafty bathroom.

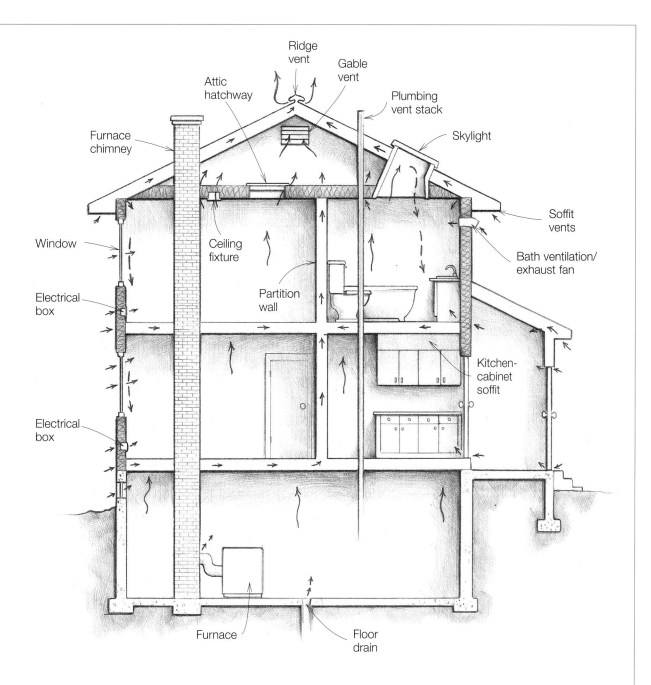

Ridge vent

Gable vent

Attic hatchway

Plumbing vent stack

Furnace chimney

Skylight

Window

Ceiling fixture

Soffit vents

Electrical box

Partition wall

Bath ventilation/ exhaust fan

Electrical box

Kitchen- cabinet soffit

Furnace

Floor drain

Air infiltration is the primary cause of heat loss in the typical home. Heated air pressurizes a house (a bit like a balloon) and escapes through any holes or cracks it can find, particularly in the ceiling. As it escapes, it draws in cool outside replacement air, creating chilling drafts. Warm rising air also cools as it comes into contact with the cool surfaces of windows and skylights and sinks back toward the floor, creating a con- vection loop that can also cause chilly drafts, which will be especially noticeable on bare wet skin.

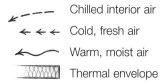

Chilled interior air

Cold, fresh air

Warm, moist air

Thermal envelope

When a bathroom doesn't get quite enough heat, a supplemental electrical heater can make it more comfortable without necessitating costly alterations to an existing system.

should be relatively low. Keep in mind that electric heat is generally the most expensive per BTU to operate; flipping a switch is easy, but you might want to do the math to find out exactly how much these heaters will actually cost to run. Don't use a portable plug-in electrical heater, though; these units don't belong in the bathroom because of the hazard of electrical shock.

Auxiliary electrical heaters can rely on either convection or radiation to distribute heat. Radiant heaters, including infrared heat lamps, are quiet and perfect for heating specific areas, like right over the tub. Convection heaters, which rely on natural air movement or a fan to circulate air over a heating element, are better for general room heating. Ceiling-mounted units, often in combination with a light and ventilation fan, are the most commonly used types of convection heaters, though there are more powerful wall-mounted units available as well (see the photo above).

Keep in mind that the surface of an electrical heating unit can get hot. Wall-mounted units shouldn't be placed where they can accidentally get bumped into or where exploring little fingers can get burned. Combination fan/light/ceiling heaters typically get placed above or close to tubs, but this isn't the best location because the blowing air will make the bather below feel chilly, even though the air is warm.

VENTILATION

One thing about my ex-wife that used to drive me crazy was that she would never turn on the bathroom fan when she was taking a shower. I understood her reservations: The fan was noisy and it seemed to make our drafty bathroom worse when it was on; and besides, she liked it nice and steamy in there. Sure, the wallpaper was peeling off, and strange things were growing up in the corners, and yes, she would try to remember next time...but still that fan stayed off.

I remember the considerable conflict of interest between the builder part of me and the husband part of me. I didn't want to make an issue out of a problem that was, in the big picture, a rather trivial one. The problem was, we were both right: The fan was too noisy to be comfortable, but the bathroom needed to be ventilated, too. Fortunately, this problem is easy to fix because there are plenty of low-noise fans that are available that can move the proper volume of air that bathroom ventilation requires without necessitating earplugs.

Not all bathrooms require mechanical ventilation. Those with operable windows that provide an open area equal to at least 10% of the floor area of the bathroom are excused by code, but not by common sense. Opening a window is a good idea and a simple way to bring in fresh air, but for children or the elderly this isn't always an option. And it's not always pleasant to have an open window on a cold winter day. So mechanical ventilation is usually a good idea, and there are ways to ensure that bath fans get used, too. One way is to couple the fan to a humidistat so that it operates whenever the bathroom environment reaches a certain humidity level (see the left photo below). This is probably the best solution. Another approach is to put the fan on a timer; this doesn't ensure that the fan will be turned on, but it does ensure that it will be turned off. A third approach is to wire the fan and main bathroom light so that they are controlled by the same switch. Of course, this solution means that the fan is on considerably more often than it needs to be, wasting resources by exhausting heated air out of the house and consuming electricity (though the current required by most fans is quite modest).

Fan noise is rated in sones—the lower the sone rating, the quieter the fan. According to the Home Ventilating Institute (HVI), the noise level of a quiet refrigerator in a quiet kitchen is equal to about 1 sone. In technical terms, a sone is equal in loudness to a tone at 1,000 cycles per second (cps) at 40 dB above the threshold of hearing. A sone rating of 2 is twice as loud as a sone rating of one; a sone rating of 4 is 4 times as loud as a sone rating of 1. Some of the quietest fans are now rated at less than 1 sone (see the right photo below), while anything louder than 3 sones is probably just too noisy for a residential bathroom.

Fans are sized according to the volume of air they can move in cubic feet per minute (CFM). Research by the HVI indicates that the optimal air-change rate for most residential bathrooms is 8 per hour. This means that mechanical or natural ventilation systems should be capable of completely exhausting and resupplying fresh air to a bathroom 8 times over the course of an hour in order to ensure that

Broan's Sensaire series of ventilating fans respond automatically to rises in humidity levels—good insurance that the fan will be turned on when the shower is. (Photo courtesy Broan.)

A noisy bath fan is annoying, but there are quiet fans. One of Broan's low-sone (0.3 to 1.5) Solitaire-Ultra Silent series fans makes less noise than a refrigerator. (Photo courtesy Broan.)

Heat-Recovery Ventilation

One of the goals of a builder is to build a tight, energy-efficient house. This means that cold outside air is supposed to stay outside, while warm inside air is supposed to stay inside. But what does a bathroom ventilation fan do? It takes warm inside air and sends it outside. This might seem counterproductive, but in an older house with a lot of air infiltration this loss isn't much of a problem because fresh make-up air is always plentiful.

In a tight house that experiences very few air changes per hour, ventilation fans pull a considerably larger percentage of a heating system's output right out of a house. Another problem is that tight houses have a limited fresh air supply due to their lack of excessive air infiltration, so a bath ventilation fan can actually pull in outside air from combustion-appliance exhaust vents, a dangerous condition known as backdrafting.

Heat-recovery ventilators are designed to both exhaust stale indoor air and supply fresh air, and they have become increasingly important for maintaining air quality and minimizing heat loss in a tight house. They draw in cool fresh air from outside with one blower, while removing warm and moist inside air with another. The two air streams pass through a heat-exchange-core, transferring the heat energy from the outgoing warm, stale air to the incoming cooler, fresh air.

Operating at around 75% efficiency, heat-recovery ventilators are available in a number of sizes ranging from room size to whole-house size and are particularly cost-effective in northern climates.

Heat-recovery ventilators (HRVs) transfer heat that is normally lost from stale outgoing air to fresh incoming air. There are several different types of heat-exchange cores used in HRVs, but the flat plate core is the most common. HRVs are available in sizes to fit a room to those that fit the whole house.

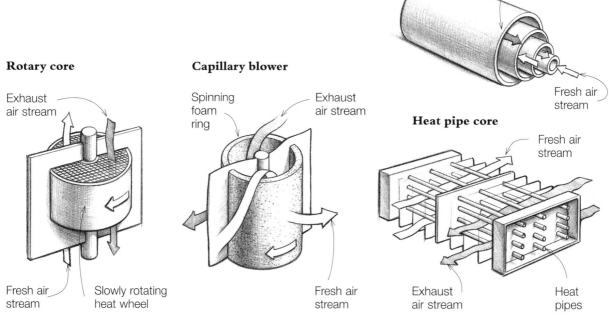

Concentric tube core

Exhaust air stream

Fresh air stream

Rotary core

Exhaust air stream

Fresh air stream

Slowly rotating heat wheel

Capillary blower

Spinning foam ring

Exhaust air stream

Fresh air stream

Heat pipe core

Fresh air stream

Exhaust air stream

Heat pipes

Heat-recovery ventilators are available with a range of capacities and are well suited for ventilating bathrooms in a tight, energy-efficient house. (Photo courtesy American Aldes Ventilation Corp.)

Flat plate core (counter flow)

Fresh air stream

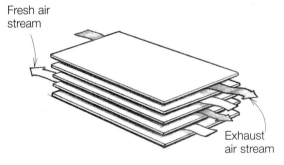

Exhaust air stream

Flat plate core (cross flow)

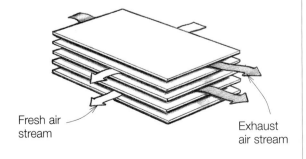

Fresh air stream

Exhaust air stream

odors and humid air are properly eliminated. To calculate the CFM capacity needed for a given-size bathroom, first determine the floor area and multiply that number by the factor 1.07 (assuming an 8-ft. ceiling). For example, 5 ft. by 9 ft. = 45 sq. ft. (floor area). Multiply that by 1.07 and you get 48.15, so the recommended fan capacity would be 50 CFM. When sizing a ventilation system, keep in mind that extensive duct runs and corners dramatically decrease the fan's efficiency and may require that a larger-capacity exhaust fan be specified.

Another variable to consider in calculation includes the length and type of the duct run. Flexible duct is easier to snake around obstructions but creates considerably more air resistance than rigid duct. Again, duct runs with many turns and corners require a stronger fan to move the same volume of air than a relatively straight run. When installing the ductwork for a ventilation system, avoid the commonly available flexible plastic duct. This stuff is quick and easy to install, but I've seen too many of these installations where there are holes and leaks, or where the plastic has deteriorated. Galvanized aluminum or rigid plastic ABS or PVC ductwork is a far better choice in the long run.

There are a number of different types of ventilation fans on the market, including those that are combined with lights and/or heaters in the same housing. Another option is to use a remotely mounted ventilator with multiple intake ports. These units are suitable for either intermittent or continuous ventilation; some are designed for use in a single bathroom, while others can ventilate a number of rooms simultaneously (see the photo on p. 96). Remotely mounted ventilators are generally quieter because they are isolated from the area

Multiport ventilators have powerful fans to handle long duct runs and can ventilate a number of rooms simultaneously. (Photo courtesy Fantech.)

being ventilated, though the HVI currently has no sone ratings available for these units. They are usually able to handle longer duct runs and can often can be located so that servicing them is easier.

LIGHTING

Most builders don't think a lot about bathroom lighting because it tends to fall on the design side of the design/build equation. But lighting principles aren't that hard to understand, and it doesn't take an architect or an interior designer to come up with a workable and thoughtful lighting plan for a bathroom. Generally speaking, a well-lit bathroom relies on a combination of appropriate natural lighting—supplied by windows or skylights—supplemented by artificial task and general lighting—supplied by well-placed light fixtures.

Natural light

Natural light is always desirable. Besides being more energy-efficient than a room that relies totally on artificial light, a room well lit by natural light provides a psychological boost, and a good bathroom design will include appropriate windows and/or skylights. Of course, in new construction, window placement is often dependent on the other windows of the exterior elevation, so that there may not be a lot of flexibility there. And in a remodel, oftentimes the window locations are predetermined. To compound the difficulties, bathrooms are usually fairly small rooms with a lot of big fixtures to fit in, so finding an appropriate spot for a window can be a challenge. But there are some window options that address the special needs of the bathroom.

Privacy is one of the big issues, and a bathroom with a lot of glass in a highly visible location might feel too exposed. To avoid this, plan (if possible) for window placements that are relatively high on the wall—arched-top windows are good in this situation—or that readily accommodate treatments like blinds (see the left photo on p. 98). Frosted or etched glass treatments might be appropriate in this situation, as might one of the new electrically controlled glass frostings that can transform clear glass into translucent glass. Some windows have integral blinds between the inner and outer glass, a good choice for reduced maintenance.

I have to admit a certain ambivalence about roof windows, or skylights. On one hand, they can introduce five times the light of a regular window with the same size opening, and they can do this while not compromising privacy. Also, any chance of breaking up the flat plane of a ceiling is a good idea, and light shafts that connect the ceiling to the roof are dramatic. Skylights can admit natural light to a bathroom without an outside wall, and an operable skylight is a great natural ventilator, especially in warm weather. On the other hand, skylights are prone to condensation, particularly in the

Windows and skylights can provide natural light and ventilation, as well as a dramatic view. (Photo © Carolyn Bates.)

high-moisture environment of the bathroom. Even the most energy-efficient ones contribute significantly to heat loss, and the area under a skylight can feel drafty because of convection currents created by the close proximity of cool and warm air.

If you do install a skylight, be aware that skylights in different roof locations will produce different types of light. North-facing exposures will always generate a soft, diffuse light. East-facing exposures introduce plenty of morning light, great for waking up to. South- and west-facing exposures have the potential of introducing too much light (and heat gain) into a bathroom. Make provisions for shades and appropriate glass coatings to reduce unwanted heat gain in this type of installation. The shape of the shaft will also influence how much light is admitted by a skylight. While straight shafts are the easiest to frame, insulate, and finish, I prefer flared shafts because they introduce more light and are more interesting architecturally.

While large windows like this arch-topped eyebrow dormer window offer a dramatic view, privacy can be an issue when choosing and placing windows.

A tubular skylight's glare-free natural light and R-22 insulation make it a good choice in the bathroom because it won't have problems with drafts and condensation. (Photo courtesy Tubular Skylight.)

As an alternative to a traditional skylight, consider installing a tubular skylight (see the right photo above). These skylights are essentially highly reflective shafts with a clear plastic dome that admits natural light on the top and a diffuser lens on the base. They look and install a bit like a metalbestos chimney and range in size from 8 in. to 21 in. in diameter. While they don't ventilate like an operable skylight, they do have an R-22 insulation rating and admit a glare-free natural light. Tubular skylights are a particularly good choice in a bathroom with no exterior walls and a long distance between the bathroom ceiling and the roof because the light shaft can range from 10 ft. (for the 8-in.-diameter model) to 30 ft. (for the 21-in.-diameter model) in length. The diffuser lens looks like a contemporary light fixture and is less intrusive than a regular roof-window shaft.

Glass block is another alternative to traditional fenestration and can let in plenty of light while maintaining privacy. Installations can be as simple as a conventional window opening that has been retrofitted with glass block or as elaborate as an extensive glass-block shower surround with one wall on the exterior that lets in light. Glass block is versatile, but it isn't particularly energy efficient, with an R-value of about 1.8 (less than a good insulating-glass window), so it should be used sparingly on exterior walls in cold climates.

A Comparison of Vanity Lighting

The most common vanity lighting—a single light source above the mirror—provides the worst illumination, creating shadows under the eyes, nose, and chin (left). For more natural lighting, mount fixtures on either side of the vanity at eye level, preferably with frosted bulbs. Called vertical cross-illumination, this type of lighting eliminates unnatural looking shadows on the face (right).

Bad

Good

Task and general lighting

Most of us need all of the help we can get when looking at our reflection in the bathroom mirror first thing in the morning. But unfortunately, the configuration of a lot of bathroom lighting leaves us looking like Boris Karloff in a scary movie, casting shadows under our eyes, nose, and chin—a discouraging way to start the day.

Light fixtures mounted overhead—either above the mirror or on the ceiling—cause this unpleasant effect (see the left drawing above). Translucent diffusers on the fixtures can help soften the shadows, and spreading the light out with multiple lamps helps too. But a better solution is to mount fixtures at eye level at least 30 in. apart on either side of the vanity mirror (see the right drawing above). Vertically mounted light bars with frosted lamps do the best job of lighting the face evenly, but two translucent fixtures work almost as well. Lighting designers call this vertical cross-

illumination. Frosted bulbs work better than clear ones to diffuse the light and reduce glare, and including a dimmer to control the light level is a good idea.

This specific task lighting usually needs to be supplemented by general lighting, unless the bathroom is fairly small—a powder room, for example—and finished in light colors. This kind of illumination is often supplied by a ceiling-mounted light, often in combination with a bath fan and/or blower heater. For general illumination, $\frac{1}{3}$ watt to $\frac{1}{2}$ watt of fluorescent light or 1 watt of incandescent light per square foot is recommended for surface-mounted fixtures located on the ceiling. Recessed fixtures require more light to achieve the same level of illumination, typically $2\frac{1}{2}$ watts to 4 watts of incandescent light per square foot or $\frac{1}{2}$ watt of fluorescent light per square foot, but tend to reduce the effect of glare since the upper corners of the room are shadowed.

I'm not that fond of overhead lighting; to me it feels vaguely industrial and too utilitarian, just one step up from a bare lightbulb mounted in a porcelain socket. I think that in many cases one or two wall-mounted fixtures, such as a wall sconce, can provide a much more pleasant general light while achieving the same level of illumination. Light bouncing indirectly off of a light-colored ceiling is much more diffuse and natural than a glaring beam of light from above.

If a bathroom is compartmentalized, be sure that each area has an adequate light source. Again, a wall sconce in a separate toilet area provides plenty of light but doesn't create that feeling of being on stage. Bathtub and shower areas require plenty of light, too, and most codes specify that the fixture used in this area be approved for use in wet and damp locations. Ceiling-mounted recessed fixtures or flush-mounted fixtures with a slightly projecting diffuser are typically used in this situation.

Remember that lighting not only serves a utilitarian purpose but it can also help to sculpt the mood of the environment. It doesn't make sense to spend thousands on a whirlpool tub without thinking about the reason that it is there: relaxation. Most people would equate lying back under a single glaring overhead light with a visit to the doctor's or dentist's office rather than a visit to a spa. Again, indirect lighting sources with adjustable light intensity can create a much more relaxing environment for those times when you take a long soak in the whirlpool. Be sure to pay attention to codes when choosing lighting for this space, however. Recessed lighting is okay; track lighting or fixtures with cords or switches within reach of someone standing in the tub are not. And accent lighting that highlights architectural features of the bath—a garden window or some other feature—can heighten the drama of the bath.

Don't forget to make accommodations for nightlighting. Many find the simple plug-in nightlights perfectly adequate. Others prefer to simply turn the intensity way down on a dimmer-controlled circuit, or sometimes integrated light/fan combinations have a nightlight setting. Another option is to install a low-voltage linear lighting system in the toekick space beneath the cabinets. Nightlighting may seem like a trivial matter, but an accident in a dark bathroom in the middle of the night is no fun. Neither is having sleepy eyes rudely awakened at 3:00 A.M. by a bathroom full of mirrors and bright chrome and lights as bright as daylight.

Bulbs and color temperature

The increasing use of fluorescent lamps in residential settings is a direct response to the increasing cost of energy. Quite simply, fluorescent lamps save energy and money. Though initially more expensive to purchase, they last far longer than incandescent bulbs and produce many more lumens of light per watt of electricity consumed.

Forget about the old tube-type fluorescent lamps, though. They're fine for a basement or a workshop, but their light is too unpleasant for bathroom use. Some of the new compact fluorescents contain the lamp, ballast, and socket all in one unit and will easily replace conventional 40-watt to 75-watt incandescent lamps. Other compacts require an adapter base or clip directly into a fixture designed to hold fluorescent lamps. A drawback to fluorescents is that they can't be easily dimmed.

Tungsten-halogen incandescent lamps are another energy-efficient alternative to standard incandescent lamps, providing 25% more lumens per watt and having more than twice the average life span. Their bright white light is ideal for highlighting colors and architectural

A Comparison of Different Types of Light Sources

Lamp Description	Watts*	Lumens	Life**	°K	Annual Cost***
Incandescent globe	25	210	1,500	2,550	$ 3.75
Incandescent "A"	60	870	1,000	2,800	$ 9.00
Halogen mini-can	75	1,200	2,000	3,000	$11.25
Fluorescent compact twin	13	825	10,000	2,700	$ 2.10
Fluorescent compact quad	26	1,800	10,000	2,700	$ 4.80
Fluorescent tube (1 in. by 48 in.)	32	3,050	20,000	3,000	$ 5.40

* Includes ballast wattage for fluorescents
** Average number of hours a light source is expected to burn
*** Calculated at 10¢ per KWH based on average residential use of 1,500 hours per year (includes ballast wattage)

Chart courtesy American Lighting Association

details. Halogen bulbs are also more compact, permitting installation in smaller fixtures. Low-voltage halogen minilights that operate on a 12-volt system are finding a niche as decorative and accent lighting; this type of system requires a transformer. Both 120-volt and 12-volt halogen lamps are easily dimmed.

Despite their high operating cost, incandescent bulbs are popular because they are readily available and inexpensive to purchase and because the light that they emit has a warm character. The color temperature of different types of bulbs can be measured in degrees Kelvin (°K), with incandescent bulbs at the warm end of the scale (2600°K to 3400°K) and daylight at the cool end of the scale (5000°K). The yellows and reds contained in incandescent light give it its warmth, while natural light has a lot of blue. Fluorescent lamps used to produce light in the cool 3600°K+ range, but the newer lamps are available in warmer temperatures that duplicate the look of incandescent light. Halogen lights average around 3000°K, a relatively neutral temperature.

The Effects of Color Temperature

Warm (2600°-3400°K)	Natural (3500°K)	Cool (3600°-4900°K)	Daylight (5000°K)
Friendly Intimate Personal	Friendly Inviting	Neat Clean Efficient	Bright Alert

Chart courtesy American Lighting Association

Chapter 6

CHOOSING FINISH MATERIALS

FLOORS

WALLS AND CEILINGS

PRIMERS, PAINTS,
AND WALL COVERINGS

SURFACING MATERIALS

Wouldn't it be great if bathrooms came with some sort of self-cleaning mechanism to keep them in showroom condition? The touch of a button would clean and dry the floors, scrub the toilet, tub, and sink, and send soap scum and toothpaste gunk right down the drain. In the real world, though, this work has to be done by real people who make real messes. From kids splashing in a tub to adults hurrying through their morning ritual on their way to work, bathrooms are hard-working spaces. They shouldn't need to be handled with kid gloves, though.

The simple truth is: The bathroom environment can be a harsh one. Floors, walls, and ceilings are subjected to wide swings in humidity levels, and moisture in some form or another—splashes from a tub, spray and humidity from a shower, condensation dripping from a toilet—is inevitable, even when there is an adequate ventilation system. And surfaces that come in direct contact with water—often on a daily basis—like countertops and tub and shower surrounds, need to be able to withstand not only the water but also the sometimes-harsh chemicals and abrasive cleaners that are often used in the bathroom. Choosing which material to use, as well as an appropriate finish, often means juggling factors like appearance, availability, affordability, and durability, as well as ease of installation. The following is an

Because bathrooms are subjected to high traffic and a lot of moisture, finish materials should be chosen for their durability, as well as for their appearance. (Photo © Carolyn Bates. Courtesy The Snyder Group.)

overview of the various finish materials commonly used in the bathroom, as well as some notes about their specific applications.

FLOORS

The performance of a finish floor depends in large part on the adequacy of the subfloor beneath it. Usually in residential construction this means a floor system composed of closely spaced (typically 16 in. o.c.) 2x floor joists and a ⅝-in. or ¾-in. plywood subfloor (see the drawing on p. 104). In some cases, you'll find an engineered floor system with wood I-joists, parallel-chord floor trusses, or even steel-trussed joists, all of which will still have a plywood subfloor. If the house is timber framed, you might find a plank-and-beam floor system, and

in an older house you'll likely find a plank subfloor. The subfloor might even be a regular or radiant concrete slab. In all these cases, you'll have to identify the floor system and determine the adequacy of the framing and subfloor for the particular type of finish flooring. (See Chapter 8 for more about floor framing.)

Because the subfloor and finish floor work together as a system, making sure that one is compatible with the other (particularly in renovation work) is important. For example, a resilient floor without properly prepared underlayment will telegraph nail heads, cracks, and imperfections right through the surface. A ceramic tile floor on a too-flexible subfloor will soon develop cracks in the grout and loose tiles.

Typical Wood-Joist Floor System

While other types of floor systems—concrete slab, plywood I-joists, or wood trusses—may also be found in residential construction, wood-joist systems are by far the most common. Joist size depends on the required span, species of framing lumber, design load of the floor, and the depth needed for insulation and/or utilities.

Size	Spacing	Span*	
		Live load= 40 lbs./sq. ft.	Live load= 60 lbs./sq. ft.
2x8	12 in. o.c.	12 ft. 10 in.	11 ft. 5 in.
	16 in. o.c.	11 ft. 8 in.	10 ft. 5 in.
	24 in. o.c.	10 ft. 3 in.	9 ft. 2 in.
2x10	12 in. o.c.	16 ft. 1 in.	14 ft. 5 in.
	16 in. o.c.	14 ft. 9 in.	13 ft. 2 in.
	24 in. o.c.	13 ft.	11 ft. 6 in.
2x12	12 in. o.c.	19 ft. 5 in.	17 ft. 4 in.
	16 in. o.c.	17 ft. 9 in.	15 ft. 10 in.
	24 in. o.c.	15 ft. 8 in.	13 ft. 11 in.

*Allowable spans can be increased by as much as 2 ft. depending on the species and grade of the framing material being used.

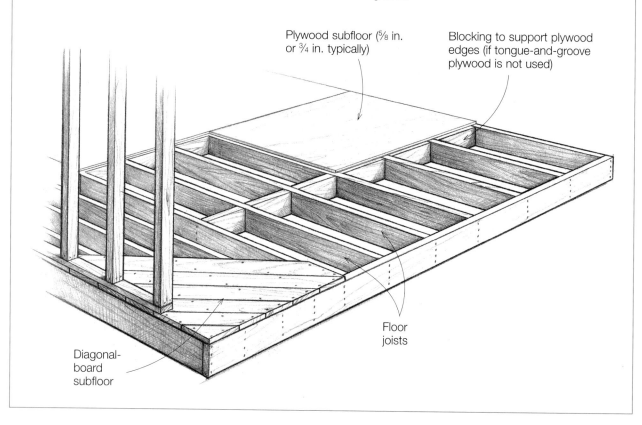

Plywood subfloor (⅝ in. or ¾ in. typically)

Blocking to support plywood edges (if tongue-and-groove plywood is not used)

Floor joists

Diagonal-board subfloor

Other types of finish floor materials—whether natural wood, cork or rubber, or even carpeting—also depend on an adequately prepared subfloor.

Of course, finish floor choice is largely a matter of personal preference. Some may like the durability of ceramic tile, while others may feel that it is too cold and too hard, preferring instead the look of a natural wood floor. Others may feel that wood requires too much care and opt for a low-maintenance vinyl floor. Knowing the characteristics of the various types of flooring available will make it easier to recommend one over the other, depending on the particular installation, and to make sure that it has an adequate subfloor.

Resilient flooring

Resilient flooring enjoys continued popularity in the bathroom, as well as the rest of the house, and for good reason. Its cost is relatively low (ranging from about $5 per square yard to over $40 per square yard); it installs quickly and easily; it resists moisture well and is easy to clean; it's available in an enormous range of patterns and colors; and it's durable. Because this flooring gives under foot, it is well suited for use on concrete-slab floors. Conventionally framed floors will require additional underlayment on top of the existing subfloor.

The term resilient flooring actually includes several different types of flooring materials, including vinyl, linoleum, and cork. Vinyl flooring, either in sheet-goods form or as vinyl tile, is by far the most popular type of resilient flooring. New vinyl tile designs that imitate granite, marble, and ceramic tiles are becoming increasingly popular, but sheet goods still account for the lion's share of the vinyl market. Vinyl tile is more susceptible to moisture damage than sheet goods are because of the seams, but this is more of a problem with self-adhering tiles than with those set in a trowelled-on adhesive.

Vinyl floor coverings fall into two broad categories: printed pattern (or rotovinyls) and solid vinyl. Rotovinyls consist of a backing material, a cushioning layer, a thin vinyl layer printed with the pattern and color, and a urethane wear layer. Sheets of this relatively flexible vinyl are widely available in widths up to 12 ft. Solid vinyl is stiffer, generally comes in either tile form or in 6-ft.-wide sheets, and is made by fusing together tiny vinyl chips or granules under heat and pressure. The color of this type of tile is richer because it goes all the way through the tile, and dents or damage doesn't show up very readily. Vinyl floor coverings range from $\frac{1}{16}$ in. to $\frac{1}{8}$ in. thick, but the more durable coverings will be at least $\frac{3}{32}$ in. thick.

So what's wrong with vinyl? For many people, nothing. While I don't really care for vinyl flooring that tries to mimic other products like wood or natural stone, many of the new patterns and colors are quite striking. Despite the improved realism that recent improvements in manufacturing processes and materials have produced, vinyl that tries to look like something else still looks hokey. But vinyl's strengths—durability, ease of maintenance, and resistance to moisture—make it hard to beat as a flooring material in the bathroom.

But vinyl is a plastic, a petrochemically based product, and some people have aesthetic and environmental concerns about that; some chemically sensitive people even have medical problems with plastic. For those folks there are still resilient floor coverings that offer many of the same benefits of vinyl. For example, linoleum, the original sheet-goods flooring, is making a comeback. Don't confuse linoleum with vinyl (as I did for years); they are two entirely different products. Linoleum is a natural product, composed of boiled linseed oil (derived from flax plant seeds), natural resins, and filler materials like cork, limestone, and pigments. It is available in sheets or as tiles in thicknesses ranging from 2mm to 3.5mm and in 80 or more colors. Expect to pay about $3 per square foot for linoleum (not including installation).

Linoleum's natural composition makes it attractive for those with chemical sensitivities, as does its lack of a clear PVC (polyvinyl chloride) wear layer. It hides stains well because of the variations in its coloring, but because it is porous it should be sealed with an appropriate finish, such as an acrylic. Linoleum lends itself to custom installations featuring inlays with contrasting colors and designs (see the left photo below).

Cork flooring is another natural alternative to vinyl flooring. Harvested from the bark of the cork oak tree, cork flooring is environmentally friendly, has both sound- and heat-insulating properties, and is very comfortable to stand and walk on. It's available in both tiles and rolls and in thicknesses between ⅛ in. and ⅜ in. Different finishes are available, including a prewaxed or a polyurethane-coated finish, or it is available in a natural sanded finish. Vinyl-encapsulated cork with a PVC wear layer on the surface is probably the best choice in a bathroom. Prices for cork range between $3 and $5 per square foot. Cork requires a bit more maintenance, including fairly regular dry dusting and wet mopping, but its color and pattern tend to conceal staining, and its warm cushiony feel is perfect in the bathroom.

Ceramic tile

Ceramic tile is a traditionally popular flooring material, and the range of colors and patterns that can be achieved with a tile floor is enormous (see the right photo below). Besides the fact that tile is largely unaffected by water, part of its appeal is the fact that the floor finish can be extended up the walls almost seamlessly, making the junction between the floor and the wall easier to clean. Because some glazed tiles can become extremely slippery when they get wet and because some tiles are harder than others, there are some kinds of tile that are more suitable than others for use on a bathroom floor.

Design versatility and new colors and patterns make linoleum floors, once popular in the first part of the century, a natural alternative to vinyl floors. (Designer Laurie Croger. Photo by Reese Hamilton.)

Used for floors, walls, countertops, and tub/shower surrounds, ceramic tile is an ideal bathroom surfacing material: versatile, durable, water resistant, and beautiful.

Tile-Floor Installations

Tile on plywood

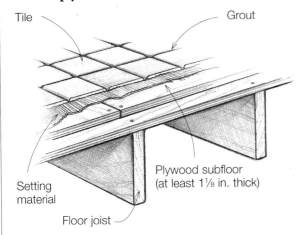

Tile · Grout · Setting material · Floor joist · Plywood subfloor (at least 1⅛ in. thick)

Joists should be adequately sized (see the chart on p. 104) and a total thickness of plywood of at least 1⅛ in. is recommended. Use exterior-grade plywood, leave a ⅛-in. gap between sheets for expansion, stagger the joints, and fill the gaps between sheets with the tile-setting adhesive.

Tile on slab

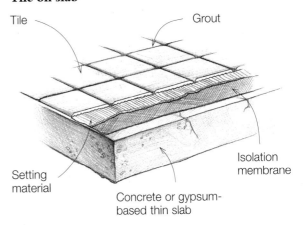

Tile · Grout · Setting material · Concrete or gypsum-based thin slab · Isolation membrane

Both concrete and gypsum-based thin slabs (typically used with radiant floors) offer a stable substrate for setting tile. If there are unstabilized cracks in the concrete, an isolation membrane like NobleSeal T/S should be applied for concrete, and gypsum-based thin slabs should have a sealing/waterproofing membrane.

Tile on mortar bed

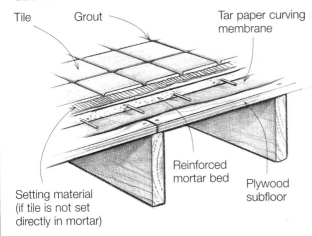

Tile · Grout · Tar paper curving membrane · Setting material (if tile is not set directly in mortar) · Reinforced mortar bed · Plywood subfloor

For tile that isn't uniformly thick or for irregular substrates that need to be leveled out, traditional 1-in.-thick mortar bed installations reinforced with wire mesh are a good alternative.

Tile on backer board

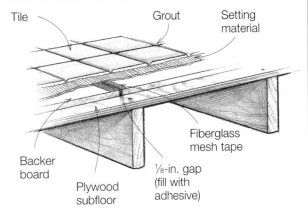

Tile · Grout · Setting material · Backer board · Plywood subfloor · ⅛-in. gap (fill with adhesive) · Fiberglass mesh tape

Cementitious backer boards are unaffected by moisture and can be applied to a number of different substrates. Sheets should be gapped ⅛ in., and joints should be taped with fiberglass mesh tape and filled with setting material.

In general, high-gloss glazed tiles are the easiest to clean but also the most slippery. A better choice for floors are either vitreous (non-water absorbing) or non-vitreous (water absorbing) tiles with a matte or slip-resistant texture. Most tiles also have an applied surface glaze that makes them impenetrable to moisture, so non-vitreous glazed tiles are generally perfectly suitable for bathroom floors and walls. The hardness of the glaze can vary, so softer tiles are more susceptible to wear than harder tiles. Tile manufacturers have adopted something called the Mohs scale to indicate glaze hardness. A tile rated at 10 will resist a diamond scratch, while a tile rated at 1 is very easily scratched. Most tiles intended for floor use fall around 6 or 7.

Ceramic mosaic tiles (typically made of pigmented vitreous porcelain) are another good choice for floors. Because of their small size, they are typically mounted on sheets to make spacing more consistent and installation easier. They're extremely hard, which makes cutting them difficult, but they're almost impervious to staining or cracking. What makes them particularly appealing for floors is their unglazed matte surface (though they are available glazed as well), which makes them naturally slip resistant. I've had good luck using them for shower floors because their small size lets them conform to the slope of the floor, and their slip resistance makes them safer under foot. Pavers and quarry tiles also are good for bathroom floors, though they both will need to be sealed to help prevent straining.

No matter what kind of tile you use, it puts more demands on floor-system installation than any other type of floor finish (see the drawing on p. 107). Tile isn't flexible, and neither is grout, so a floor system has to be rigid enough to support whatever loads are encountered in the bathroom without appreciable flexing. Concrete slabs are ideal for tile installations, whether cast on-grade or as part of an above-grade radiant floor. If you're planning a tile installation on a conventionally framed floor (either with dimensional or engineered floor joists), you'll need to make sure that the floor meets minimum standards for deflection under load, and that the substrate thickness is adequate (typically $1\frac{1}{8}$ in. of substrate is required, or two layers of $\frac{5}{8}$-in. plywood).

Wood

There are quite a few people who advise against installing a wood floor in a bathroom, citing primarily the potential problems that moisture can cause. I'm not one of them, though. I think that, in many situations, wood floors are perfectly appropriate for bathrooms. Though moisture—both in liquid form and as water vapor—can cause problems in wood floors, the presence of enough water to damage a wood floor indicates a more severe problem that will eventually cause problems with any type of floor. For example, if there is a leak around a toilet's closet bend or excess condensation dripping from the tank, then that water will eventually work its way into the subfloor anyway, regardless of the floor covering.

Choosing the right type of wood flooring and paying close attention to installing and finishing it correctly are the keys to a successful wood-floor installation in the bathroom. (See Chapter 11 for more information on installing a wood floor.) I've had good luck with red oak, maple, and cherry, all of which are common hardwoods here in New England. Walnut, teak, and some of the increasingly available but lesser-known stable tropical hardwoods would also be good choices. Narrow strip flooring is better because wider boards shrink and swell more with swings in humidity than strip flooring and will be more likely to show gaps between the boards. Flooring that is less than 3 in. wide is best.

While narrow hardwood strip flooring is generally more stable and less apt to open up gaps, don't discount using wider planks of both hardwood or softwood. Here in New England there are plenty of old houses with antique wide-board floors, many of which have been painstakingly reclaimed from attempts at modernization. These floors are very attractive and serviceable, despite their gaps between boards. In some regards the gaps are a good idea because they allow the floor to breath.

No matter what type of finish will eventually be used, prefinishing the ends, edges, and backs of the flooring will go a long ways toward minimizing water absorption and will help keep the flooring from cupping. I've used both oil-modified urethane and waterborne urethane with good success, and while I've found oil-modified urethanes to be slightly more durable than the waterborne urethanes that I've tried, VOC (Volatile Organic Compound) regulations intended to improve air quality by reducing the amount of toxic VOCs allowed in paints and stains have discouraged their use. (VOCs evaporate as a paint or stain dries, can be inhaled or absorbed into the skin, and contribute to ozone pollution.) Avoid using penetrating oils and finishes because they don't provide enough protection against spilled water.

Other flooring options

Laminate flooring is a relatively new product in the U.S. market, though it has enjoyed wide-spread popularity in Europe for several years. This flooring is produced by thermofusing melamine-saturated photographically imprinted decorative paper to a substrate (typically medium-density fiberboard, or MDF). It can resemble wood-grain plank flooring, marble, ceramic tile, and even stone and is remarkably realistic. I've used decorative laminate panels for years in cabinetry and have found the material to have many very good qualities. Unfortunately, moisture resistance isn't one of them. The melamine-coated surface is fine, but the substrate swells when it picks up moisture, which could lead to problems in a bathroom installation.

Slate's durability and subtle coloring make it a good choice for the floor and tub deck in this bath-house. (Photo by the author.)

But why not choose the real thing instead of a look-alike. The relatively small floor area of a bathroom means that options like marble, slate, or other natural stones would not be prohibitively expensive. Slate, a softer sedimentary stone, is a good choice when a durable but unobtrusive stone floor is desired (see the photo on p. 109). Granite, an igneous rock, is much harder and resistant to scratches and staining. Its veining (from other minerals contained within it, like quartz and mica) makes it a more distinctive floor material. Steer clear of polished granite for flooring; it looks dramatic, but it's very slippery when wet. A better choice is a matte finish. Polished marble is also very slippery, and etched or honed marble is better for flooring. Marble is also susceptible to stains and scratching because it is a porous and soft type of limestone.

Don't overlook other flooring options. I've seen elaborately painted plywood floors that look

Commercial rubber tile floors are comfortably cushioned and virtually maintenance free.

While vinyl's durability and low-maintenance make it an ideal bathroom floor covering, don't discount the use of carpet in the right situation. (Designer Baylis Brand Wagner Architects. Photo by Charles Miller.)

quite nice, and one of the high points of visiting my grandmother's house as a child was the warm, thick carpet that she had in her bathroom. Of course, carpet would have been a disaster in our own house, with seven children using the facilities, but for retired folks where warmth underfoot is a real issue, carpet might make sense (see the right photo on the facing page). What our bathrooms could have used instead was commercial rubber tile, a virtually indestructible and maintenance-free flooring.

This widely available flooring isn't commonly seen in residential settings, but it's attractive, comes in a wide range of colors, and its durability makes it a good choice for bathroom floors (see the left photo on the facing page).

WALLS AND CEILINGS

Before talking about some of the more specialized wall treatments and surfacing materials that are available for use in the bathroom, it is worthwhile to look at the

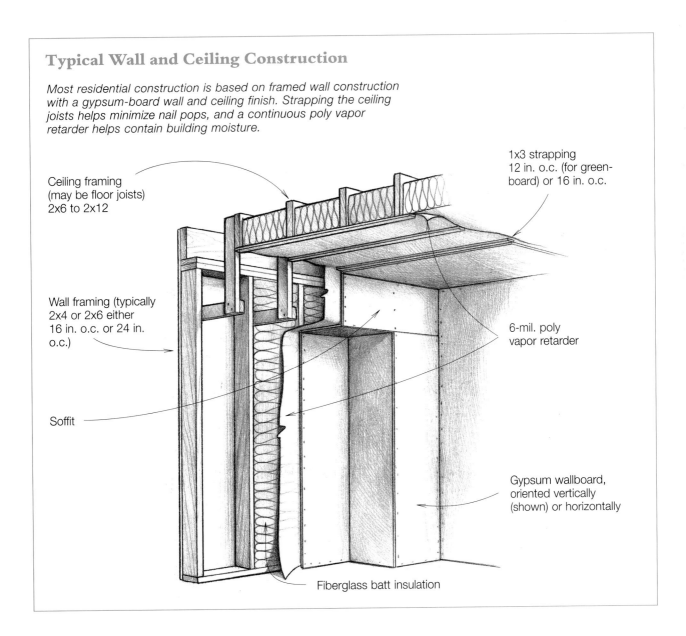

Typical Wall and Ceiling Construction

Most residential construction is based on framed wall construction with a gypsum-board wall and ceiling finish. Strapping the ceiling joists helps minimize nail pops, and a continuous poly vapor retarder helps contain building moisture.

Ceiling framing (may be floor joists) 2x6 to 2x12

1x3 strapping 12 in. o.c. (for greenboard) or 16 in. o.c.

Wall framing (typically 2x4 or 2x6 either 16 in. o.c. or 24 in. o.c.)

6-mil. poly vapor retarder

Soffit

Gypsum wallboard, oriented vertically (shown) or horizontally

Fiberglass batt insulation

structure of the walls and ceilings themselves (see the drawing on p. 111). In most parts of the country, 2x stud walls filled with batt insulation (on exterior walls) and covered with drywall have become the standard for wall construction. In an older home, however, you may find solid plank walls covered with lath and plaster; I've even worked on walls with cavities that have been filled with bricks. Some timber-frame homes use panelized wall construction, where rigid foam is faced on the outside with exterior sheathing and on the interior with gypsum-board drywall, forming a monolithic panel that is then attached to the framing. You also might find steel-stud framing in the walls, or a solid masonry wall, typically reinforced concrete block.

Ceiling construction is usually comparable to wall construction, although it will be important to identify whether there is living space above the ceiling, an attic, or if the ceiling is part of the roof. Occasionally you'll find a dropped ceiling, with a suspended frame supporting acoustic ceiling tiles. Whatever the construction method, you'll need to identify it and make sure that it supplies the specific structural needs that a bathroom has, including appropriate blocking, adequate air sealing and insulation, and properly routed mechanical systems.

Cement-based backer boards like Durock are well suited as substrates for stone and tilework, particularly for tub and shower surrounds.

Drywall

While standard ½-in. gypsum-board drywall is adequate for most other rooms of the house, moisture-resistant (MR) drywall should be used in bathrooms. MR drywall, also called greenboard because of its green paper covering, has asphalt emulsions in its gypsum core, which makes it heavier and helps it to resist moisture. But the asphalt emulsions also make the board less rigid than regular drywall; that is why it should only be used on ceilings when the framing is 12 in. o.c. rather than the standard 16 in. o.c. to prevent sagging. Also, MR drywall isn't waterproof, only moisture resistant, and will in fact fall apart if it gets a constant soaking.

I've pulled out enough deteriorating tile jobs that used MR drywall as a backer to know that it shouldn't be done, at least in wet areas.

Textured patterns can also be created on regular drywall. I've never been especially fond of them because they complicate the job of repairing and patching that comes with renovation, not to mention the difficulty of wall-papering over them at a later date. But they do offer an alternative to the monolithic look of drywall. Drywall textures can be sprayed on with either manually operated or air-powered spray texture guns (usually available at a local equipment rental operation) rolled on with a regular paint roller, or trowelled on, or a combination of all three.

Backer boards and mortar beds

In wet areas under a tile installation, like in a shower surround, a cement-based backer board or a traditional floated mortar bed should be used rather than MR drywall. Compared to a traditional mortar bed, fiber-mesh-reinforced cement backer boards are lightweight and install essentially like gypsum board, being either screwed or nailed to the framing. They can be scored like gypsum board and snapped to size or cut with a masonry blade mounted in a circular saw (a very dusty process). These boards aren't affected by water, and they don't shrink or expand with changes in temperature or humidity, making them an ideal substrate for tile. (For more on installing backer boards, see Chapter 10.)

Plaster

While drywall has largely replaced traditional lath and plaster as a wall and ceiling covering because of its quick installation and finishing, plaster has a subtly different look and feel than drywall that many people prefer. Traditional three-coat plaster—consisting of an initial scratch coat to adhere to the lath, a brown coat that levels the surface, and a finish coat—is labor-intensive and thus expensive, typically costing at least twice as much to install per square foot as standard drywall. While the old-timers installed wood lath, nowadays metal lath is commonly used because it installs more easily and provides a better substrate for the base coat (see the drawing below).

Plaster Wall Systems

Plaster over metal lath

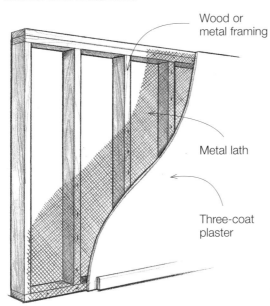

Wood or metal framing

Metal lath

Three-coat plaster

Metal lath is available in different types and weights for different applications. Typically three-coat plaster is used with metal lath, though two-coat plaster can also be used.

Plaster over gypsum lath

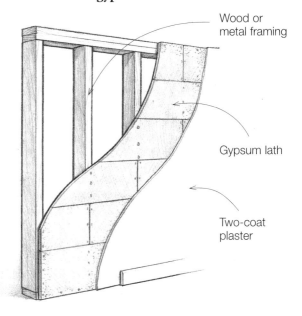

Wood or metal framing

Gypsum lath

Two-coat plaster

Gypsum lath is available in both ³⁄₈-in. and ¹⁄₂-in. thicknesses and is typically used with two-coat plaster systems.

Two-coat plaster over gypsum lath (sometimes called veneer plaster) is a more user-friendly plastering system, but it is still more expensive than drywall. Gypsum lath is similar to drywall but comes in 2-ft. widths and in varying lengths and is attached to the wall framing in the same way. Alternatively, veneer plaster can be applied over regular drywall, which is more widely available. A base coat and finish coat are then trowelled on. Both two-coat and three-coat plaster finishes depend on the skill of the finisher and can have a variety of textures ranging from smooth to swirling.

Wood

Wood has a warmth and texture that makes it an appealing wall-surfacing material in the bathroom, but its sensitivity to moisture is a liability unless it is carefully protected with an appropriate finish (see Wood on p. 108). Another liability is its coloration: Extensive use of a relatively dark finishing material like wood in the confines of the bathroom can result in a space that feels claustrophobic. But if naturally colored wood is protected with the right finish and used in moderation, the results can be dramatic.

For example, wainscoting usually extends about 36 in. up from the floor, a prime area for dirt. A painted or urethaned surface here is more durable and easily cleaned than drywall and can provide a decorative accent to a bathroom. An elegant formal bathroom might have raised-panel wainscoting, while beaded tongue-in-groove boards are simpler to install and more informal. A clear urethane finish will protect the wood and allow its particular coloration to dominate the room, while a light-colored painted surface will keep the room looking brighter and larger and be less intrusive (see the photo at left).

PRIMERS, PAINTS, AND WALL COVERINGS

Like floor coverings, wall and ceiling finishes are usually chosen for their decorative effect, though they actually serve both decorative and functional purposes. In addition to appearance, a good bathroom finish should be durable, cleanable, and air and moisture resistant, particularly around high-traffic areas. Paints or

Whether painted or treated with a clear finish, wood wainscoting provides an attractive and durable accent to a bathroom.

wall coverings are the two most common residential wall finishes, while the right type of primer underneath is the best insurance that your walls and ceilings will remain looking good for years to come.

Primers

I used to be indifferent to primers and usually bought the cheapest one available, figuring that it was going to be covered by paint anyway. But primers can make a lot of difference in the quality of the final finish, and the difference in price between the cheap ones and the expensive ones is minimal, especially when a good primer can sometimes save you an extra coat of paint. For woodwork, I don't know of a better primer than Benjamin Moore's Underbody (see Resources on p. 209). Available in both an alkyd and a latex formula, this primer has a lot of body for smoothing out imperfections, and it's sandable. I use B-I-N, a fast-drying shellac-based primer, for spot-priming knots and stains or for priming end grain in the field. B-I-N also makes a water-based primer that I've used in both interior and exterior applications and that is good at hiding stains.

While PVA (polyvinyl acetate) primers for drywall are cheap and easy to put on, they don't do anything to stop vapor transmission. For plaster or drywall in the bathroom, it makes sense to pay a bit more for a primer that is specifically intended to inhibit vapor transmission, like Benjamin Moore's Alkyd PrimeSeal. There are also primers intended specifically for use under wall coverings.

Paints

I've worked on a lot of old houses, so I've come to appreciate the ability of a flat latex paint to hide flaws in the walls and to go on quickly and easily. But if you've ever lived in a household with small children, you know how hard it can be to keep painted walls clean. Especially

bathroom walls. So I've also come to appreciate semi-gloss enamels for their durability and cleanability.

The glossiness of a paint is determined by the ratio of resin to pigment, so flat paints with proportionally more pigment are better at hiding bumps and patches, while glossy paints with more resin have a harder surface that gives up fingerprints and crayon marks more readily. If you don't like the wet, shiny look of a high-gloss paint but still want a cleanable surface, paint manufacturers offer a range of sheens with names like semi-gloss, satin, and egg-shell that are washable and yet non-reflective.

In general, alkyd (or oil-based) enamels are more durable and abrasion resistant than latex enamels. I've always preferred alkyd enamels for trimwork because of the smooth, hard surface that they leave, as well as their ability to hide brushmarks. But latex enamels are easier to work with because they dry more quickly, they don't have an overpowering smell, and they clean up with soap and water.

An important factor to consider when choosing a paint for the bathroom is its permeability, or the degree to which water vapor can pass through the paint membrane. Both alkyd enamels and latex enamels are vapor resistant to a varying degree, depending on the particular paint, but in general, alkyd enamels are better vapor retarders. Some paints and primers are even sold as vapor retarders and used to add another protective barrier against water vapor (see the sidebar on p. 116 for more about vapor retarders).

Wall coverings

While the unrelieved flat surface of drywall can be boring, especially in a large room, it isn't as much of an issue in a bathroom, and it's perfect for applying wallpaper. Unfortunately, wallpaper

A Word about Vapor Retarders

I've always appreciated the idiosyncrasies of drywall hangers and tapers, figuring that anyone handling drywall all day every day was entitled to a few. But I have to admit that I was more than a little puzzled when I saw one crew pull out utility knives just before starting to hang their drywall and proceed to slash the 6-mil. polyethylene vapor retarder that my partner and I had just carefully installed on a large ceiling. When I asked them what they were doing, they said that the poly would ruin the drywall, making it droop and sag, and that this was SOP.

Vapor retarders—typically a continuous membrane of polyethylene film—are supposed to keep moisture in the form of water vapor from permeating through porous wall and ceiling surfaces. What the drywallers were trying to prevent was moisture condensing between the poly and the back of the drywall.

Slashing the poly will help save the drywall, but water vapor that makes it all the way into wall cavities and attics presents an even worse problem, one that may not be immediately visible but that will have more dire consequences.

Many building experts consider a poly vapor retarder to be unnecessary *if* there is a continuous and monolithic wall and ceiling surface like drywall (board siding and suspended ceilings don't count) and *if* the walls and ceiling are painted with appropriate low-permeability primers and paints. Most paint manufacturers make low-perm paints and primers and clearly label them. I still recommend putting up the poly in addition to using low-perm paints and primers. A little extra protection never hurt anyone, and maybe the drywallers will only use their knives to cut drywall.

Warm interior air is pressurized relative to cooler outside air and will permeate porous walls and ceilings through cracks and openings, condensing on cold framing and sheathing.

Vapor retarders—in the form of continuous polyethylene film and continuous drywall with low-permeability paint applied, for example—will contain the bulk of this moisture, which should be exhausted properly with adequate mechanical ventilation.

Water vapor

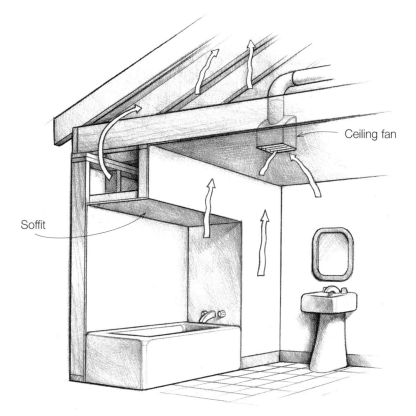

Ceiling fan

Soffit

isn't always perfect for a bathroom, especially those with high moisture levels that aren't controlled adequately by mechanical ventilation. The moisture will attack the seams and eventually loosen the paper, a condition that I've found in many otherwise very nice bathrooms.

The best wall coverings for a bathroom are of fabric-backed vinyl, installed over walls prepared with an oil-based primer. The vinyl will help prevent moisture from penetrating to the backing, and the oil-based primer will help prevent moisture from penetrating to the paper covering of the drywall. In a powder room or half-bath, of course, a broader range of wall coverings is suitable because moisture isn't an issue (see the photo at right).

SURFACING MATERIALS

Unlike other rooms in the house (with the exception of the kitchen), a bathroom needs protective materials that are impervious to water and cleaning chemicals, as well as able to stand up to some pretty heavy physical abuse. These surfacing materials are used for countertops and tub and shower surrounds, and in addition to being able to take a punch or two, they need to look good doing it. Some options, like tile and stone, have been around for years and still do a good job. But there are some new kids on the block, too—materials like Corian and Avonite—that look good, are relatively easy to work with, and that can stand up to some hard use.

Ceramic tile

In practice, I've found that most tile works fine for bathroom, shower, and tub walls. In fact, I've found that most of the standard 4x4 wall tiles have a softer nonvitreous body and a relatively soft glaze. This makes them easier to score and cut, particularly around tricky spots like shower valves and drains. The weak link of a tile job is the grout, for it is usually here that tiled walls begin to leak as grout lines develop cracks. Water that penetrates hairline cracks in

The most durable wall coverings in bathrooms with showers are of vinyl with a fabric backing, but sometimes it doesn't hurt to improvise. This bath is papered with sheet music that has been decoupaged.

the grout can also remain long enough for mold to start forming, not a pleasant situation. Cracking is not as much of a problem for cement-based grouts as in the past because of new additives like latex, acrylic, or epoxy that provide more flexibility. Epoxy grouts are also available that use epoxy resins instead of cement for their strength. I don't particularly enjoy working with these kinds of grouts, but I am sold on their desirability for bathrooms (see the sidebar on p. 173). They are highly resistant to moisture and staining and have a high degree of flexibility, making them more able to resist cracking. (For more information on selecting tiles, adhesives, and grouts, see The Taunton Press' *Setting Tile* by Michael Byrne.)

Glass block offers design versatility and is well suited for both decorative and structural use in the bathroom. (Photo © Carolyn Bates.)

Natural stone

Closely related to ceramic tile are gauged tiles of marble, granite, slate, flagstone, and other natural stones. Terrazzo is a mixture of marble and other decorative stone chips and cement that is highly polished and shaped into slabs or smaller tiles. These stone tiles are cut to consistent dimensions and are usually polished, making them easier to clean. While stone is generally quite hard and resistant to scratches, it is a good idea to seal these tiles to keep them from developing stains. Marble is relatively soft and is particularly vulnerable to staining. Stone tiles are generally applied and grouted in a similar manner as ceramic tiles.

Glass block

Glass block is an interesting addition to the palette of wall-covering materials because it provides both structure and surface and it lets light through. While simple enclosed panels of block can be made, entire walls are also possible and can make a dramatic architectural statement, particularly when the walls are curved. Different types of block are available for different looks (see Pittsburgh Corning Corporation in Resources on p. 209). (See pp. 182 and 183 for more about building a glass-block wall.)

Decorative laminates

Decorative laminates have already been mentioned in connection with their use as a flooring option, but there are other types of decorative laminates as well, including high-pressure (HP) decorative laminate and color-through laminates. Standard HP decorative laminate consists of a core made up of several layers of phenolic resin-saturated kraft paper, a decorative layer of melamine resin-saturated paper with either a solid color or gravure print, and a protective overlay of melamine, all bonded by heat and high pressure. Color-through laminate uses melamine color sheets instead of the phenolic resin core of regular HP decorative laminate. This gives the laminate a uniform color and texture throughout, rather than a thin veneer of color on top. It also means that the seams are less visible because of the absence of the dark lines of the underlayers and that scratches don't show as easily (see the top photo on the facing page). Even at twice the cost of regular plastic laminate, it's still a good buy.

HP decorative laminate is available in sheets of various sizes and in two grades for custom fabrication. Vertical-grade laminate is 0.03 in. thick, while horizontal-grade laminate is 0.05 in. thick. Both grades are available in a flexible version (called forming laminate) so that they can be bent more easily in the process known as post-forming, which produces those countertops with the integral seamless backsplash, slightly raised front edge, and curved nose. Part of the appeal of HP laminate, besides the tremendous variety of patterns and colors, is that it is relatively easy to work with on-site and in the shop. Countertops, cabinetry and shelving, and other finish surfaces can be fabricated without a huge investment in specialized tools.

HP decorative laminate can also be used as a combination tub/shower or shower surround material, though this is relatively uncommon (see the photo below). Sheets of the material are available as large as 5 ft. by 12 ft., and some fabricators who specialize in working with

Countertops that are durable and appear seamless can be economically constructed using color-through high-pressure laminate.

HP laminate wall surrounds are seamless and are available for both tubs and showers in a wide range of standard styles and colors. (Photo courtesy Wilsonart International.)

decorative laminate have bending machines that can custom-form the laminate to your exact dimensions. The resulting one-piece surround is seamless, minimizing the potential for leaks.

Composite panels are another type of decorative laminate. These typically consist of a substrate of particleboard, MDF, or plywood to which is laminated a protective and/or decorative surface. This surface can vary in weight and durability, according to the specific type of composite panel, from the light-duty micropapers (or "rice papers") to heavier thermofused melamine. Because of its hard, durable surface, melamine is

Composite panels like Nevamar's LamMates offer the look of more-expensive HP laminates but are used in less-critical applications, such as cabinetry and shelving. (Photo courtesy International Paper Decorative Products Div.)

more resistant to moisture and abrasion than the more decorative micropapers or foils (another medium-weight composite panel), and so is more suitable for use in the demanding environment of the bathroom. Typical uses for composite panels include bathroom cabinetry and light-duty vertical and horizontal applications, though they aren't suitable for use as countertops or in damp-wall locations (see the photo below).

Solid-surface materials

One of the attractions of solid-surface materials like Corian is that they have the appearance and characteristics of stone yet can be worked with common woodworking tools. First introduced over 20 years ago, now there are a number of manufacturers that offer their own versions that are similar to one another, yet slightly different. None of them are manufactured exactly alike using the same materials; acceptable fabricating processes vary from manufacturer to manufacturer, and appearance and characteristics also vary from brand to brand. But there are enough similarities to make some generalizations.

The first is that solid-surface materials is repairable, whether it gets scratched or stained, because the color and pattern are consistent throughout the material. All of the various products are nonporous, so they're hard to stain in the first place, except perhaps by harsh chemicals like paint removers or oven cleaners. But if they do happen to sustain damage, sanding with a fine-grit sandpaper and a follow-up buffing will restore the surface.

Another attribute of solid-surface materials is that pieces can be joined together almost seamlessly. This means that sink bowls of the same material (if available) can be added to custom-cut countertops with a watertight and

Solid-surface veneers (SSVs) that are ⅛ in. thick are an economical choice for tub and shower surrounds yet offer the performance of regular solid-surface materials. (Photo courtesy Wilsonart International.)

virtually invisible joint. They are all thermally sensitive to a degree, so accommodations should be made for expansion and contraction. Most solid-surface manufacturers offer fabricator training, and in some cases will only sell sheet stock to fabricators certified in their particular process. Besides DuPont's Corian, some of the other major brands of solid-surface materials include Avonite, Surell, Gibraltar, and Fountainhead.

Solid-surface materials are available in a number of thicknesses and sheet sizes and are well suited for countertops and shower and tub surrounds. Some manufacturers, responding to concerns about the relatively high cost of solid-surface materials, are now offering thinner ⅛-in.-thick sheets—called solid-surface veneers, or SSVs—which are more economical for use in shower and tub surrounds (see the photo above).

Chapter 7

PROVIDING BATHROOM STORAGE

VANITIES
AND CABINETS

SPECIALTY STORAGE

When you think about all of the items that a family uses in the bathroom, it's no wonder that there never seems to be enough room for everything. In addition to towels, extra toilet paper, medicine, and cosmetics, bathrooms need storage space for cleaning supplies and scrub brushes, soaps and shampoos, even bathtub toys for the kids. Some items are big and bulky, while some are small and fragile; some items are used frequently, while others are used only occasionally. Part of a good overall bathroom plan is to make sure that there is reasonable access to all of these items, as well as a good place to put them when they aren't being used.

The reality of many bathrooms, however, is a marginally adequate two-part storage system: a big box under the sink (the vanity-base cabinet) that is already half-filled with plumbing pipes and a tiny cabinet over the sink that is suitable for small items like medicine and cosmetics but not much else and that is all but inaccessible for children or wheelchair users. A drawer or two in the vanity improves the situation, but quite often there isn't any room because the sink and its associated plumbing take up too much space.

Rather than be satisfied with minimal storage, there are a number of ways that a designer or builder can optimize the available storage space in a bathroom. The solutions range from simply adding shelving and making sure that vanities have drawers to stock or custom-built wall systems (see the photo at right).

VANITIES AND CABINETS

A vanity-base cabinet offers a convenient way to add storage space in a relatively compact bathroom. In fact, in a 5-ft. by 7-ft. full bath, the area below the sink might be the only available space for storage, making the sink/vanity cabinet combination unit a more attractive option than a pedestal sink (with its lack of storage space). But vanity cabinets aren't always an ideal storage solution. Their low height and deep depth isn't very convenient when it comes to retrieving regularly needed items, which are better stored in the range between 15 in. and 48 in. off of the floor (see the drawing on p. 124). Too often, the vanity cabinet becomes simply a convenient box on which to mount a countertop and sink, and the storage area below is really an afterthought.

Most stock vanity-base cabinets are typically about 30 in. high by 21 in. deep. With a sink mounted on top and extending 8 in. or so below the countertop, there simply is no room for the drawers that would make this awkward space more usable. But simply making the vanity taller helps, particularly if there is another shorter vanity available for use by children or the disabled. Most adults are more comfortable with countertop heights between 32 in. and 36 in. tall, and cabinet manufacturers are now making available bathroom vanities that are a little taller. The few extra inches might not seem like much, but it can mean enough room for a drawer. Often a 30-in.-tall vanity will only have doors, while a taller vanity will

While cabinet manufacturers offer a broad range of bathroom cabinetry, custom-built wall units can offer advantages like adjustable shelves and extra drawer space to maximize storage.

Optimizing Bathroom Storage

According to the NKBA, the optimal height for storing regularly needed supplies is between 15 in. and 48 in. above the floor. While not always practical because of space limitations, making provisions for storage between countertop and mirror level will result in a more functional bathroom.

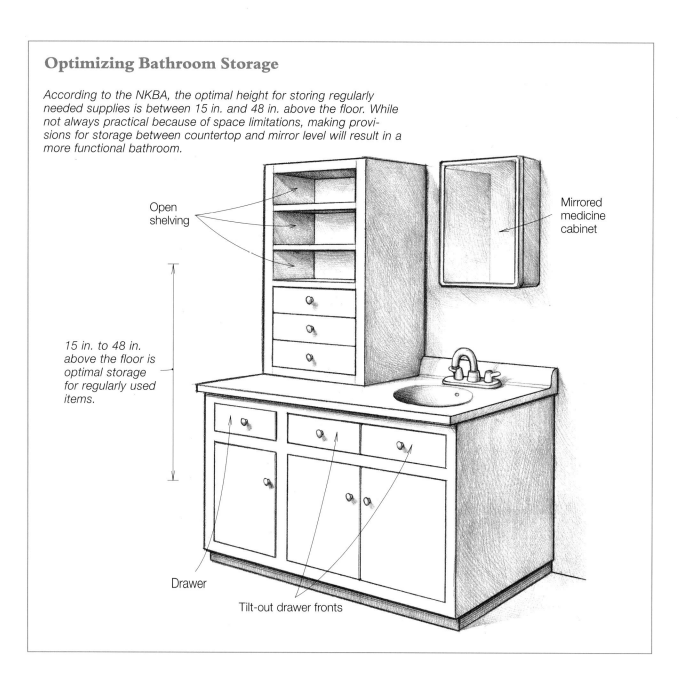

Open shelving

Mirrored medicine cabinet

15 in. to 48 in. above the floor is optimal storage for regularly used items.

Drawer

Tilt-out drawer fronts

usually have false drawer panels as well. Adding tilt-out hinges to the false drawer panels just below the sink can create extra room for small items like toothpaste and toothbrushes (see the photo on the facing page).

Offsetting the sink in the vanity cabinet provides room for a stack of drawers either to the side of a single-sink vanity or in the center

of a double-sink vanity (see the drawing on the facing page). While this won't work with a single base less than 30 in. wide, wider vanity bases should have room for both a reasonably sized sink and a set of drawers. In a double-vanity configuration, this will usually require three cabinets: two sink bases and a center drawer cabinet. Drawers admittedly add extra expense to a vanity, but I've found that several drawers—including both shallow and deep ones—make a lot of difference in bathroom storage and are well worth the extra money.

Cabinet construction and materials

Custom cabinetry in a bathroom is a nice touch, but with custom-built cabinets costing twice as much and more as stock cabinets, they can be a potential budget-breaker. Granted, you don't need nearly as many cabinets in a bathroom as you would in a kitchen, which makes bathroom cabinet upgrades relatively more affordable. But still, when it comes down to a decision between a whirlpool tub and a custom-built bathroom vanity, I think that the whirlpool will generally win out. Not that this will result in a horribly

A tilt-out tray mounted on an unused false drawer panel can add extra storage for often-used items like toothbrushes and toothpaste. (Photo courtesy Feeny/ Knape & Vogt Manufacturing Co.)

Making Room for Drawers

While drawers add to the expense of vanity cabinets, they add considerably to the utility of a bathroom. Shown here are suggested dimensional requirements for a single-sink vanity with drawers (right) and a double-sink vanity with drawers (below).

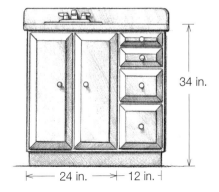

34 in.

|← 24 in. →|← 12 in. →|

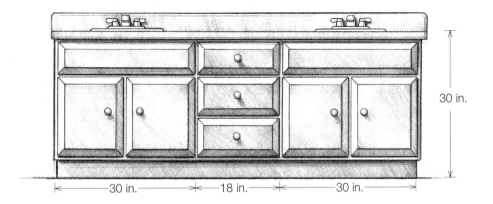

30 in.

|← 30 in. →|← 18 in. →|← 30 in. →|

The Difference between Stock, Semi-Custom, and Custom Cabinetry

In the world of cabinet manufacturers, I've found that the difference between the terms stock, semi-custom, and custom is not as clear-cut as you might think. Semi-custom, in particular, has always seemed ambiguous to me.

Stock cabinets are pretty straightforward. They're manufactured in standard sizes and supplied through distributors to places like The Home Depot, local lumberyards, and specialty kitchen and bath shops. Their carcases are typically of particleboard, though their doors, face frames (if they have them), and drawer fronts are usually of hardwood. Manufacturers keep the cost of their stock cabinets down by using simplified drawer construction and thinner paper-laminated particleboard in areas of the cabinet that aren't readily visible.

Semi-custom and custom cabinets often have the same hardwood drawer fronts, doors, and face frames as their less expensive stock cousins, but their carcases and drawers are usually of a higher-quality construction. While a stock-cabinet drawer might have particleboard sides stapled directly to the drawer front, better cabinets will have four-sided drawer boxes, often dovetailed, of solid hardwood screwed to the drawer front. Also, better cabinets will have sturdier carcases built of veneered plywood rather than particleboard (although MDF with either a melamine or high-pressure laminate surface is often used in high-quality face-frame and frameless cabinets).

Both semi-custom and custom cabinets are made to a specific customer order, rather than premanufactured, and require a sometimes-substantial lead time of between 3 and 12 weeks for delivery. For the close to 25% more that you can expect to pay for custom vs. semi-

A good way to judge the quality of a cabinet is by taking a careful look at its drawers. Dovetailed joints and solid wood construction indicate a drawer that is built to last.

custom cabinets, you'll see minor upgrades: ⅝-in. vs. ½-in. drawer stock, for example, or extended stiles rather than wood filler strips. In some cases, custom cabinets can actually be made slightly larger than standard size, though this varies from manufacturer to manufacturer.

Will one grade hold up better than another in the sometimes-hostile bathroom environment? The major functional difference between the three types of cabinets is in the type of drawer that they have. If Kitchen Cabinet Manufacturers Association (KCMA) certified, it's unlikely that installed custom-cabinet carcases will last any longer than KCMA-certified stock carcases, and in most cases the door frames and drawer fronts will be virtually identical. But the drawers are where the differences will show up over time.

For all three types of cabinets, you're limited to styles and sizes listed by the manufacturer, though in some cases custom cabinets can be ordered with an over-size stile to fill in a gap (rather than having to rely on a screwed-on filler strip) or even in a slightly larger size. Other differences are usually minor and depend upon the manufacturer.

ordinary bathroom; there are plenty of fine-looking stock cabinets around that are reasonably priced and well made.

The most reliable and economical source of bathroom cabinetry will be manufacturers who are members of the Kitchen Cabinet Manufacturers Association (KCMA) (see Resources on p. 209). Cabinets carrying KCMA certification labels meet standards for general design and construction, strength, finish, function, and hardware. Of course, this still leaves a lot of leeway; in cabinetry, as in most other things in life, you get what you pay for. Quality details like dovetailed drawers and mortise-and-tenon face frames are more expensive; so, too, are cabinet carcases of plywood and MDF rather than less-expensive particleboard, from which screws and staples are more likely to pull out.

Two Types of Cabinets

Frameless cabinets

Frameless cabinetry offers slightly more accessible storage space and simplified construction. A key part of frameless construction is the concealed cup hinge, which is strong, adjustable, and invisible when the door is closed. Frameless construction is adaptable to a number of different styles of cabinetry.

Face-frame cabinets

Face-frame cabinetry is strengthened by the hardwood frame, an advantage when the cabinet carcase is constructed of thin particleboard but redundant if the carcase is constructed out of better-quality ½-in. or ¾-in. sheet goods. Typical hinges for face-frame cabinets can be a liability because they aren't adjustable, making doors difficult to align both initially and after years of wear and tear.

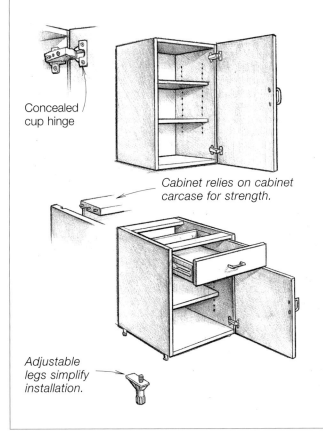

Concealed cup hinge

Cabinet relies on cabinet carcase for strength.

Adjustable legs simplify installation.

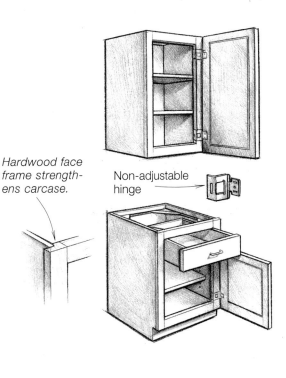

Hardwood face frame strengthens carcase.

Non-adjustable hinge

Choosing one particular style of cabinetry over another is largely a matter of personal taste. I have a preference for traditional frame-and-panel wood doors and face-frame cabinets, but I've found that flat full-overlay doors on Euro-style frameless cabinets offer better accessibility and are a little easier to keep clean (no corners for dust and dirt to settle in). Though I like the look of natural wood, cabinetry with a light-colored melamine or laminate interior is a great choice for bathrooms. The light coloring makes it easier to find things even when they are shoved toward the back, and the hard, durable surface is easy to clean and resists water and stains. Cabinets with this type of interior are available in either frameless or face-frame construction (see the drawing on p. 127).

Usually cabinets from one of the many major cabinet manufacturers can be configured to fit in almost any bathroom, but sometimes a cabinet built on-site or from a local woodworking shop is the only solution to a particular space and design problem. I've built a number of different styles of cabinets, both on-site and in my shop, and I've worked with cabinets built by local cabinetmakers. While I've been pleased with the results, these are expensive options; for any given level of quality, it's difficult to compete in price with a large-scale cabinet manufacturer.

Types of bathroom cabinetry

The *kind* of storage that a bathroom has is as important as the total *amount* of storage it has. Medicine cabinets are fine for holding small items, while a vanity cabinet (when there is one) is fine for holding bulkier items, like cleaning supplies and toilet paper. I've always wondered why medicine cabinets don't come with locks as standard issue. After all, they usually contain some potentially lethal stuff. But while most of them don't have locks, there is an enormous range of styles and sizes, some of which are designed to match other cabinetry in the bathroom (see the photo on the facing page).

Cabinets from Components

One way to offer fairly economical cabinetry that looks custom-built is to build your cabinets from components. Manufacturers who specialize in building cabinet doors, drawers, and carcases offer high-quality products at extremely competitive prices, certainly for less than I've found I can build them for on a time-and-material basis. For example, I don't build enough custom cabinets to justify the expense of having on hand the different shaper bits required to build the range of panel profiles, edge profiles, and frame profiles that I can get from the different door manufacturers. By ordering doors from one of these suppliers, I can offer new styles and profiles, usually in just about any wood that I want.

I've found components particularly helpful in bathroom renovation work. In many cases, a cabinet carcase can be built on-site around existing plumbing, a face frame can be attached to the carcase, and then doors, hardware, and drawers can be added later. While building a cabinet this way involves a fair amount of fitting to get doors and drawers to align properly, the result is a relatively economical built-in.

The carpenter side of me shudders when I see metal cabinets, but they do have a few advantages that make them a good choice in this particular situation. For one thing, they have more usable space inside than a wood cabinet of the same outside dimensions and are good for recessed installations because the sides of the cabinet will be hidden in the wall. Metal cabinets are also good for unobtrusive recessed installations when a vanity is set into a mirrored alcove; the metal cabinet can provide storage in the side wall to compensate for the fully mirrored surface directly behind the vanity (see the drawing below).

So the typical storage gives you places for the little stuff and the bulkier stuff you want hidden, but where do you put extra towels and washcloths? A linen cabinet or built-in linen closet is a good way to provide storage for this type of item. In many cases, a linen cabinet can be accommodated by making the vanity smaller

Medicine cabinets can be either recessed or surface mounted and come in a range of styles and materials, including this furniture-grade wood cabinet with beveled-glass doors. (Photo courtesy Omega Cabinets, Ltd.)

Finding More Room for Storage

A recessed medicine cabinet mounted in a side wall can provide unobtrusive storage and still allow for a large mirror over the sink. A shallow shelf extending behind the toilet adds additional countertop area, yet doesn't interfere with access to the low one-piece toilet.

A full-height linen cabinet placed next to a vanity doesn't take up much floor area but provides plenty of storage area at more convenient heights than a vanity-base cabinet. (Photo courtesy Omega Cabinets, Ltd.)

and placing a matching full-height cabinet right next to it (see the photo on the facing page). Large countertops just tend to collect clutter anyway, while a linen cabinet's smaller vertically arranged shelves are more efficient and make more items easily accessible.

If there will be a recessed medicine cabinet centered in front of the sink, I've found that it pays to make room for it while doing the framing, whether or not an actual decision has been made at this point about cabinetry. While larger cabinets will need an appropriately sized rough opening (and advance planning), at the very least lay out studs so that a standard 14-in. recessed cabinet can fit where it is supposed to without having to tear into framing again. A little foresight can save a lot of aggravation later if plans about cabinetry change and can help ensure that a plumbing vent won't have to be rerouted around the recessed cabinet.

Cabinet accessories

There are a number of different cabinet accessories available to help make bathroom cabinetry more user-friendly. As I've mentioned, the depth and low location of most vanities means that storage there is often poorly utilized, but a roll-out drawer that mounts on the bottom of the cabinet makes it easier to reach items like cleaning supplies or extra rolls of toilet paper that might otherwise get shoved to the back of the cabinet (see the top photo at right). A roll-out or tilt-out hamper is another good way to utilize this space (assuming that the plumbing doesn't interfere with its operation), and it provides a convenient place to throw dirty laundry (see the bottom photo at right). I prefer tilt-out hampers mounted on a bottom-hinged door because they require only one motion to open.

Other cabinet-door-mounted epoxy-coated wire racks are available for items like toilet paper and cleaning supplies, and there is even a magazine

Accessories like this sliding shelf, which operates automatically as the door is opened or closed, are easily fitted to new or existing cabinetry. (Photo courtesy Blue Heron Enterprises, Inc.)

Other options to make bathroom storage more useful include this pull-out laundry hamper. (Photo courtesy Feeny/Knape & Vogt Manufacturing Co.)

rack that mounts on the side of a toilet tank. Also available are plastic drawer inserts to help organize cosmetics (see the left photo below). None of these accessories are particularly expensive or difficult to install, and they add a useful and custom touch to stock cabinetry.

SPECIALTY STORAGE

There are a few other ways to maximize the utility of a bathroom. For example, deck-mounted whirlpool tubs need access panels to their pumps and plumbing, and it isn't hard to build a shallow, easily removable cabinet to fit in that space. Or if the panel is hinge mounted like a cabinet door rather than more permanently attached, that area underneath the tub can also be used for storage. Sometimes there might be a wall cavity (behind a kneewall, for example) that can be used for extra storage space, though it might require some creative carpentry and odd-shaped cabinets.

While nooks and crannies can be converted by a clever carpenter into bathroom storage space, open shelving is usually an easier and more economical storage solution. Items like towels and bathtub toys look good on open shelves, adding color and texture to the bathroom.

Drawer inserts fit stock or custom cabinetry and help organize small items like cosmetics. (Photo courtesy Feeny/Knape & Vogt Manufacturing Co.)

Open shelving recessed into a wall is an efficient way to provide storage for frequently used items like towels.

A Vertical Towel Rack Recessed into a Stud Bay

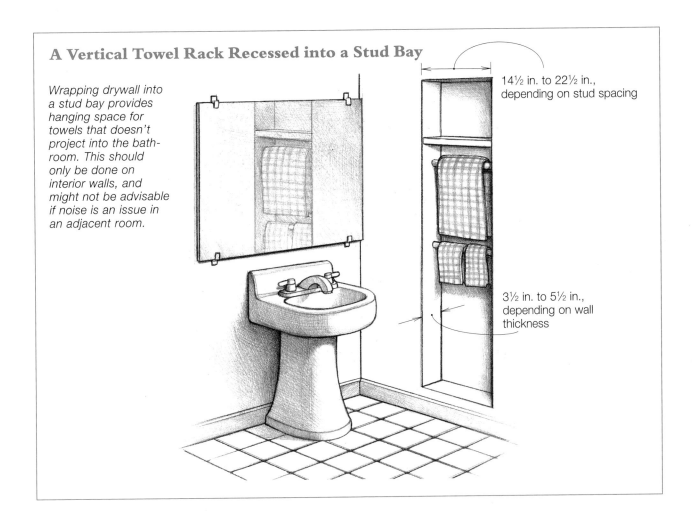

Wrapping drywall into a stud bay provides hanging space for towels that doesn't project into the bathroom. This should only be done on interior walls, and might not be advisable if noise is an issue in an adjacent room.

14½ in. to 22½ in., depending on stud spacing

3½ in. to 5½ in., depending on wall thickness

Simple wood or melamine shelves supported by track-mounted brackets install quickly and are good for underutilized areas like above the toilet. Other options include shallow shelving recessed into a wall cavity (see the right photo on the facing page) and bookcase-style shelving coordinated with other bathroom cabinetry.

Is there a good place for an ironing board in your house? If you can't think of one (I certainly can't), why not mount a cabinet-mounted ironing board on the bathroom wall. At as little as 16 in. wide by 48 in. tall by 4⅝ in. deep, these cabinets don't take up much room, and even when lowered into position the ironing board will still be useful in an average-size bathroom.

And finally, one thing I like to see in a bathroom is plenty of hooks from which to hang clothes and towels. The back of a door is a good place to put hooks, as is right near the entry to the tub or shower; these are locations that aren't always ideal for a full-size towel bar. Of course, plenty of towel bars are desirable too, though most bathrooms have a limited amount of wall space for them. A towel rack that is mounted on the wall is one solution to this problem; another is to wrap drywall into a stud bay and mount bars above one another between the studs (see the drawing above). Another option is to install an electric or hydronic panel radiator, which combines the functions of a heater and a towel rack in one unit.

Part Two

CONSTRUCTION

Chapter 8

FRAMING

There's an old saying that a roof is only as good and as straight as the foundation supporting it. This is true for bathrooms as well. But besides the literal building foundation (which may or may not be adequate—always a good thing to verify), the bathroom's foundation is also its superstructure, or shell. This includes the floor, wall, and ceiling framing, as well as the plumbing, electrical, and mechanical systems that service the room. Whether in new construction or in remodeling work, a successful and functional bathroom depends in large part on a good foundation of solid framing.

There are two ways to approach framing a bathroom: just like any other room or as a special space with specific needs. Both ways take about the same amount of time and essentially the same materials, and if the only responsibility you have toward the house is the framing, then it won't really make much difference to you. By the time the plumber starts pulling out his reciprocating saw to remove parts of joists, studs, and blocking that are in his way, you'll be long gone. But if you're like me, you'll be around when the plumber is there cursing and chopping away at lumber. You'll also be there when it comes time to lay tile, and if the walls aren't plumb or straight, you'll know about it. Both situations can produce a major headache, so I like to try to follow the second approach and frame a bathroom with its function in mind.

FLOOR JOISTS

A floor plan will indicate the location of major plumbing fixtures like toilets and tubs, and simply paying attention to fixture locations when laying out floor joists so that they don't need to be moved or chopped away later can save a lot of aggravation. For example, the closet bend for a toilet is pretty bulky and needs a lot of room—about a 6-in. square space—to drop down through the floor system. Sometimes the floor-framing plan takes this into account and shifts joists so that the closet bend falls into an open bay. If it doesn't, though, it isn't a hard problem to fix. Since the closet bend is usually centered 12 in. from the finish wall, center the first floor joist either no farther than 8¼ in. from the finish wall or so that it leaves at least 3 in. of clearance from the center of the drain (see the drawing below). The next joist can then be laid out so that it too has 3 in. of clearance from the center of the drain, which will leave 6 in. of clearance for the closet bend. Blocking around the toilet will stiffen the floor considerably under the toilet, reducing the chance of leakage around the wax ring later on. The remaining floor joists can be laid out normally from either the first floor joist or the second floor joist.

Framing to Accommodate Toilet Plumbing

Bathroom floor joists should be laid out so that they don't have to be cut later on to make room for the toilet's closet bend.

- Toilet outline
- Finish wall
- 2x studs
- 6 in. (min.)
- 8¼ in.
- 12 in.
- 16 in. o.c.
- 3 in.
- 4-in. closet bend

Framing to Accommodate Bathtub Plumbing

Framing should be planned to make it easier to run plumbing and to minimize cutting and notching of joists. Floor joists in particular should be laid out so that they don't interfere with the bathtub drain, while stud layout in the shower-valve wall should leave plenty of clearance for the shower valve and related supply lines.

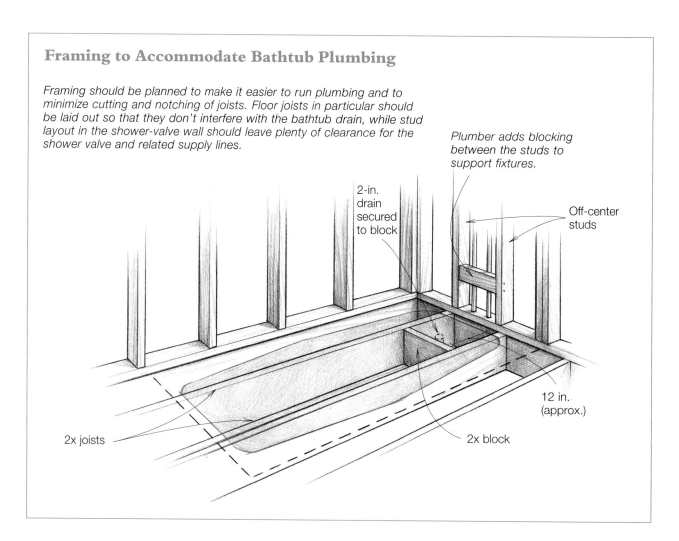

Plumber adds blocking between the studs to support fixtures.

2-in. drain secured to block

Off-center studs

12 in. (approx.)

2x joists

2x block

While the larger 4-in. toilet drain certainly requires more framing clearance, the bathtub drain will also need to have room to drop through the floor. The best way to do this is to find the center of the drain and lay out the floor joists equidistant from that on their 16-in. centers (see the drawing above). If the floor joists are running perpendicular to the length of the tub, try to avoid having any joists closer than 12 in. from the valve wall. If the joist layout works for one fixture but not another, don't be afraid to add an extra joist or two; the added cost will be minimal compared to the cost of coming back later and chopping stuff up and moving it.

Another way to help framing and plumbing cooperate is to use metal bridging or 1x X-type bridging for floor joists instead of solid 2x blocking. Snaking plumbing and wiring through the bridging is much faster and easier than chopping through solid blocking with a reciprocating saw. If you do cut blocking for high-traffic plumbing areas, it's a good idea to leave the nails slightly protruding so that they can be more easily pulled and removed. This gives the plumber more flexibility in running his pipes, but you must remember to come back later to nail them home. Another note about nails: Try to keep them out of places where plumbers and electricians will be drilling holes. When nailing plates down, pay attention to where it looks like supply or drain pipes might be dropping through, and don't nail all the way home so that the nails can be easily pulled and moved later on. When nailing plates, try to nail into floor joists rather than into just subfloor because plumbers don't usually try to bore holes there anyway and because it's a better place to nail in general.

Finally, it's worthwhile to think about how large plumbing lines are affected by joist layout. Remember it's not easy to figure out how to route 3-in. and 4-in. pipe through the framing and then face drilling the series of large holes that it might require. You can often avoid running the pipe through framing by simply rotating floor joists 90° so that a drain can run along a joist bay instead of having to travel perpendicular to the joists.

WALL FRAMING

According to the Tile Council of America (TCA) (see Resources on p. 209), walls that are 8 ft. high (typical bathroom wall height) should be no more than ⅛ in. out of plumb if they are to be tiled without taking corrective measures. That isn't a lot of leeway, but it's a good goal to shoot for when framing bathroom walls. Even when tile isn't specified, plumb walls make installing other items—like combination tub/shower units—a whole lot easier. If you take a look at the sliding glass doors on a combination tub/shower and notice that there is a big gap at the top or bottom when the doors are closed, that's because the tub was installed in an inaccurately framed and out-of-plumb rough opening. Tile that is installed on severely out-of-plumb walls will look crooked because the cuts will have to be tapered to compensate for the faulty wall.

If there is a combination tub/shower unit planned, the framed opening for it should be ⅛ in. longer than the actual measured length of the tub (which may differ from the manufacturer's spec sheet). Frame any end walls about 5 in. longer than the width of the tub, which will leave enough room to wrap drywall and corner bead, as well as make it easy to tape with a 6-in. knife. Blocking will be needed where grab bars are located, along the top flange of the tub, and around plumbing. Insulation will be needed on exterior walls and will make the shower quieter if it's added to interior walls as well.

Walls also need to be straight, and if you've noticed the quality of 2x framing lumber lately you'll see that this isn't always so easy to do. Typically when I frame walls I like to make sure that all of the studs are crowned (the slight bow that most dimensional lumber has) in one direction, usually outward. In bathrooms I'll try to take this one step further and work with the straightest studs possible, eliminating any framing with anything more than a slight crown. While I've never worked with light-gauge steel studs, they might be a reasonable option for interior walls in a bathroom; they certainly would be straight. If you end up with crooked framing anyway, a portable power plane is a handy tool for straightening it. (See the sidebar on pp. 140-141.)

Pay special attention to making sure that walls are parallel or perpendicular to each other in a bathroom when you lay them out. If there is any kind of flooring with a geometric pattern—like tile or many kinds of resilient flooring—walls that are out of square will be really noticeable. Don't hesitate to use a framing square and a 3-4-5 right triangle to verify

Fixing Existing Framing Problems

Because remodeling accounts for more than two-thirds of the amount spent annually on construction, it isn't enough for a small builder to be able to put a bathroom together from scratch. He also needs to be able to analyze an existing bathroom and pinpoint its problems.

Besides the typical framing problems of working with an existing structure, the biggest hurdle in most renovation bathroom projects is making room for changes, which often requires demolition. I always approach demolition with two competing impulses. One is to totally gut the room and cart everything away to the dump, while the other is to try to remove as little as possible. Though expensive and messy, gutting gives you the most control over the final product and is often the only way to fix problems like sagging or rotting joists and studs. Sometimes, though, surgical demolition is a less-expensive and more efficient alternative, particularly if the character of the bathroom is worth saving.

If you are remodeling a bathroom, you'll need to take a close look at the framing, which may be difficult depending on where the bathroom is located in the house. In some cases, framing problems begin at the foundation, so be sure to check its condition. An out-of-level floor indicates that there may be some problem that needs to be addressed, like undersized joists, but finished floors and ceilings may make it difficult to determine the exact problem until you can open things up. Bouncing in place on the floor should give you a rough idea of its load-bearing capacity.

When checking the floor system, keep in mind the proposed finished floor; tile is less forgiving of structural deficiencies than resilient flooring. Fixing a structurally inadequate floor may mean replacing or sistering on floor joists to beef up the floor system or providing other means of structural support.

Walls need to be checked to make sure that they are plumb and straight. Commonly you'll find the insulation in the walls is inadequate. Many times there are voids caused by careless insulation installation, but you won't know this unless you open up the walls. If you do open up walls, be sure to add blocking for grab bars and look for (and fill with caulk) holes in the exterior sheathing.

If you notice a stud that is bowed, it can be brought back into alignment by cutting a notch in it to accept a 2x4 that extends to the adjacent studs. Nail one side of the 2x4 to one of the studs, then push back on the other end until the offending stud is in alignment again, toenailing it as necessary (see the drawings on the facing page). Of course, if the stud is accessible at the top and bottom, it might be easier just to replace it. Another method of straightening crooked walls and ceilings is to fur the walls out with 1x strapping and appropriately placed shims, a technique that I regularly use in renovation work.

Ceilings shouldn't be neglected either. Cracks in plaster or openings around fixtures or ceiling fans allow warm moist air to escape into the house framing or attic, and they should be sealed off. A suspended ceiling is notorious for allowing warm air to escape, though you'll often see them installed in old houses with high ceilings in the theory that the lower ceiling will make the room easier to heat and more comfortable. It's better to frame a new ceiling with 2x4s or 2x6s and use regular drywall, which is effective at stopping air movement and vapor transmission. And if the ceiling is also an attic, be sure that a complete blanket of insulation is up on top.

Straight walls are critical in a bathroom, particularly if there will be tilework. Sometimes bowed framing is easily replaced, but in some cases it is easier to straighten it using one of the techniques below.

Bowed-in stud

Toenail crossmember as deep as needed to remove bow.

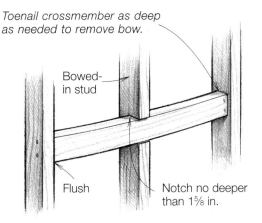

Bowed-in stud

Flush

Notch no deeper than 1⅝ in.

A stud that bows into a room can be straightened by notching it, adding a crossmember, and nailing it as shown until the bow is removed.

Bowed-out stud

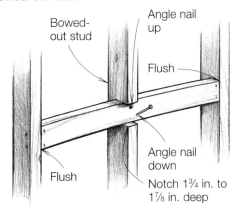

Bowed-out stud

Angle nail up

Flush

Flush

Angle nail down

Notch 1¾ in. to 1⅞ in. deep

A stud that bows away from a room can be brought back into plane by making a deeper notch than the thickness of the crossmember, nailing the crossmember flush with the two adjacent studs, then nailing through the crossmember into the bowed stud until it is pulled back into alignment.

that the walls that you are laying out in the bathroom are truly square (see the drawing on p. 142).

When framing a valve wall for a conventional tub, don't forget that there will be a big shower valve located right in the middle of it. But since tubs are usually about 32 in. wide, a lot of carpenters just lay out the studs from the back wall and plunk a stud on its 16-in. center...right in the middle where it shouldn't be. It's better to use an extra stud and divide the space into equal thirds, leaving a clear bay for the plumber

Plumbing the shower valve wall is easier if there is an open stud bay centered on the shower valve.

Determining If Corners Are Square

Accurate layout will help ensure that walls are parallel and corners are square. A framing square can help with short walls (as long as it is accurate), but the most accurate method is to use a 3-4-5 right triangle, where $c^2=a^2+b^2$ (see below).

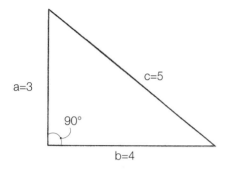

This basic relationship can be used to establish square wall layout, as well as to check after the fact to plan for installing any geometrically rigid flooring material (like tile). In the example below, if any of the measurements don't correspond to the basic 3-4-5 right triangle, then one wall is not exactly perpendicular to the other wall.

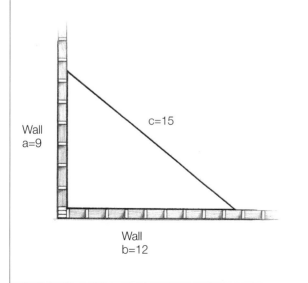

A continuous drywall ceiling is the best way to prevent warm, moist air from escaping into the ceiling.

to run his supply and drain pipes and install the shower valve (see the photo on p. 141).

It's important to make sure that the exterior walls and the ceiling of a bathroom form a continuous barrier against air movement into building cavities. The best way to do this behind any prefabricated enclosure is to first hang drywall, taking care to tape joints (see the photo above). Besides being a more durable barrier to air movement than 6-mil. poly, drywall will also function as a fire-stop, which may be required by code in some areas.

HOLES AND NOTCHES

The building codes are very clear about the size and placement of notches and holes in joists and studs. Most plumbers know these rules, but if you are doing your own plumbing (or part of it), you'll have to follow them too. Basically, holes can't be drilled within 2 in. of the top or bottom edge of the joist, and they can't be larger than one-third the depth of the joist (see the drawing on the facing page). Notches can't be deeper than one-sixth the joist depth and can't be put in the middle one-third of the span; if they are located at the end of the joist, they can't be deeper than one-quarter the joist depth.

Cutting Notches and Holes in Joists

The major building codes are in agreement about the size of notches and holes that won't compromise the strength of solid-wood floor joists. Don't cut or notch engineered joists without consulting their manufacturer or an engineer.

Studding

Plates

Notches not more than $\frac{1}{6}$ joist depth and not in middle third of span

Holes should be same size as pipe, not much more than $\frac{1}{3}$ joist depth, and not within 2 in. of top or bottom edge at the joist.

Joist

$\frac{1}{3}$ $\frac{2}{3}$ $\frac{3}{3}$

No more than $\frac{1}{4}$ joist depth

Splice

Sometimes cutting and notching is unavoidable, but usually framing can be laid out to make it easier to run plumbing and wiring.

Codes are also specific about cutting into studs, allowing holes no greater than 40% of the total width of the stud (or about 1½ in. in a 2x4 and 2¼ in. in a 2x6). Nonbearing or bearing studs that are doubled can have holes up to 60% of their width. The edge of the bored holes should be at least ⅝ in. from the edge of the stud to minimize the chance of penetration by drywall screws. Pipes that pass through these holes should be protected by 1½-in.-wide by ⅛-in.-thick steel plates nailed with no fewer than six 16d nails.

It will be tempting to bore oversize holes to make it easier to pull wire and run pipe, but don't do it. Fire-prevention provisions of most building codes dictate that bored holes should be the same size as the pipe or conduit passing through it. The fit shouldn't be so tight that the pipe binds, but it shouldn't be so loose that small creatures can pass through.

Chapter 9

ROUGHING-IN SYSTEMS

PLUMBING

ELECTRICAL

HEATING

Once the superstructure of a bathroom is in place, it's time to turn attention to the systems that bring water, electricity, and heat into the room. Like other small builders that I know, I rely on subcontractors to do much of this work. But on many small jobs it's more expedient to run an extra electrical circuit or sweat a few copper joints myself rather than trying to schedule an electrician or a plumber. But whether you subcontract the work or do it yourself, builders need to be well informed about the rough-in requirements of a bathroom's plumbing, electrical, and heating systems. Chapter 2 presented the basic components of typical bathroom systems while highlighting some important design issues that should be considered and some of the requirements of the various codes. In this chapter, we'll take a look at how these systems get put in place.

PLUMBING

Installing water-supply and DWV systems in a house isn't rocket science, and it isn't beyond the capability of a competent nonprofessional, but I can guarantee that it will take a nonprofessional at least twice the time to do the same job as an experienced plumber, not to mention the general aggravation. If you've ever peeked in the back of a plumber's van, you'll notice that they carry *a lot* of small parts; these parts are what you won't have when you're trying to do your own plumbing. For more information on doing your own plumbing, check out Peter Hemp's *Plumbing a House* (The Taunton Press, 1994).

I rely on the plumber to bring supply and drain pipes into the bathroom, but it's up to me to make sure that everything goes to the right locations. Because I usually work with a subcontractor that I've worked with before, I have confidence that he'll meet or exceed code in sizing pipes and in his level of workmanship.

And he knows that I'll supply him with specific information about the fixtures to be installed, including stubout locations and unusual details on shower and tub configurations. In order to do that, I need to either have the actual fixtures (preferably) or the manufacturer's specifications (at the very least). Most important, we work together, which is the key to approaching plumbing installation.

Sinks
You'll need to know the type of sink (or sinks) planned for a bathroom and its exact location. A pedestal sink, for example, will require an exactly centered drain, while a vanity sink is

---

Sink Rough-In Dimensions

The drain and hot and cold supplies for a bathroom sink should be roughed in about 19 in. to 23 in. above the subfloor. Offsetting the drain will allow room for the trap to make a clean connection.

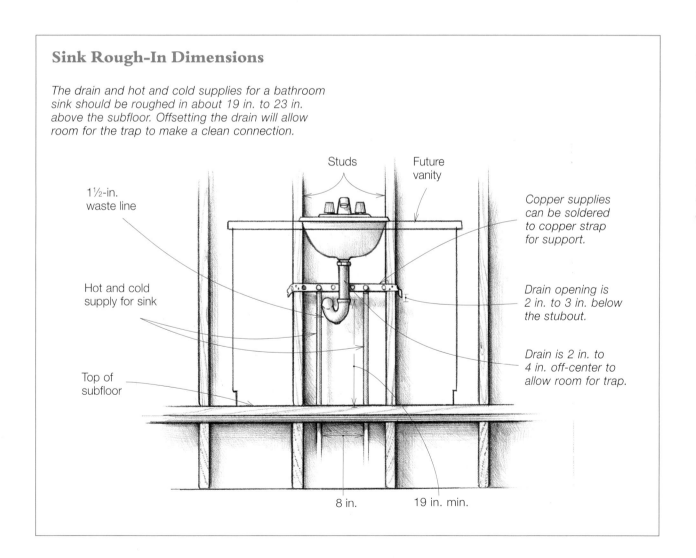

Studs

Future vanity

1½-in. waste line

Copper supplies can be soldered to copper strap for support.

Hot and cold supply for sink

Drain opening is 2 in. to 3 in. below the stubout.

Drain is 2 in. to 4 in. off-center to allow room for trap.

Top of subfloor

8 in.   19 in. min.

better off with a drain offset a few inches from centerline. Hot and cold supply lines should be centered 8 in. apart and end slightly above the drain opening (see the drawing on p. 145). Some plumbers will nail copper strap, which has ½-in. and ¾-in. holes spaced at regular intervals, to the framing to help space and securely hold copper supply lines, which can be soldered directly to the strap.

Toilets and bidets

The vast majority of new toilets now requires the flange to be roughed-in at 12 in. o.c. from the finish wall, or 12½ in. o.c. from the framed wall if the finish walls will be drywall (see the drawing below). Of course, it might be possible that the finish wall will be thicker than standard ½-in. drywall (for example ¾-in. wood wainscoting or tile set in a thick mortar bed); this detail will need to be verified before the

Toilet Rough-In Dimensions

The toilet flange should be roughly level with the finish floor and centered at least 12 in. from the back finish wall. One-piece toilets require a lower cold-water-supply stubout, while two-piece toilet supplies can be located higher on the wall.

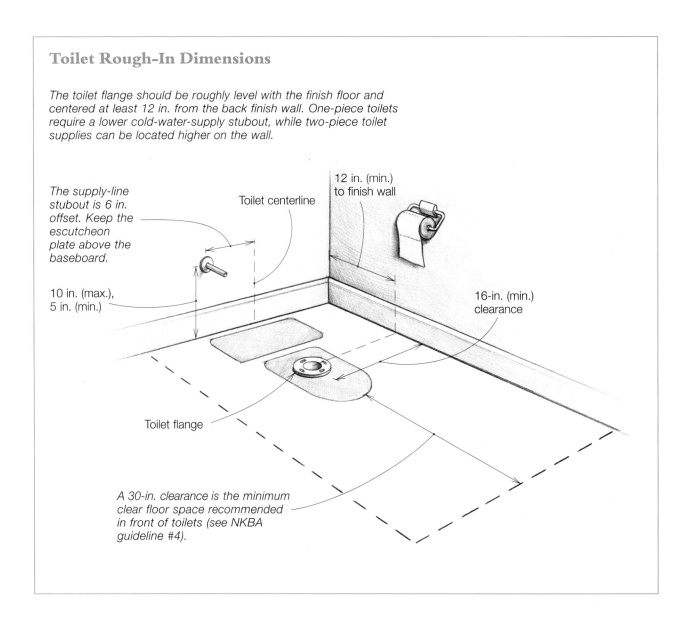

The supply-line stubout is 6 in. offset. Keep the escutcheon plate above the baseboard.

Toilet centerline

12 in. (min.) to finish wall

10 in. (max.), 5 in. (min.)

16-in. (min.) clearance

Toilet flange

A 30-in. clearance is the minimum clear floor space recommended in front of toilets (see NKBA guideline #4).

toilet flange can be accurately roughed-in. Many plumbers will rough-in at 13 in. o.c. from the framed wall, which leaves 1 in. for finish wall material and dimensional variations in the fixture.

The top of the flange should ideally lie flush with the finish floor, so you'll have to take account of the finish floor material when setting the flange in place. Anything more than ¼ in. off in either direction can cause problems, but it is better to be a little low than too high. If the finish floor will be ¾-in. wood flooring or tile set in a thick mortar bed, block up the flange with a ½-in. or ¾-in. plywood ring to the estimated height of the floor.

If the cold-water supply comes through the wall, it should be placed high enough above the eventual height of the baseboard so that neither the baseboard nor the escutcheon plate around the pipe will need to be cut or trimmed. Low-profile one-piece toilets require a lower supply pipe, while higher two-piece toilets work fine with supply pipes up to 10 in. above the finish floor. If the supply pipe enters from the floor, offset it enough from the framed wall to provide clearance for the escutcheon plate and baseboard. Whether the supply enters from the floor or the wall, it should be offset 6 in. from the centerline of the toilet. Wall-hung toilets and urinals will require a manufacturer-specific installation.

Bidets present far more rough-in variables than toilets, which for the most part are now standardized (see the drawing on p. 48). While most bidets have a self-contained P-trap that connects directly to a sanitary tee via a long trap arm, the manufacturer's specifications for the particular bidet that will be installed should be consulted to determine the type and location of the drain opening. Valve systems for bidets also vary, with some mounted on the wall and some mounted on the bidet itself. Again, the manufacturer's specifications will need to be consulted to establish the rough-in locations for the water supplies.

Tubs and showers

Tubs and combination tub/shower units are usually set in place before any DWV connections are roughed-in. It's easier to verify the exact location of the drain opening this way, especially because manufacturer's specifications often differ from the drain opening's actual location on individual units. But before you set the unit, cut a 12-in. by 12-in. cutout in the subfloor, centered underneath the tub's approximate drain location, to leave plenty of room for the waste and overflow (W&O) tee and tailpiece. (If you followed the framing guidelines in Chapter 8, this area should already be clear of floor joists; if it isn't, you'll have to do some cutting and headering.) After the tub is in place, the tub W&O fitting can be assembled, installed, and connected to the P-trap and DWV system. If the tub will be set on a slab, there should be a tub box, or opening in the slab, with a P-trap and drain already waiting to be connected to the tailpiece of the W&O fitting (see the drawing on p. 148). In this case, the W&O will already be installed before the tub is set in place, though making the final connection will be a little tricky.

Many builders set tubs and shower stalls early in the construction process, before the finish floor is installed, but I think it's better to have the finish floor run underneath the tub than stop at the edge. This helps prevent water from penetrating through the inevitable seam that will open up and into the subfloor, where it can cause rot. Besides, a caulked joint here looks

Setting a Tub on a Slab Floor

Tub W&O fittings will need to be installed before a tub is set on a slab floor because of the limited access to the underside of the tub once it is in place. For regular wood-framed floor construction, the connections can be made after the tub is set in place.

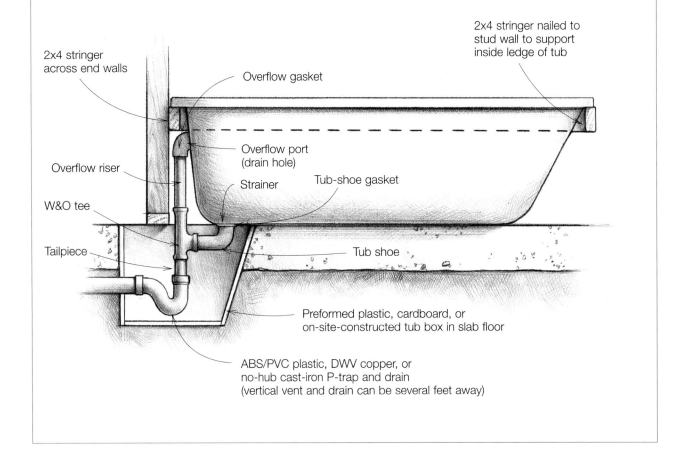

2x4 stringer nailed to stud wall to support inside ledge of tub

2x4 stringer across end walls

Overflow gasket

Overflow port (drain hole)

Overflow riser

Strainer

Tub-shoe gasket

W&O tee

Tailpiece

Tub shoe

Preformed plastic, cardboard, or on-site-constructed tub box in slab floor

ABS/PVC plastic, DWV copper, or no-hub cast-iron P-trap and drain (vertical vent and drain can be several feet away)

terrible (see the photo on the facing page). This will mean taking extra care of the finish floor, and will complicate hanging drywall, but it will result in a better looking and more waterproof bathroom.

Hopefully the valve wall will have been framed to leave an empty stud bay centered over the tub drain (see the drawing on the facing page). Blocking will eventually be needed to securely

attach both the shower stubout and the faucet body to the framing, and it can be either a piece of 2x cutoff or a scrap of ¾-in. plywood (which is less likely to split). The blocking will have to be set at the correct height for both the faucet and the showerhead. A typical faucet height is 30 in., and a typical showerhead height is 72 in., but these can be varied according to personal preference.

Consider installing tub and shower units after the finish floor to prevent this ugly joint that is vulnerable to water and dirt from opening up. (Photo by the author.)

Setting the blocking at the correct depth in the wall is a little trickier and depends on the particular type of faucet, as well as the type of finish wall. Some faucets have a limited degree of adjustability (sometimes less than 1 in.), while others are more adaptable to different wall-surface depths. Some manufacturers offer extensions, a feature that you'll appreciate if your client changes his or her mind about a shower wall-surface material, like from a thin Corian to a thick mortar-bed-and-tile surface. Many faucets come with plastic setting gauges that indicate the correct mounting depth for the valve.

Tub/Shower Valve Rough-In

Shower valve and stubout heights can vary depending on the requirements of the people who will be using them. ADA guidelines give a range of between 38 in. and 48 in. above the floor for the control area in a shower stall, but for someone seated in a tub this is probably too high. A better height might be around 30 in. A showerhead stubout is often set 72 in. above the floor, but for a short adult or child this might be too high, while a tall adult would have to duck down to be immersed in the shower stream.

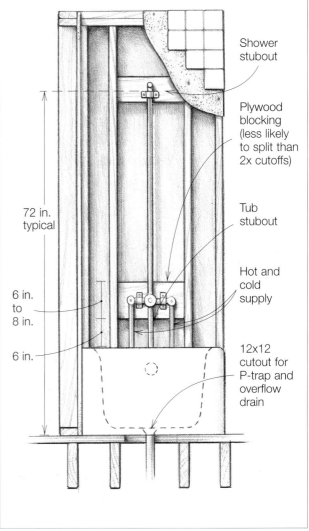

Shower stubout

Plywood blocking (less likely to split than 2x cutoffs)

Tub stubout

Hot and cold supply

12x12 cutout for P-trap and overflow drain

72 in. typical

6 in. to 8 in.

6 in.

A potential problem with one-piece or two-piece tub units and shower stalls is that the valves and stubouts can get in the way of sliding the unit into the framing. If the valve is on a sidewall instead of a back wall (see Chapter 2 for layout considerations), the protruding stubouts will mean you won't be able to slide the unit into place very easily, if at all. In that case, you'll have to wait until the unit is in place to install blocking and to attach the plumbing to the blocking because you'll need to be able to pull everything back into the stud bay to slide the plastic tub or shower unit in place. If the valve wall is an exterior wall (not a good idea in a cold climate), then you may have to access the wall from the exterior of the building. (For more on installing tubs and showers, see Chapter 10.)

Atypical tub/shower set-ups, like walk-in showers, need to be roughed-in to accommodate their particular water-supply and drain system needs. For example, a tiled shower floor with a waterproofing membrane will require a two-piece clamping drain set high enough to accommodate a sloped mud floor, the waterproofing membrane, mortar or adhesive, and tile. If there will be multiple showerheads or valves, they too will have to be roughed-in according to the needs of that particular installation, and will probably require the expertise of a plumber to ensure adequate water pressure and temperature.

ELECTRICAL

Compared to the plumbing, electrical system rough-in can be a breeze. Romex cable and the associated boxes and connectors that electricians use are clean, lightweight, and easily maneuvered. The holes that electricians need to make are small, and even though they may have to fish some cable through finish walls and climb into attics and shimmy into crawl spaces, they don't have to deal with heavy cast-iron pipe or the waste that flows through it. At the risk of sounding repetitious, though, I'd like to reiterate a precaution about working with

electrical systems. Any work that you do on an electrical system is potentially dangerous, and while much (if not all) of the rough-in electrical work is within the ability of any careful and conscientious builder, this book is no substitute for either a qualified electrician or general knowledge and experience with residential wiring. If terms or procedures are unfamiliar or unclear, then you should seek help. For a good practical introduction to residential electrical systems, you might try Rex Cauldwell's *Wiring a House* (The Taunton Press, 1997).

Circuitry and cable

There should be at least two circuits to the bathroom, with at least one being a 12-gauge 20-amp GFCI-protected outlet circuit; the other is the switched-lighting circuit, which can be a lighter 15-amp circuit but which is more commonly a 20-amp circuit as well. If there is a fan or light in the shower (considered to be a wet area), it will need to be on a GFCI-protected circuit; otherwise, bathroom lighting needs to be separated from GFCI-protected circuitry so that the lights don't go out if the GFCI trips. If there are any other appliances in the bathroom, such as an in-wall electrical heater, a whirlpool, or a steam generator, they too will need their own appropriately sized circuits, and in the case of the whirlpool, the circuit will have to be GFCI-protected as well.

In most cases, type NM (Romex) cable—with two or more insulated wires, a bare grounding wire, and paper insulation all protected by a thermoplastic jacket—will be the cable of choice. Type NM 12-2, which has two conductors and a ground, is commonly used for most general outlet and small-appliance wiring, though some situations (such as three-way switches) will require 12-3 cable (with three conductors and a bare grounding wire). While codes usually permit 14-gauge 15-amp circuits for general-purpose lighting and receptacles, most electricians I've worked with prefer to use 12-gauge cable consistently throughout the

Different Types of Electrical Cable

BX or armor–clad (AC) cable

Designed for small (less than 30 amp) circuits, the spiral metal armor serves as both conduit and ground. It's used for interior circuits only.

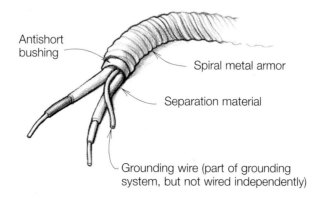

Antishort bushing

Spiral metal armor

Separation material

Grounding wire (part of grounding system, but not wired independently)

Romex (type NM, or nonmetallic-sheathed) cable

This is the most common cable used for home wiring. It's available in different types for different applications like routing behind walls, ceilings, and floors.

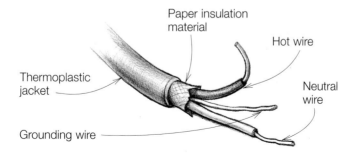

Paper insulation material

Hot wire

Thermoplastic jacket

Neutral wire

Grounding wire

house, unless heavier cable (and larger-capacity circuits) is required.

Armor-clad (AC) cable, often called BX cable, is used far less commonly now in residential construction than it used to be. I occasionally run across it in renovation work, and I cringe when I do because it is harder to work with than Romex, requiring anti-short bushings and special boxes. In some areas and in some types of construction BX cable is specified by code because the flexible metal jacket serves as a conduit and protects the cable within. But rather than try to tie in with BX circuitry, I usually run new branches to the bathroom with Romex. If I come across old knob-and-tube wiring, of course, I'll pass by that circuit altogether, since it isn't grounded. And if it gets too complicated, I'll call my electrician.

Code requires that cable should be stapled at a maximum of every 4½ ft. in the center of studs (1¼ in. minimum on either side of the cable to the edge of the stud) and within 12 in. of a metallic box (8 in. from a plastic box). Like plumbing, cable needs to be protected by metal plates where it passes through notches or through holes closer than 1¼ in. from the edge of a stud or plate. Be sure to unwind the cable from the spool so that it lies flat instead of twisted in coils, and nail staples so that the cable lies individually rather than stacked on top of other cable and flat instead of on edge.

Receptacle boxes

There are many different sizes, shapes, and materials for receptacle boxes, but if you want to make things easier for yourself, always use the deepest box you can find that will fit. Trying to stuff too many wires and connectors into a box is not only frustrating, but it will also probably

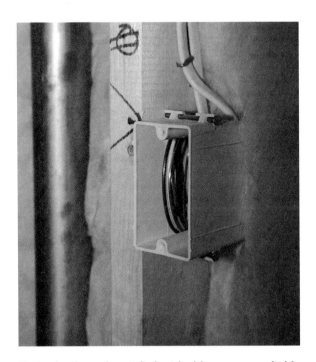

Both plastic and metal electrical boxes are suitable for new construction. They come in different styles and sizes for different applications.

result in a violation of code and be unsafe. Nonmetallic, or plastic, boxes are cheaper, faster to install, nonconductive, and preferred by drywallers who cut their wall openings with those tiny, whining mini-routers (see the photo below). Most electricians prefer them too, though there are still a few who swear by metal boxes, which used to be the industry standard. I like metal boxes, too, because they feel more substantial (they don't bow or bend when you attach them to a stud, for example), have better clamps, and are reusable. Both metal and plastic boxes are available in different configurations for different applications; knowing which box to use when is almost a subspecialty.

The few receptacle boxes that are in the bathroom will need to be placed carefully. Blocking might be needed near the entryway framing to keep the switches and switchplate cover out of the way of the door casing, and you'll need to account for the height of the vanity backsplash in determining the location of the vanity outlets. Double sinks should have either one outlet placed in between the sinks or two outlets—each placed within 12 in. of either side of the sink. Because some medicine cabinets have integral lights and are hard-wired, you may not need a fixture box for the cable; if that's the case, you can just run cable long and hard-wire it into the cabinet when it is mounted later on.

Lights and fans

Vanity and ceiling lighting, which is pretty much everything other than hard-wired medicine cabinets with integral lights, will require mounting either fixture boxes (for surface-mounted lighting), recessed-light housings, or combination fan/lights or fan/light/heaters. A pancake box, the most common type of fixture box, is round and about ½ in. thick and 3½ in. or so in diameter, though slightly larger diameters and depths are available. The light fixture mounts either directly to the pancake box or to a mounting plate that is screwed to the box, and boxes can be mounted either on the wall or on the ceiling. (By the way, don't use plastic receptacle boxes for ceiling-mounted fixtures because they aren't strong enough.) In most cases, the pancake boxes don't even need to be recessed and can be mounted directly on the wall or ceiling and screwed to the framing underneath because they are usually totally covered by the fixture.

Recessed lights generally have their own self-contained wire-connection box. They are usually attached to the framing with metal hangers, with the bottom face of the housing flush with the bottom of the framing. Some recessed-light housings are rated for contact with insulation (called IC-fixtures) and can be used in attic spaces. Thermal housings (called T-fixtures) have a thermal protector to disrupt the electrical connection if the unit gets too hot, and they need to be kept at least 3 in. from any covering insulation.

Like recessed-light housings, combination fan/light housings fan/light/heaters usually mount to the framing with metal hangers. These units aren't usually mounted in the immediate shower area unless they're rated for use in wet locations. If the ventilation fan is a remote unit, it can be mounted later if the location is accessible, though provisions for duct runs and electrical connections will have to be made (see the photo below).

After recessed lights and ceiling-mounted fan units are in place, it's time to install drywall. Securely fasten support arms to the housing and caulk points of metal-to-metal contact to minimize vibration and reduce fan noise.

HEATING

Depending on the type of heating system, much of the installation work for it will be done during the plumbing and electrical rough-ins. The extent of the rough-in might range in complexity from simply running electrical cable to a wall-mounted electric heater to locating and installing a toekick heater to laying down tubing for a radiant floor and pouring a slab. (For more information on the different types of heating systems, see Chapter 5.)

The responsibility for the heating-system installation usually lies with the heating subcontractor, who in most of the work I do is also responsible for the plumbing. I don't try to tell these guys how to do their job, but there are always ways that we can help each other out.

Because I feel responsible for the overall quality of the finished bathroom, making suggestions about and helping with details such as radiation or duct placement is part of my job.

Hydronic heat

Despite all of their attributes, hydronic radiant-heat systems are easily the most labor-intensive (and expensive) to install, which is the primary reason you don't see more of them. Most above-grade radiant systems are installed in 1½-in.-thick slabs, so all other rough-ins, including things like the toilet flange, sink stubouts, and wall switches, will need to raised up 1½ in. to accommodate the higher floor (see the photo below). Plates for partition walls and enclosures should also be nailed in place before the tubing is laid and the floor is poured. If the tubing

The hydronic radiant concrete slab hasn't yet been poured for this bathroom. Note the raised elevation of the toilet flange. (Photo by Steven Lowther.)

circuit that the subcontractor has laid out doesn't indicate tubing under the tub or shower stall, you might point out that it should. The minimal extra expense of adding tubing there will more than pay for itself in comfort.

If the hydronic system is a conventional one, there will either be a baseboard radiator, a wall-mounted panel radiator, a toekick heater, or some combination of the three. In the case of the toekick heater, you'll have to know the exact dimensions and location of the vanity cabinet; drawing the footprint of the cabinet (particularly if it has nonstandard dimensions) on the subfloor will help the plumber accurately stub-in the heat and remind the electrician to run power there. The hydronic system might have a conventional design that calls for baseboard radiation behind the toilet, which is probably the worst location for it. Try to talk your plumber into another location (if there is one) or a wall-mounted panel radiator instead.

Forced-air heat

Unless they are quite large, most bathrooms don't have a return-air intake, but you will have to find a location for a supply register. Ceiling-mounted diffusers are available (see the photo above), but for bathrooms in cold to moderate climates, the best location for a supply register is on or near the floor. Keep in mind that moving air—whether warm or cool—will chill bare skin, so try to locate any supply registers so that they don't direct air right at a bather or someone seated on the toilet.

If there is a vanity cabinet and local building code allows it, the toekick cavity underneath can be converted into a wood plenum by running the ductwork up through the floor into the cavity, sealing the joints with caulk and cutting a register into the cabinet base. If this isn't allowed, regular metal 3-in. by 10-in. duct will also work, but you might have difficulty making the right angle turn into the cavity.

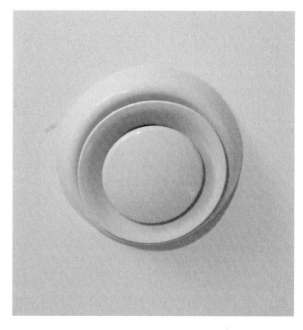

Some grills are suitable for both supply and exhaust applications, diffuse air evenly, and are adjustable.

Electric heat

Electric baseboard radiators have the same placement problems as hydronic baseboard radiators: They rust when they come into contact with moisture. But rough-in and installation simply involve running cable for the unit and wiring in a thermostat. Recent installation innovations—electric panel radiators, drywall-like heating panels that can be installed on walls and ceilings, and electric cables, meshes, films, and fabrics that are installed under a finish floor—make electric heat a viable alternative for a bathroom. For each type of installation, an appropriately sized electrical circuit will be needed, as well as a thermostat, which is typically located 48 in. above the floor and on an interior wall away from the heat source it controls.

Chapter 10

INSTALLING TUBS AND SHOWERS

Never underestimate the determination and ingenuity of a carpenter. I was reminded of this not too long ago when I was invited over to see a friend's recently purchased house. It had undergone some extensive remodeling a few years before; some of the renovations were nicely done and in keeping with the Greek Revival origins of the house, but some of them were a little funky.

On the requisite house tour, my friend was anxious to show me the upstairs master bath, an odd-shaped room shoehorned into a larger odd-shaped room. Immediately on walking into the bathroom I noticed a pronounced bump or seam extending around the entire perimeter of the fiberglass one-piece tub/shower about 5 ft. up. Obviously, the unit had been too big to fit somewhere on its journey up the stairs, around corners and through doorways, and into the room. So rather than return the unit for a two-piece or three-piece one that would have fit, the remodelers had simply lopped off the top with a circular saw and reattached it after the newly created two-piece tub had arrived at its destination. A little creative fiberglass repair, and the unit was as functional as ever...albeit with a major cosmetic blemish at right about eye level.

I don't recommend this approach; I think that it's easier to order the right kind of bathing or showering fixture right from the start. Before ordering any bulky bathroom fixture, make sure that it will fit into the intended space, and make sure that you have a route mapped out to get it to its final destination. One-piece units usually fit without too much trouble into new construction, but most remodels will require multipiece units that can be broken down and reassembled. Fastening systems will vary from manufacturer to manufacturer, so it's important to follow assembly directions carefully.

Chapters 8 and 9 presented some of the rough-in requirements for typical installations. Now it's time to start putting fixtures in place and hooking them up. This chapter will outline the procedures for installing a basic tub, as well as a whirlpool tub and a combination tub/shower unit. It also includes information on how to install a prefabricated shower and different types of shower receptors. And it includes information about site-built showers and surrounds, in addition to some facts about faucets.

BASIC BATHTUB

Depending on what material the tub is made of, it will usually require additional support when it is installed against a wall; this information will be specified in the manufacturer's installation literature. Generally, a 1x4 or 2x4 nailed horizontally at the correct height and absolutely level at the back wall is the basic requirement, though some manufacturers also specify a vertical 2x4 at either corner of the tub.

You'll need to make a decision at this point about whether to install the finish floor before installing the tub or afterward. I prefer to install the floor first because it looks better and adds another protective waterproofing layer above the framing and subfloor, but it does mean that extra care will have to be taken to protect the floor during installation and while finishing the rest of the bathroom walls. (For information on installing floors, see Chapter 11.) Cast-iron tubs, which can weigh close to 300 lbs., are particu-larly unwieldy and will require more than rosin paper to protect the flooring. A protective layer

of ¼-in. plywood or Masonite on top of rosin paper might seem like an unnecessary expense, but it will give you peace of mind and is a lot more economical than a big gouge or scratch in the floor. Before laying the rosin paper down, carefully vacuum the floor to pick up scraps of debris that might scratch it. Overlap the seams of the rosin paper, and after laying down the protective sheathing, tape the joints with duct tape to keep debris from falling through the cracks.

Easing the tub into place requires both brute strength and finesse. You'll need at least one other helper for a plastic tub and two or three for a cast-iron tub. A couple of 2x4 runners will make it easier to slide the tub into position and will also help protect the floor. If you've cut one of the protective sections of Masonite to fit the footprint of the tub, then you can just remove that section before installing the tub and pull back the rosin paper. (Don't tear off the rosin

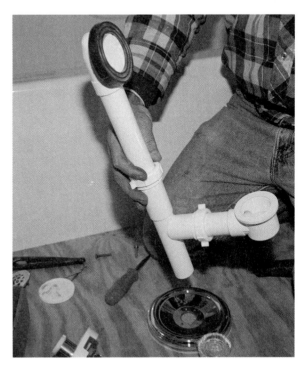

After the tub has been set in place, the W&O fitting can be assembled and installed.

paper, though. When the tub is in place, let the rosin paper lap up onto the tub apron to help protect it in the later stages of construction.)

If the tub is fiberglass or acrylic, setting it in a bed of mortar about the consistency of damp sand will help to deaden sound and give the tub a firmer feel under foot. Be sure that the mortar doesn't raise the tub off its front edge or back ledger; if it does, pull the tub out again, remove some of the mortar, and reset the tub. After the tub has been set in place in its framed opening, verify that it is level both front to back and side to side before you attach it to the framing. I like to use a screw gun and galvanized screws rather than a hammer and nails to secure plastic tubs to the wall because an errant hammer blow can do a lot of damage to fiberglass and enameled cast iron.

Unless the tub W&O fitting was assembled before the tub was installed, now is the time to do it (see the photo on p. 157). There are different types of W&O fittings, and each will require a certain amount of fitting and trimming before it will fit the tub and function properly (see the drawings at right), so follow the manufacturer's installation instructions carefully. After the W&O fitting has been assembled and attached to the installed tub and functions smoothly, the brass tailpiece can be connected to the P-trap and the tub drain, and the tub can be filled with water and checked for leakage.

WHIRLPOOL TUB
While whirlpool tubs are typically bigger, deeper, and heavier than ordinary tubs, their installation is similar, whether they are set against a wall or designed to be set in a deck. This section will discuss the installation of a whirlpool tub in a deck and will highlight the particular plumbing and electrical needs of a jetted tub, but the general installation guidelines are the same for both.

W&O Fitting Options

Pop-up stopper brass W&O fittings
These fittings have the largest internal passageways and drain the most quickly. They are recommended for inaccessible installations (e.g. over a slab) where durability is important.

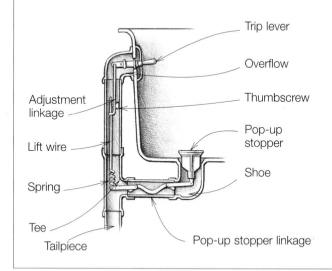

Trip lever
Overflow
Thumbscrew
Pop-up stopper
Shoe
Adjustment linkage
Lift wire
Spring
Tee
Tailpiece
Pop-up stopper linkage

Connecting W&O to the Drain System

One of the tricky parts of residential plumbing systems is that oftentimes dissimilar materials in different diameters are being connected to one another. Shown here are various possibilities that may be encountered when connecting a tub to the drain system.

No-hub iron

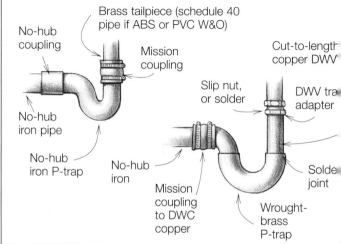

No-hub coupling
Brass tailpiece (schedule 40 pipe if ABS or PVC W&O)
Mission coupling
Cut-to-length copper DWV
Slip nut, or solder
DWV trap adapter
No-hub iron pipe
No-hub iron P-trap
No-hub iron
Mission coupling to DWC copper
Solder joint
Wrought-brass P-trap

Lift bucket W&O fittings

These fittings are generally less expensive than pop-up W&O fittings and don't drain as quickly due to their smaller drainage area. The drain is open when the bucket is lifted and closed when it's lowered.

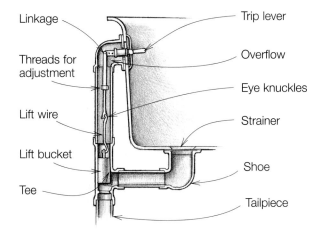

Linkage

Trip lever

Threads for adjustment

Overflow

Eye knuckles

Lift wire

Strainer

Lift bucket

Shoe

Tee

Tailpiece

Toe-tap W&O fittings

These fittings are typically made of ABS or PVC plastic and have no internal fittings. Steer clear of thinner lightweight plastic tubing and stick with regular schedule 40 pipe, which is less likely to break or come apart at the joints.

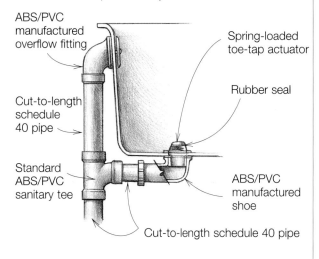

ABS/PVC manufactured overflow fitting

Spring-loaded toe-tap actuator

Cut-to-length schedule 40 pipe

Rubber seal

Standard ABS/PVC sanitary tee

ABS/PVC manufactured shoe

Cut-to-length schedule 40 pipe

ABS or PVC

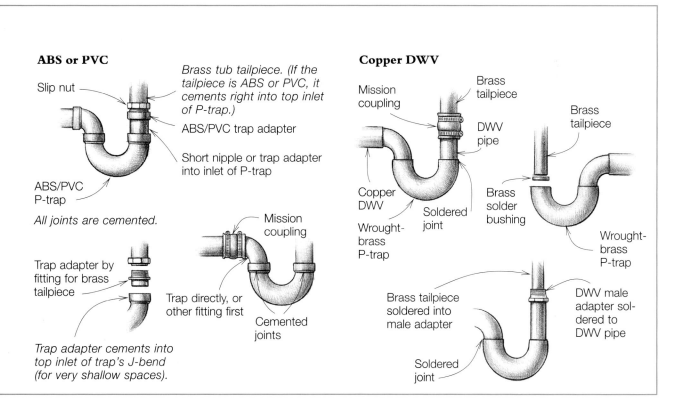

Slip nut

Brass tub tailpiece. (If the tailpiece is ABS or PVC, it cements right into top inlet of P-trap.)

ABS/PVC trap adapter

Short nipple or trap adapter into inlet of P-trap

ABS/PVC P-trap

All joints are cemented.

Trap adapter by fitting for brass tailpiece

Mission coupling

Trap directly, or other fitting first

Cemented joints

Trap adapter cements into top inlet of trap's J-bend (for very shallow spaces).

Copper DWV

Mission coupling

Brass tailpiece

Brass tailpiece

DWV pipe

Copper DWV

Brass solder bushing

Soldered joint

Wrought-brass P-trap

Wrought-brass P-trap

Brass tailpiece soldered into male adapter

DWV male adapter soldered to DWV pipe

Soldered joint

Floor framing under a whirlpool tub—which can weigh over 800 lbs. when loaded with 50 to 60 gallons of water and two adults—should be strong enough to support a load of at least 60 lbs. per square foot. Sometimes sistering on 2x joists to existing framing will provide the needed strength if the existing floor system is inadequate. It may be worthwhile to get the opinion of a structural engineer if you are unsure about the strength of an existing floor system or the integrity of previously cut and notched joists. As a quick test, jump up and down on the floor. If it feels springy, chances are the framing will need to be beefed up.

Tubs can either be set on a raised platform or recessed at floor level. If a tub is recessed, you'll simply need to frame an opening in the floor system by headering off joists in the appropriate location. You will also need to provide support framing beneath the tub, since the edges alone won't be enough to support it.

A tub platform is conventionally framed with 2x4s, making sure that there is easy access for the jet pump (see the drawing below). The height of the platform should be about an inch more than the overall height of the tub so that there is room for shims and mortar underneath when the tub is set in place. If the tub is extra deep, you should think about creating a recess for the tub base to drop into rather than having it sit at floor level because it's difficult for a bather to climb over a tub wall that's much over 2 ft. high, while some tubs are close to 3 ft. deep. Verify the location of the tub drain before

Deck-Mounted Jetted-Tub Installation

Whirlpool tubs can weigh a lot, so floor framing should be adequate to support 60 lbs. per sq. ft. (see the drawing on p. 104) and reinforced if necessary. The deck itself can be conventionally framed, and while the installation won't require the waterproofing of a typical shower surround, the framing should be protected with the use of a water-resistant building paper such as Tu-Tuff or with regular 15-lb. asphalt felt paper.

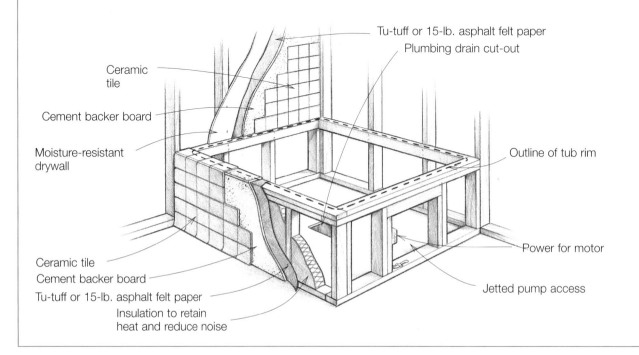

Ceramic tile

Cement backer board

Moisture-resistant drywall

Ceramic tile
Cement backer board
Tu-tuff or 15-lb. asphalt felt paper
Insulation to retain heat and reduce noise

Tu-tuff or 15-lb. asphalt felt paper
Plumbing drain cut-out

Outline of tub rim

Power for motor

Jetted pump access

making the 12-in. by 12-in. drain cutout, since it may be in the middle of the tub, as well as at either end.

If at all possible, try to apply finish material to the deck and surrounding walls (if any) before dropping in the tub. While it is common to cut in tile to fit around an installed tub, this leaves a vertical joint around the rim of the tub that is vulnerable to water and that is too reliant on caulk for its integrity. It also subjects the tub to considerable job-site wear and tear as workers try to finish off the areas around the tub. I've tried installing the tub proud of the surface, leaving enough room to slide tile underneath, but I haven't been too happy with either the process or the result (see the photo at right).

Jetted tubs will require a GFCI-protected dedicated circuit; check with the manufacturer's literature before sizing the circuit. Large tubs should also have ¾-in. rather than ½-in. supplies; otherwise, the tub will take forever to fill up. In some cases, a tub will also need its own hot-water heater to supply the 50 or more gallons of hot water the tub will need per fill.

COMBINATION PLASTIC TUB/SHOWER

Because plastic combination tub/showers are so big and bulky, any reinforcing that has been attached to the unit for shipping should be left in place until just before the unit is installed. Also, carefully inspect the unit for damage when it first arrives because damage during shipping isn't uncommon but can be hard to spot.

Assuming that the rough opening has been properly framed—about ⅛ in. oversize, insulated and air sealed, and with blocking in place—slide the unit into the opening while protecting the finish floor. Don't force the unit if it doesn't fit; instead, back the tub out and use a chisel or a power plane to make the opening bigger. If you force the tub, it might crack later from the stress of being shoved into too small of an opening.

If a drop-in tub is installed before the deck's finish material, a wood shim can hold the tub proud of the deck, allowing room for tile to be slipped underneath later.

You may have a problem installing both combination tub/shower units and prefabricated shower stalls because usually the plumbing wall is in the side rather than the back, which makes it difficult to slide the unit past the valve and spout or showerhead nipples. One approach is to hold off fastening the blocking holding the plumbing to the framing until after the unit is in place, allowing everything to be pulled back into the stud bay as the tub is slipped into the opening.

Sometimes this isn't possible though, such as when the valve wall is on an exterior wall. In this case, framing the enclosing wall after the unit is in place may be the better option. The unit can then be set against the plumbing wall to get valve locations, pulled away to drill the openings, then set back in place, all without worrying about the enclosing wall making things too tight. It's a good idea to go ahead and lay out and install the sole plate while the rest of the framing is being done, though; it won't be in the way when moving the stall around, and it will ensure that the wall is square and in the right place when it does get framed.

After the unit is in place and is plumb and level, temporarily screw it to the framing through the flange in either corner. Then locate the plumbing openings by drilling small (i.e. ⅛-in.-diameter) holes through the back wall. After the locations have been marked, unscrew the unit and remove it far enough from the framing to freely drill holes for the plumbing. Then drill the proper-size holes from the finish side only, using the small holes as pilots for the larger bits (see the photo below).

The unit can now be set in place again. Rather than relying on nails and my good aim with a

Once their locations are marked with small-diameter pilot holes from the back, plumbing cutouts are best made from the finish side with the proper-diameter hole saw in order to avoid chipping and tearout.

hammer, I like to predrill countersunk holes through the flange (about six or so per side) and use a screw gun to fasten galvanized drywall screws through the flange into the framing. I also think that it's a good idea to lay down 15-lb. felt paper on the finish floor under the base of the tub and bed the unit in mortar. When it's spread just thick enough to support the underside of the tub, mortar will help support the base and give it a more solid feel; it will also help dampen the vibrations of a whirlpool jet motor if the tub has one. If the tub is plumb and level, the front edge sits flush to the floor, and the plumbing openings all line up, go ahead and screw the unit to the framing.

PREFABRICATED SHOWER STALL

Nowadays, many fiberglass and acrylic shower stalls are almost as bulky as full-size tub/shower units. Because they are so large, they are often manufactured as two- or three-piece units and are assembled on-site before installation. Usually, reassembled multipiece units—whether tubs or showers—are well engineered and watertight without relying on caulk. However, beads of silicon caulk with an anti-mildew additive applied to the joints and seams of these will help to prevent mildew-causing water and soap scum from collecting (see the left photo on the facing page).

Whether or not the shower stall is one piece or multipiece, its installation is very similar to the installation of combination plastic tub/shower units (see p. 161). Of course, there won't be a W&O fitting to contend with, and unless the stall will be set on a slab, the shower drain can be fitted after the stall is in place. In any case, it's a good idea to hold off on the drain rough-in since the actual drain location on a stall can vary significantly from a manufacturer's tech sheet. It's better to just cut out a 12-in. by 12-in. hole in the subfloor, roughly centered on the drain opening (assuming, once again, that the framing has been laid out so that a joist isn't right in the way).

Multipiece shower and tub/shower units require assembly before installation. Caulking assembled joints will help keep out mildew-causing water and soap scum.

Tile-Redi waterproof shower modules come in various sizes, are installed and function like prefabricated shower receptors, and are ready for tile installation. (Photo courtesy Tile-Redi.)

The biggest headache will be maneuvering the stall past the plumbing as it slides into its opening. As with combination tub/showers, leaving the valve unattached to the framing and pulling it back into the stud bay as the unit is slipped into place is one option, while another is to frame up the enclosing sidewall after the unit is in place.

PREFABRICATED SHOWER RECEPTOR

Setting a shower receptor is considerably easier than setting a tub because there is no W&O fitting and because it is smaller and lighter. Again, it's a good idea to verify the drain-opening location from the actual unit because small variations can make the hookup to the DWV system a little difficult, particularly if the receptor is being installed on a slab. No matter what material the receptor is made from, the heavier and more rigid it is, the less likely it is that it will flex under foot, which could eventually cause leakage around the drain fitting. Setting the receptor in mortar is still a good idea and will help reduce flexing, but it isn't a substitute for quality construction in the first place.

I think that shower receptors, like tubs, should be installed on a finish floor. After cutting out a 6-in. square opening roughly centered below the pan drain opening, the receptor can be set in its framed shower enclosure. In some cases, particularly corner showers, there won't be an enclosure, and the receptor will be attached directly to the wall framing. Be sure to level the receptor if necessary with shims, and if you use mortar underneath, be sure it's is bedded down securely. Use screws instead of nails in predrilled and countersunk holes to attach the nailing flanges to the framing.

Shower receptors either have integral drain fittings cast out of the same material as the pan itself, or a separate plastic or brass fitting, which is either cast into the receptor or installed later on. The 2-in.-diameter waste pipe extends into the shower-drain fitting and is sealed with a rubber bushing (see the drawing on p. 164).

Shower-Receptor Installation

Shower receptors can be made out of a number of different materials, some more rigid than others. In most cases, receptors will benefit from a supporting layer of mortar, which will make the receptor feel more rigid under foot and prevent flexing that will eventually cause the drain connection to loosen, creating leaks. Proper detailing of the shower surround will help prevent leakage (see inset).

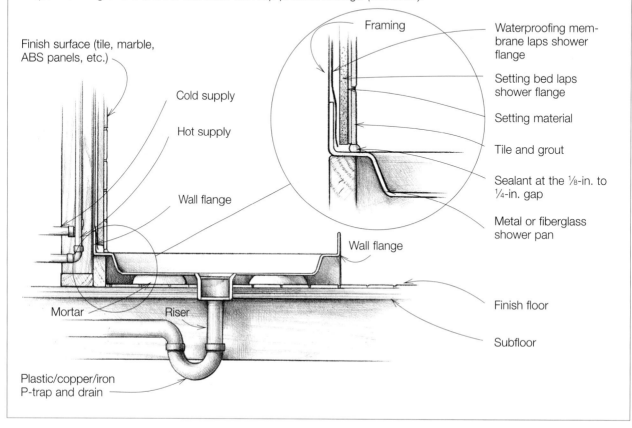

Finish surface (tile, marble, ABS panels, etc.)

Cold supply

Hot supply

Wall flange

Mortar

Riser

Plastic/copper/iron P-trap and drain

Framing

Waterproofing membrane laps shower flange

Setting bed laps shower flange

Setting material

Tile and grout

Sealant at the ⅛-in. to ¼-in. gap

Metal or fiberglass shower pan

Wall flange

Finish floor

Subfloor

SITE-BUILT SHOWERS

For unusual spaces and custom installations, a site-built shower is the best option. Rather than trying to fit a square peg (a prefabricated shower) into a round or irregular-shaped hole, the site-built shower allows for the creative use of space and materials, like a functional sculpture. Functional, of course, is the key word: A site-built shower that leaks can be a nightmare for both the builder and his clients. So while the surface materials of a shower might elicit oohs and aahs, it's the underlying construction and waterproofing and the details that make the shower work.

The heart of any site-built shower is the pan, or waterproofing lining that keeps moisture where it belongs. For many years, site-built showers utilized metal or hot-mopped pans to ensure that water wouldn't leak through the enclosure floor and into the subfloor and framing. While occasionally you'll still meet an installer who swears by these pans, more often now the pan will be made of a plastic material, and for good reason: The new plastic membranes are more durable and leak proof, and they have a much longer projected life span, usually more than 50 years. The two basic types of membrane materials are CPE (chlorinated polyethylene) and PVC (polyvinyl chloride). While these materials are available in different thicknesses, most local codes require the 40-mil.-thick variety. Chloraloy is the most widely used CPE membrane that I know of, while Composeal and Permaguard are two of the most widely used PVC liners. Most plastic-pan manufacturers also offer solvents, cements, accessories like preformed corners, and good technical support with their product (see Resources on p. 209).

A two-piece clamping drain (also called a subdrain assembly) works in conjunction with the plastic shower pan to contain and direct water into the DWV system (see the right photo below). The lower half of the drain attaches to a nipple extending from the shower's P-trap, while the upper half bolts onto the lower half, clamping the membrane in between. Weep holes allow water that has seeped through the grout and into the mortar bed to run into the drain.

The floor of the shower needs a ¼-in.-per-ft. slope to the drain, both for the surface water and for water that works its way down to the pan liner. So the pan should be installed on a sloped subfloor before the rest of the mortar bed is poured. This can be done either with a shimmed plywood subfloor, or by first floating a cement subfloor, using a 4:1 sand/cement mix and a latex additive (see the drawing on p. 167). In addition, 2x12 blocking should be installed between the studs around the perimeter of the shower. If the shower walls will have a cement backer board, then the bottom of the studs should be notched slightly so that the surface of the membrane won't sit proud of the framing and bow the backer board inward when it is attached.

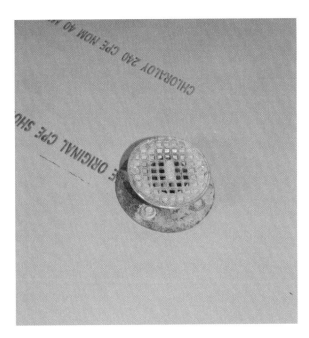

Site-built showers offer tremendous design flexibility but also require considerable knowledge of different building materials and techniques.

Key elements of a waterproof site-built shower include a plastic shower-pan liner and a two-piece clamping drain.

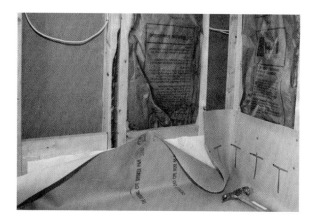

A "pig's ear" fold is watertight and folds flat, ensuring that corners of the liner remain flat and square.

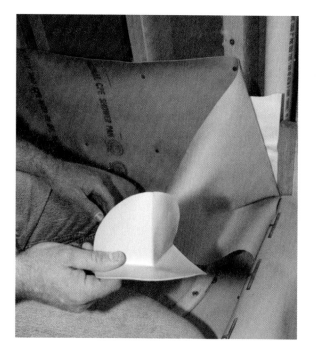

Preformed corner patches help make tricky outside corners easy.

After the framing, subfloor, and bottom half of the subdrain assembly are in place, the pan material can be laid out. Many showers are larger than the 60-in. width that many of these pan materials are available in, so you may have to carefully weld together two pieces of material together before laying the piece in place on the shower subfloor. Follow the manufacturers'

instructions carefully for solvent-welding these two pieces together, and leave plenty of time for the weld to dry (preferably overnight). When cutting the material to size, leave enough so that the membrane will extend about 10 in. up the wall (or at least 3 in. above the height of the finish curb), and be sure that there is enough material to totally wrap the curb. Before actually laying the material down, smooth away any sharp or rough edges and carefully sweep the subfloor clean.

Corners are the tricky part. Inside corners should be folded tightly into a "pig's ear" fold, using plenty of solvent to ensure that the corner lies flat (see the top photo at left). Outside corners, such as those found on curbs, will need some cutting and patching with solvent. Some manufacturers offer preformed corner patches to help make this joint more easily (see the bottom photo at left). Staples are the easiest way to secure the membrane to the framing, but be sure not to put any staples below the height of the finish curb.

The final step in preparing the pan is to cut out the drain opening and make a small incision to push the bolt heads through the membrane. A double bead of butyl caulk—one on the inside and one on the outside of the bolts—between the bottom half of the clamp and the underside of the membrane should keep the drain/ membrane assembly from leaking after it's clamped together. Be sure to test the pan by plugging the drain, filling it with water to an inch or so above the drain, and leaving it overnight. If there is a leak, it's better to know about it now rather than later.

After the pan has passed the leak test, the mortar bed can be floated, again making sure that it maintains the ¼-in.-per-ft. slope. Wire mesh—typically 20-gauge galvanized 1-in. mesh—will reinforce the mortar and help prevent cracking, as will a latex additive. A waterproofing additive like Anti-Hydro (see

Site-Built Shower

The heart of a custom shower is the waterproofing membrane and the two-piece clamping drain, which when properly installed will ensure that the shower doesn't leak. The drawing below details a tile installation, but the same general waterproofing principles hold true when other surround materials, such as natural stone, are used.

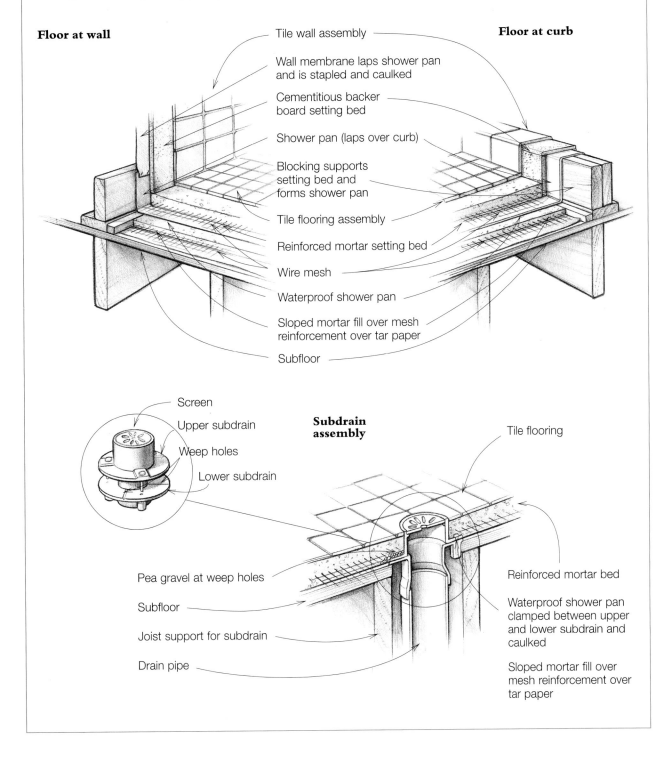

Floor at wall

Floor at curb

- Tile wall assembly
- Wall membrane laps shower pan and is stapled and caulked
- Cementitious backer board setting bed
- Shower pan (laps over curb)
- Blocking supports setting bed and forms shower pan
- Tile flooring assembly
- Reinforced mortar setting bed
- Wire mesh
- Waterproof shower pan
- Sloped mortar fill over mesh reinforcement over tar paper
- Subfloor

- Screen
- Upper subdrain
- Weep holes
- Lower subdrain

Subdrain assembly

- Tile flooring
- Pea gravel at weep holes
- Subfloor
- Joist support for subdrain
- Drain pipe
- Reinforced mortar bed
- Waterproof shower pan clamped between upper and lower subdrain and caulked
- Sloped mortar fill over mesh reinforcement over tar paper

Resources on p. 209) will significantly reduce the water-absorbing capability of the mortar bed. Before floating the mortar, place pea stone, tile chips, or some other similar-size object in front of the weep holes to ensure that water has a free passageway into the drain. Alternatively, a porous filter specially designed to be placed over the weep-hole openings is also available (see Dallas Specialty & Manufacturing Co. in Resources on p. 209).

SITE-BUILT TILE SURROUNDS

There are plenty of different materials from which to build a tub or shower surround, but the basic idea is to use something that will keep the water where it belongs, won't fall apart from constant contact with water, can be scrubbed clean without scratching or fading, and looks good year after year. (See pp. 74-77 for a look at surround materials.) Tile is one popular choice, and this section will summarize the important components of a tile installation, though the underlying principle—a sound substrate that will resist damage from the moisture that will inevitably penetrate behind the finish surround—is the same for other surround materials as well, such as fiberglass panels, solid-surface materials, or HP laminate.

Installation techniques for different types of surround finishes other than tile will depend on the type of material that you choose. Most commonly, MR drywall will be the substrate of choice, to which the surround material will be attached with adhesive caulk. No matter what the type of surround material, rarely is leakage a problem through the material itself except through seams. And while one material may be more durable, last longer, and look better than another, functionally the key is properly installing the material, making sure seams are properly caulked and sealed, and carefully detailing and caulking the joints between the material and the tub edge or shower pan. (For more on caulks, see Chapter 13.)

Beauty is more than skin deep: The surround substrate needs to be detailed to prevent moisture from penetrating into building cavities, which in this case means a trowelled-on waterproofing membrane applied to the shower seat.

The substrate

The traditional way to install wall tile is on a floated mortar bed. This method is great for uneven surfaces and provides a high-quality base for tile, but it is labor-intensive and tricky to do correctly. A simpler method is to use one of the cementitious backer boards like Durock or Wonder-Board, which have a mortar core sandwiched between layers of reinforcing fiberglass mesh. Other new backer boards include Dens-Shield, which has a gypsum core with a fiberglass-matte face and a waterproof coating, and Hardibacker, a ¼-in.-thick cementitious sheet that is used in conjunction with plywood. Tile can be set on other surfaces as well, like drywall and plywood, though these materials are susceptible to moisture damage. While neither Durock nor a traditional mortar bed are affected by water, neither are they waterproof, so for a wet installation like a tub or shower surround some method of waterproofing either the substrate itself or the framing beneath the substrate will be needed (see the photo above).

There are actually several waterproofing options, depending on the substrate used. For example, a 30-mil. CPE membrane like NobleSeal (see Noble Co. in Resources on p. 209) can be applied over almost any clean and smooth surface, making even conventional drywall a suitable substrate in a wet location. First, a latex thinset adhesive is combed on with a notched trowel, and then the membrane is applied over the adhesive and smoothed out with a roller. After about 24 hours of curing time, the membrane is ready for a regular thinset tile installation. There are also other trowel-applied membranes that are installed in a similar fashion, like Laticrete 9235, which consists of a liquid latex into which a layer of fabric is embedded (see Resources on p. 209).

An economical way to protect framing beneath backer board is with 15-lb. or 30-lb. asphalt-saturated felt paper. Embedded in trowelled-on cold-patch roofing cement, with 2-in. overlapped joints also sealed with cement, the felt-paper membrane will protect the framing from moisture migrating through joints, seams, cracks, and nail holes. The roofing cement helps seal around staples and screws and helps keep the paper lying flat against a substrate. Tar paper can also be secured directly to studs, and roofing cement should be used wherever there might be a leak. Be sure to completely bed the bottom edge of the tar paper in a continuous layer of roofing cement spread around the top edge of the tub or shower pan, since caulk won't stick to tar paper.

Although not a product that I've used for this purpose, some builders use a cross-laminated poly sheeting called Tu-Tuff (Sto-Cote Products, Inc.) as a moisture barrier beneath backer board. It's more durable and puncture resistant than regular 4-mil. or 6-mil. polyethylene sheeting, and it installs much more cleanly than tar paper and roofing cement because there are no noxious fumes and sticky mess to deal with (see the photo above).

A protective waterproofing membrane of either a material like Tu-Tuff or common asphalt-saturated felt paper is needed beneath backer board to prevent moisture damage to framing and sheathing.

Like drywall, backer board can be scored with a regular utility knife and snap-cut, though this leaves a fairly rough edge and eats up knife blades pretty quickly. Still, blades are cheap, and the edges can be cleaned up with a Surform plane, and snap-cutting creates a lot less dust than cutting with a circular saw mounted with a masonry blade. Smooth cuts are nice to have, but joints and seams should be taped with fiberglass mesh tape and sealed with thinset anyway. Backer board can be nailed in place with galvanized roofing nails, but I prefer to predrill countersunk holes and drive in galvanized drywall screws. While countersunk holes aren't absolutely necessary, I find that without them screw heads sometimes will sit slightly proud of the backer board and that edges are less likely to split and crumble with a predrilled hole. Holes for plumbing are best cut with carbide-tipped hole saws or with a jigsaw, though I've seen some installers simply score a hole with a utility knife and punch it out with a hammer. I fill the gap where the backer board meets regular drywall with Durabond and tape it with fiberglass mesh tape, leaving a smooth and durable transition point for tile.

Layout

Assuming that there is both a properly installed waterproof substrate and appropriate tile, a good tile surround also depends on a good layout and a secure bond. To my mind, the layout is the trickier part. It depends on such factors as the size and shape of the field and trim tile, the configuration of the walls, and unusual features in the area to be tiled, such as window openings. Tile is unforgivingly geometrical; you can't just start installing it and depend on "fudging" to make vertical and horizontal lines meet in the right places without planning. So good layout depends on being able to project the tile's grid—the pattern of individual tiles and grout joints—onto the walls so that you'll know exactly where every course of tile will end up before you actually start setting the tile. A tub surround is a pretty straightforward introduction to the principles of tile layout.

Before starting any kind of tile layout, first get an accurate measurement of the tile and its grout joint. The width of one tile and one grout joint is the module that your layout will be based on, and the most accurate way to find this is to actually lay out enough tile (with spacers) to fill about a 2-sq.-ft. area. For example, 4-in. square tile is often actually $3\frac{7}{8}$ in. wide, leaving room for a $\frac{1}{8}$-in. grout joint; 18 tiles will fit in exactly 2 sq. ft. Unless the tiles are quite large, I feel comfortable working in about a 2-sq.-ft. area when I'm setting them.

Once I know the tile module and the exact size of the comfortable working area (the area in which I apply adhesive at one time), I'll find the exact centerline of the back wall. Then I'll measure over from the centerline to the sidewall to verify where the last full tile course will lie.

Tweaking the layout by shifting it right or left is usually necessary to ensure that an equal tile cut will be made on both ends of the back wall. A full vertical course of tile on one end of the back wall and a cut vertical course of tile on the other will look unbalanced. If exactly half a tile needs to be cut on either end, then I'm in luck: I can shift the whole layout either to the right or to the left one-half a tile, eliminating any cut tiles for the back wall. In general, try to avoid layouts that leave courses of tile with more or less than half their width cut off (see the left photo on the facing page).

Usually I'll try to start horizontal courses with a full tile right at the back edge of the tub, but experience has taught me not to assume that a tub is level, particularly if I haven't installed it (and on at least one occasion when I did). Now I always check both front-to-back and side-to-side level, and if the tub isn't exactly level, I'll use a 4-ft. spirit level and mark a level reference line on the back wall above the tub. If the tub isn't too far off level, you can just let the gap widen slightly between the tub and the tile from one end to the other, knowing that this joint will be caulked anyway. If the tub is severely out of level in either plane, it will be necessary to start with a half course and individually cut each tile to follow the slope of the tub—a time-consuming procedure. When I know my starting horizontal and vertical lines, I carefully mark reference lines to establish the grid, using whatever multiple of the tile module that will leave me with approximately 2-ft.-sq. grids (see the top right photo on the facing page).

Sidewall tile layout is usually less fussy. The horizontal line has already been established off the back wall, and unless trim tiles need to be placed at a specific point, the first vertical course next to the back wall can usually be a full course. I like to finish off both the top and outside courses with bullnose trim tile, lapping over the backer-board substrate onto the smoother MR drywall.

Tile placement shouldn't look random. Try to avoid layouts that require cutting more than half a tile.

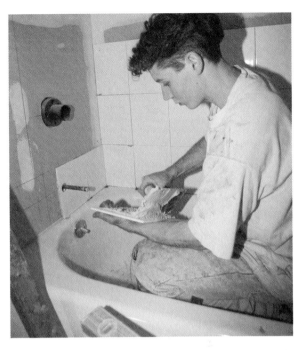

Walls should be divided into a layout grid with plumb and level reference lines to help keep tiles on course. The tub should be checked for level from front to back and side to side before layout lines are established.

Cutting tile can be a snap (literally) or a real pain in the keister, depending on the type of tile you're trying to cut and the tools you have to do it with. Most straight cutting is easily done with snap cutters, which score the face of the tile and then apply pressure to either side of the scored line, snapping the tile in two. Nippers can be used to make curved or irregular cuts in tile, and work by removing small bits at a time; they are good for cutting out around valves. Neither of these tools is very good for making particularly smooth or right-angle cuts, though; for that you'll need a diamond-blade wet saw (see the bottom photo at right). For installations requiring many cuts, the time and aggravation that you'll save by using one of these saws will more than make up the cost of renting or buying one. For softer-bodied tile, I've found that a carborundum blade mounted in a table-mounted jigsaw is an economical alternative to a wet saw; with it, I can do both straight and curved cuts. Another option is a dry-cutting diamond blade mounted in a right-angle

While snapcutters and tile nippers are adequate for many simple tile cuts, a wet saw is essential for critical or complicated cuts and leaves a smoother edge.

grinder, though I think that this setup is a little dangerous, if versatile. Makita makes a cordless 12-volt glass- and tile-cutting saw that is equipped with a 3⅜-in. diamond blade and a water source. Though I've never used this saw, it looks like an economical and highly portable alternative to a bulky wet saw.

For holes, a carbide-tipped hole saw mounted in a drill works pretty well, at least in softer tiles, though higher speeds and harder tiles are more likely to result in cracking. For smoothing out cuts and rough spots on tile, a handheld tile grindstone is a handy item to have.

Grouting tile

After the tile has been properly bedded into the adhesive and allowed to cure, it will need to be grouted. Traditional portland-cement-based grouts are now available with additives like latex, acrylic, or epoxy that make them more flexible and less likely to crack. Joints narrower than ⅛ in. need an unsanded grout, while joints ⅛ in. and larger should have a sanded grout to add strength and reduce shrinking. For my money, though, I think that it is hard to beat a 100%-solids epoxy grout, such as Latapoxy 210 (from Laticrete International, Inc.). While it doesn't make grouting (a job I'm not particularly fond of) any easier, the resulting grout joints are remarkably flexible, durable, stain resistant, colorfast, and seemingly impervious to the problems that sometimes plague conventional grouts, like cracking and mildew growth (see the sidebar on the facing page).

Before doing any grouting with either a traditional portland-cement-based grout or with epoxy grout, make sure that grout joints are cleaned of excessive adhesive and that any spacers have been removed (see the photo above). Uniform joint depths are critical for color consistency with portland-cement-based grouts. Vacuuming thoroughly afterward will clean out the debris that can get stuck in the joints. Keeping the tile slightly damp and at a

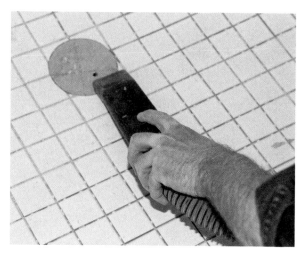

Before grouting, joints should be cleaned of spacers and excess adhesive, and the tile thoroughly vacuumed.

cool temperature (between 65°F and 75°F) with a sponge or mister and clean water will keep portland-cement-based grouts from drying out too quickly and make grouting easier. Epoxy grouts, on the other hand, require a bone-dry surface. For both types of grouts, proportioning, mixing, and slaking instructions should be followed carefully before starting to pack it in.

TUB AND SHOWER FAUCETS

For the most part, tub and shower valves are installed within a wall before the tub or shower is set in place. This means that the handle(s) and escutcheon plate(s) will need to be installed after the shower or tub is in place. Most have a neoprene gasket that keeps water from penetrating behind the plate, but some will also need a bead of silicone caulk. If I use caulk, I'll leave an opening at the bottom of the plate to allow water that gets in behind to drain out. If there are conventional fluted stems and handles such as you might find on an older shower valve, it isn't a bad idea to apply some waterproof valve-stem grease to help prevent corrosion.

Plastic tub spouts that slip over a ½-in. copper tube aren't very strong, but often they need to

Using Epoxy Grout

My first experience with epoxy grout was a disaster. I assumed that I could use the same soft-rubber grout trowel that I'd used with portland-cement-based grouts, that I could grout at the same pace and with the same techniques, and that I could mix up and use an entire batch at once. I was wrong on all counts.

Instead of working like, well, grout, the stuff was like a sticky peanut butter, and my trowel wasn't stiff enough to cut away excess grout after the joints were packed. The realization that this stuff was epoxy and wouldn't easily clean off the face of the tile once it cured made me panic and concentrate all the more on getting every last bit off, which made my progress even slower. About one-quarter of the way through the job that I'd mixed an entire batch for, the epoxy began to set up. Frustrated, exhausted by the frantic pace, and blinded by sweat pouring into my eyes from the 90°F heat, I watched as three-quarters of a batch of very expensive epoxy grout solidified in the bucket.

But I did learn some lessons from that experience. Now I mix small batches of epoxy grout at a time, keep several buckets full of clean water and a big stiff sponge for cleaning, use a stiff rubber trowel for grouting, and have on hand a good abrasive pad or two.

After a small (10 sq. ft. or so) area of tile is packed, I'll pull away the excess with the trowel held almost perpendicular to the tile and at about a 45° angle. I don't worry so much about imperfect joints or excess grout at this point; I know that in a few minutes, after the grout has stiffened, I'll be going over everything with an abrasive pad and water. The abrasive pad helps to scrub the tile clean, and water lubricates the epoxy, turning into a slurry that won't reattach to the firmer epoxy already packed in the joints. The pad needs frequent rinsing in one water bucket, and after one area has been scrubbed I'll clean off the excess epoxy and foam with the sponge, rinsing frequently in the other bucket of water.

Shaping the joints is done mainly with the pad, though I also try to clean them up with the sponge as I'm cleaning everything off. Using a cheap sponge is a mistake because it will start to deteriorate and leave fibers in the grout, and a flimsy one won't bridge the joints well. After the grout has hardened, there will be a haze that can be cleaned off with mild household detergent and water and a sponge. The grout may still be slightly sticky, in which case protect it from traffic until it is fully cured.

---

be because spouts are used as grab bars by adults (and shimmy bars by children). Brass or cast-iron nipples and chromed-brass spouts are stronger, though they can require some fussy fitting to get the right nipple length. The spout should rest flush and tightly against the finish wall, but if it doesn't, try a shorter nipple or make a copper nipple with two copper, male iron pipe adapters. Before final installation, wrap Teflon tape around the male threads of the nipple, spread pipe dope on the female threads, and pack the cavity of the spout with putty. Sometimes the spout can be tightened sufficiently by hand, but a large-diameter wooden dowel inserted in the spout hole makes a good handle for more leverage. Be careful not to tighten the spout too much, though, as the 90° elbow inside the wall can crack.

Deck-mounted faucets for tubs are installed essentially like sink faucets. Access may be a little more difficult, and anyone drilling holes in a $2,000 tub should rightfully feel a little queasy. Again, plumber's putty should be packed in faucet cavities and at the through-tub or through-deck connection.

Chapter 11

INSTALLING FLOORS, WALLS, AND CEILINGS

FLOORS

WALLS

CEILINGS

Two factors make installing floors, walls, and ceilings in the bathroom different than in any other room in the house. The first is the continual presence of moisture during the life of the bathroom, both as standing water and as water vapor. The second factor is that large built-in units like tubs confound the order of installation, often requiring that the floor be finished before some walls are even framed, let alone finished. But there are lessons to be learned in the microcosm of the bathroom that can (and should) be extended to floor, wall, and ceiling installations throughout the house.

As I mentioned earlier, it's useful to think of the finish surfaces of a room as a kind of envelope. Cracks in the envelope will allow warm air to escape the room, only to be replaced by cooler air either from another part of the house or from outside, creating annoying drafts. Worse, the escaping air carries with it the increased humidity of the bathroom into walls and ceilings, creating the potential for moisture damage to sheathing and framing as vapor condenses on their cold surfaces.

Extraordinary measures are not required to ensure that the bathroom has a tight envelope—just attention to detail. When you understand that seemingly insignificant small cracks and openings around recessed lights and other fixtures eventually add up to square feet of chimney-like passageways for escaping warm air, it's more likely you'll take the time to seal them up. So the following discussion on installation of typical bathroom finish materials focuses on creating and maintaining a continuous shell that will not only be as resistant as possible to moisture, but which will inhibit the passage of air into surrounding building cavities.

FLOORS

Like most builders, I usually prefer to install finish floors as late in the construction process as possible to protect them from wear and tear. However, in the small and complicated space of the bathroom, the floor is sometimes best installed earlier in the process. Having flooring—particularly resilient flooring that is relatively impervious to moisture—extend underneath a tub or shower rather than butting up to its front edge is a much more watertight detail, and cutting in any type of flooring around tubs and vanities is no fun. Installing flooring before anything else is in place makes for a simpler, more watertight installation of large bathing fixtures, and because the bathroom floor is rarely larger than the size of two sheets of Masonite, it isn't difficult or expensive to protect after it's installed. A careful sweep and vacuum, a layer of red rosin paper, and Masonite cut to fit with duct-taped seams will keep a finished floor safe from harm.

Resilient flooring

The next time you're in a well-lit room with a vinyl floor, take a close look and see if you can find little bumps in it. Those little bumps are nail heads that have popped slightly proud of the underlayment and are pushing up the resilient flooring that covers them. That is why it is better to screw underlayment down rather than nail it: Screws aren't as likely to pop up over time as the sheathing and framing dries and shrinks.

Underlayment should be installed over a layer of 15-lb. felt paper, which functions as a vapor barrier and prevents the wood-on-wood contact that can result in squeaking floors. Before laying down the felt, mark joist locations and plywood subfloor seams on the wall. Underlayment seams should fall on joists and should overlap subfloor seams. I try not to have a seam fall in the middle of a doorway. I always try to nail or screw into joists, keeping about a 4-in. fastener spacing around the perimeter and a 6-in. spacing in the field. Also, I leave about a $\frac{3}{8}$-in. gap around the perimeter of the room between the underlayment and the sidewalls to allow for differential expansion (see the photo below).

Plywood that is $\frac{3}{8}$ in. thick and rated for underlayment by APA-The Engineered Wood Association is a good choice under resilient

Underlayment for resilient flooring should be securely fastened to the subfloor over asphalt felt paper with nails or screws.

Smoothing out resilient flooring with a roller helps remove trapped air; move from the center toward the edges. (Photo © Carolyn Bates.)

of tubs, so the resilient-flooring tile placement doesn't look haphazard. This is, of course, more important with geometric designs than with solid-color or more abstract flooring.

Flooring subs often install sheet goods with the cut-and-fit (or freehand) method, simply laying an oversized piece of sheet goods in the room and cutting it in place. I think that the pattern method is more reliable and accurate, and the little extra time that it takes is well spent considering the high cost of some of these types of flooring. Besides, bathrooms often have a lot of nooks and crannies that make freehand installation tricky.

Almost any pattern material will do, as long as it cuts easily and can be fastened together with masking tape or duct tape. Make the pattern by laying out sections of pattern material until the entire floor has been covered, taking care to carefully follow indentations and irregular edges with material that is cut to fit. Then tape all of the material pieces together, carefully roll the pattern up, then spread it out again on the rolled-out flooring. Shift the pattern around on the sheet goods until the layout looks good—for example, lines in the pattern should be parallel or perpendicular to cut lines—tape the pattern down to keep it from shifting about, and then cut the flooring out.

Before applying mastic or adhesive, take a careful look at the underlayment for indentations or imperfections, then give it one more thorough vacuuming. Roll out the sheet goods onto the floor to test for fit, then lift one section of it up at a time and comb out the mastic with the appropriate-size notched trowel. After the floor covering is in place, roll the entire floor, moving from the center to the perimeter, to release trapped air bubbles (see the photo above). Different manufacturers and different types of resilient floor coverings have specific recommendations for the type of

flooring because it won't swell if it comes into contact with water. Other thicknesses might be more appropriate to bring the floor level up to match an adjacent floor. After the sheets are screwed down, fill in imperfections, seams, and screw holes with a nonshrinking filler, then sand everything flush after it dries. If there is an existing vinyl floor, underlayment can be placed on top of that, but anything more than two layers should be removed to the subfloor before installing more flooring.

Once the subfloor is in place, you're ready to install resilient flooring. Layout of tile-sized resilient flooring is similar to the layout of ceramic tile. Try to avoid joints over seams in the underlayment, and pay attention to visually critical areas, like doorways and the area in front adhesive to be used with their product, as well as specific laminating instructions.

Wood

If you've ever seen a wood floor with cupped boards, big gaps, or buckling, you've seen a wood floor that has responded to very wide variations in humidity. Seasonal variation is normal, but uncontrolled humidity from any number of sources—a damp basement, water spilled from a bathtub, overspray and humidity from a shower—can stress a wood floor's ability to absorb and release moisture. And because a bathroom environment is, by definition, a wet one, the bias against wood flooring there is understandable. But wood floors can be detailed to limit moisture absorption and can serve well in the right kind of bathroom.

For a wood floor in any part of the house, a felt-paper underlayment is the first line of defense against moisture getting to it from underneath. As with resilient flooring, mark joist locations on the wall before rolling out the felt paper. After the paper is stapled down with about a 2-in. overlap, I like to snap lines to indicate the joists and make it easier to hit them when nailing the flooring down. Besides keeping moisture from migrating into flooring from underneath, the felt-paper underlayment also helps to protect against squeaking floors (see the photo at right).

Cupping and buckling is caused by uneven moisture absorption, usually from the underside of the floor. The floor finish protects the surface of the wood flooring and its exposure to air allows it to dry out quickly, but the edges and underside of the flooring are usually unprotected from moisture and dry out more slowly. Prefinishing these areas with a moisture-inhibiting finish like a urethane varnish will make a big difference in the amount of moisture the flooring can absorb. Water-based polyurethane is handy because it dries quickly,

Felt-paper underlayment helps to protect wood floors from moisture and to minimize squeaking.

making the tedious task of back-priming a little easier and less messy.

It is often difficult to sand a wood floor in the tight confines of a bathroom. I've gotten good results using a belt sander and a random-orbit sander when the big floor sander just wouldn't fit. I try to use the edging sander sparingly, as it tends to leave swirls and an uneven surface that are especially noticeable in highly visible areas, such as right in front of the tub.

Ceramic tile

In Chapter 10, the basics of installing tile in a shower stall were discussed, including the use of substrates like Durock and the necessity of waterproofing membranes in wet locations. For a tile bathroom floor that isn't exposed to excessive moisture, there are a few different alternatives to preparing a substrate for tile installation. Assuming that the floor system is suitably strong and that appropriate tiles have been chosen, tile can be set on a traditional thick-bed mortar, on backer board, on plywood, or on a concrete slab. Tile can also be set on other surfaces that are in sound condition and properly prepared, including a previous tile installation and uncushioned resilient flooring (providing that there is only one layer). The type of substrate determines the type of adhesive used, though in most cases a latex thinset adhesive offers the best combination of performance and economy.

Substrates If a floor system is sufficiently strong but has surface irregularities that make tile questionable, a 1¼-in. mortar bed might be the answer. It can easily accommodate changes in level in the subfloor that would be difficult to do otherwise and is much easier to install on the horizontal surface of a floor than on the vertical surfaces of walls. Mix a 3:1 ratio of mason's sand and portland cement with a liquid latex mortar additive. Then float it over an asphalt-paper curing membrane and wire-mesh reinforcement to make a strong and smooth setting bed for tile. A latex thinset adhesive is a good choice for setting tile on a mortar bed.

A minimum ½-in. plywood subfloor that is flat and smooth can be covered with backer board to make an ideal substrate for floor tile. The backer board should be laminated to the subfloor with a wood-compatible latex thinset or waterproof construction adhesive and screwed to the subfloor on 6-in. centers with galvanized drywall screws. There should be a ⅛-in. gap between adjacent sheets of backer board, which should be filled with thinset and taped with fiberglass mesh tape, as well as a ¼-in. gap at the walls for differential seasonal movement. Joints should be staggered and fall on joists and should overlap plywood subfloor joints. Again, latex thinset adhesives are a good choice for setting tile on backer board.

Given the choice, I would always pick backer board over plywood to set tile on because it is less expensive and more consistently flat and void free. But exterior-grade CDX or AC plywood can also be used as a substrate for tile floors. Tile requires at least 1 in. of plywood underneath it if the plywood will act as the setting bed, so another layer of plywood should

With adequate structural support and the right adhesive, tile floors can be successfully installed over a number of different substrates, including plywood.

be added to the typical ½-in. or ⅝-in. subfloor, with joints staggered so they fall on joists. Fasten plywood down like backer board, using construction adhesive and screws on 6-in. centers. Leave a ⅛-in. to ¼-in. gap between sheets, which will later be filled with adhesive. Either an epoxy thinset adhesive or a latex thinset adhesive works for setting tile on plywood (see the photo above).

Concrete slabs make good setting surfaces for tile, provided the slabs are sound and uncracked. A slab that has been floated with a wood trowel has a rougher surface than a steel-troweled slab and is better for setting tile; the smoother slab may have to be roughed up a bit by grinding it with an abrasive wheel. Unfortunately, most tile adhesives don't stick well to slabs that have been treated with a form-release agent or curing compound. You can check for this by sprinkling the slab with water. If it isn't readily absorbed, then you'll need to choose another flooring material.

It's a good idea to check the surface of a slab with a straightedge to determine how flat it is. Minor depressions can be filled in with thinset, and minor humps can be ground down with an electric grinder. In some cases, it might be necessary to float an additional layer of deck mud to even out the high and low spots. If there are cracks in the concrete and structural repairs are infeasible, an isolation membrane like NobleSeal T/S (from The Noble Co., see Resources on p. 209) will help to insulate the tile from movement in the underlying substrate. Latex thinset is a good choice for an adhesive on most masonry surfaces, including concrete and gypsum-based thin slabs.

Layout and installation Taking the time to carefully plan the layout and installation of a tile floor is as important as planning the layout of a tile shower (see pp. 168-172). Finding the centerlines of each wall and checking that the room is square are the first steps, and you'll want to plan the layout so that highly visible areas—door thresholds, areas in front of a tub or shower—look symmetrical and logically laid out. Narrow strips of cut tiles at the edges are distracting and should be avoided, and the layout should try to minimize the appearance of walls that aren't parallel or square (more common of a situation than you might think). Because narrow tiles visually accentuate this problem, making sure cut tiles that are at least half-sized are used next to out-of-square walls will help. Sometimes letting the grout joint of the last course that is parallel to the offending wall widen or narrow slightly can help to minimize this problem, particularly if the grout joints are fairly wide (⅛ in. to ³⁄₁₆ in.) to begin with.

As with wall-tile layout, it's very helpful to draw your precise layout on the floor before setting tile. Then you'll know ahead of time which tiles need to be cut and you'll be able to plan your work so you're applying adhesive to only one small area at a time. Tile adhesives skin over fairly quickly after they've been troweled on, so working in small areas and having tile precut make the process go more smoothly and

Planning the layout, precutting tiles, and working a small area at a time make setting tile easier. Plastic spacers (in the box) help make joints more consistent but should be removed before grouting.

enable you to work at a productive rather than frenetic pace.

Other flooring materials

Natural stone flooring, such as marble, granite, or slate, generally is installed like ceramic tile. Cleft and unpolished stone is difficult to seal and keep clean, particularly in damp or wet locations; gauged tile (which is cut to size by the manufacturer) is more common in bathrooms and is easier to seal. During installation, both cleft and gauged stone tiles should be cut with a wet saw and are best set with a thinset adhesive. Just make sure to wipe the back before installation to remove dust or manufacturing residue. Thinset adhesives also work well with cement-bodied tile and brick-veneer tile.

WALLS

Walls not only have to be durable and look good, but they also are responsible for keeping moisture-laden air from escaping the room. Whatever type of wall surface you install, it should be detailed for both needs.

MR drywall is more resistant to water than regular drywall. Large cracks and gaps are best filled in with a setting compound like Durabond before taping with a regular joint compound.

Drywall

MR drywall is commonly used in bathrooms because it doesn't absorb water vapor like regular drywall does. I'm not convinced, though, that regular drywall with a good low-perm paint doesn't perform just as well; after all, both types of drywall will deteriorate in the presence of a real water problem. Still, the distinctive green coloring of MR drywall makes its absence noticeable, and the perception of quality by clients is an important factor in construction. Besides MR drywall, I also like to use galvanized drywall screws in bathrooms instead of nails or regular drywall screws. While regular drywall screws and nails have some corrosion resistance, I think that the slight extra cost of galvanized screws is more than offset by

the sense of security that I get knowing that rust spots aren't likely to appear if the screw heads are exposed to bathroom humidity. And screws are much less likely to pop than nails are. They hold the drywall to the framing tenaciously, even as the framing dries out and shrinks.

Using a construction adhesive to glue drywall to the framing adds a little to labor costs, but it also reduces the number of screws that will be needed to fasten the sheets to the walls. Typical screw spacing is 16 in. o.c. on walls (12 in. o.c. on ceilings), but glued drywall needs only three fasteners in each framing member—one on each edge and one in the middle. Although it doesn't do any good to glue drywall to framing that is covered with a poly vapor barrier or with the ears of kraft-paper-faced fiberglass insulation batts, a glued installation is quieter and stronger than a nonglued one.

Assuming that all of the systems are in place and that there is blocking for items like grab bars and towel bars, actually hanging drywall in the bathroom is a process that goes fairly quickly because pieces are usually short and the room is small so that there aren't a lot of them.

There is a fair amount of cutting and fitting to accommodate electrical boxes and fixtures, so I use a 4-ft. T-square for measuring and a drywall saw, utility knife, and/or a drill-mounted hole saw for cutting. Some installers use a drywall cutout tool, a small router with piloted bit, but I've seen too much nicked Romex and too many chewed up electrical boxes to be comfortable with that setup. Because the sheets are usually not full size or very heavy, the little extra handling involved in marking boxes in place and then removing and cutting them before final fitting is sometimes faster and easier than measuring out everything. A little chalk, pencil lead, or lumber crayon spread on the perimeter of the box will leave an outline on the backside of the sheet when pressed against the wall.

It isn't necessary to be compulsive about fitting drywall. Gaps and measuring errors can be easily corrected with setting compounds like Durabond, which dries by a chemical reaction rather than by evaporation and which is available with different drying times. Before taping with regular all-purpose joint compound and paper tape, fill cracks and gaps—for example, at the wall/ceiling intersection—with Durabond. I use fiberglass mesh tape with Durabond where there are seams because it is self-adhering and easy to use. And I make sure to smooth the stuff carefully because it is very hard to sand and isn't water soluble (see the photo on the facing page). Outside corners that have a metal corner bead are also a good place to use Durabond, partly because it is far more durable and resistant to bumps and gouges than regular compound, but also because even thick layers of it dry quickly, making it possible to recoat the same day. I also use Durabond to fill in gaps around plumbing cutouts, even if they will be covered by a vanity. In general, if there is a penetration through the room's envelope that will allow any air to escape, it should be filled in, no matter where it is.

The object of taping drywall is to create the illusion of seamlessness, and each taper seems to have his own specific approach to achieving that result. A small room like a bathroom is a challenge to tape well because it seems to consist of all corners and edges. If there are any butt joints (places where nontapered edges meet), I try to cleanly taper back both edges at a 45° angle with a utility knife during installation so that paper doesn't get pushed up proud of the surface and create a high spot. The joint then gets taped with paper tape (I almost never use fiberglass mesh tape except with Durabond because it isn't as strong as paper and is more likely to crack with regular joint compound), and I make the joint double width to have enough room to feather the edges so that there won't be a hump where the seam is.

Sanding is probably everybody's least favorite part of the process, but if you've taken care to feather joints and keep things smooth, it should go quickly. I use both a pole sander and sandpaper mounted in a half-sheet sanding block. There are pole sanders with integral dust-collection/vacuum systems, but I've never tried one. If it works and makes sanding easier and less messy, then it sure would be worth almost any price. I've found that a clamping work light is indispensible for finding irregularities while sanding, including paper bubbles (where the paper tape hasn't been fully embedded in joint compound), nicks, and depressions. Shining the light along the wall will highlight these imperfections, and the more light you have in the room during the taping process, the better the results. After the room has been sanded, I sweep off everything, vacuum thoroughly, and wipe everything down with a large sponge. An inexpensive sponge mop works great for this: It quickly removes dust and smooths joints and is easy to wring out in a bucket of water.

Tile

Most of the basic techniques for installing tile were covered in the previous sections on tiled tub and shower surrounds and tile flooring (see pp. 168-172 and 177-179). It should be noted that many wall-tile installations in areas that don't receive a lot of exposure to moisture perform well using MR drywall as a tile backer. This drywall is also more impervious to air movement than cementitious backer boards. A floated mortar bed can resolve many problems associated with out-of-plumb framing. But, in general, cementitious backer boards offer the best combination of economy, durability in potentially wet locations, and ease of installation for any type of wall installation.

Because walls are so visible and because various kinds of trim tiles are often extensively used on walls, careful layout is critical (see the photo on p. 182). Also, gravity sometimes works against setting tile on a wall, depending on the "hang"

Tile placement on a wall needs to be planned so that joints fall in logical places and cuts look symmetrical.

(the ability to hold tile in place before it has cured) of an adhesive. One solution is to use masking tape secured either to the wall above or to top rows of tile supported by small nails driven partway into the substrate and to tape the tiles as they're set. (This should be done for a tile surround as well.)

Glass block

Glass-block installation can range from a simple panel installed in a framed opening to extensive wall systems. In addition to traditional mortar-based techniques for laying up glass block, there are now new mortarless systems that incorporate extruded aluminum frame components and a silicone rubber sealant. Glass block isn't installed exactly like brick, regardless of whether it is a mortar system or not, but still requires extensive reinforcement with metal.

Small glass-block panels that are framed like window openings are fairly straightforward. They are laid up with a polymer-fortified mortar (with an additive for wet locations to kill mildew) in a similar fashion to brick, but also using spacers, anchors, and reinforcing from the manufacturer. The effects of expansion and contraction limit the size of these types of

panels to less than about 25 sq. ft.; a fiberglass expansion strip between the top course of block and framing will protect the glass panel from movement (see the drawing on the facing page).

Wainscoting

Wainscoting can range from simple beadboard installed vertically and topped by a chair rail to more formal cabinet-style frame-and-panel designs. Regardless of the style of wainscoting, blocking is needed at the base and at about 30 in. to catch the top of the wainscoting and the chair rail. If the wainscoting will be on an exterior wall, be sure that the poly vapor barrier is intact and that tears in it have been repaired because air will pour through all of the joints otherwise. While not common, a layer of drywall underneath wainscoting helps prevent air intrusion, but it will require a different chair-rail detail than wainscoting that is installed directly against framing.

CEILINGS

Gravity ensures that ceilings are largely unaffected by splashes of water, but they are highly vulnerable to air bypasses that can cause considerable moisture-related damage. Buoyant, warm, moisture-laden air will pour through any crack or opening in a ceiling—especially when the area above is an attic—and quickly condense on colder rafters and sheathing. So you should take this process into account and have a system in place to prevent this from happening to any type of ceiling that you choose.

In the discussion of vapor retarders (see p. 116), drywall is mentioned as an alternative to a poly vapor retarder, as long as it is coated with low-perm paint. For other types of ceilings, such as acoustic tile ceilings or any type of wood ceiling, a continuous film of 6-mil poly is essential and is the most economical way of keeping warm air and water vapor where they belong. Take the time to install the poly carefully, lapping seams generously and cutting in around any openings to maintain as continuous of a seal as possible.

A Small Glass-Block Panel Installation

While larger glass-block wall systems require extensive support and reinforcement, smaller glass panels (surrounded on four sides by framing) aren't difficult to install. Either a mortar or a mortarless system can be used, and different styles of block are available.

Mortar system

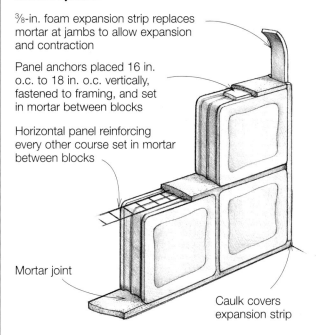

⅜-in. foam expansion strip replaces mortar at jambs to allow expansion and contraction

Panel anchors placed 16 in. o.c. to 18 in. o.c. vertically, fastened to framing, and set in mortar between blocks

Horizontal panel reinforcing every other course set in mortar between blocks

Mortar joint

Caulk covers expansion strip

Conventional framing supports the block, while an expansion strip at the header and jambs protects the panel from movement. Horizontal panel reinforcement is needed every 24 in.

Mortarless system

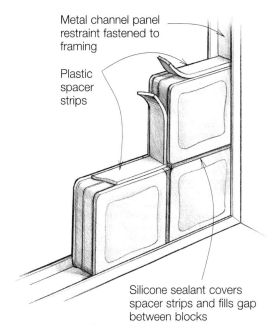

Metal channel panel restraint fastened to framing

Plastic spacer strips

Silicone sealant covers spacer strips and fills gap between blocks

A combination of plastic spacer strips and silicone sealant replaces mortar to hold the blocks together, while metal channel is used to secure the panel to the framing.

Drywall has become an almost universal ceiling material. Before installing any ceiling drywall, I like to fur out the joists with 1x3 strapping installed on 16-in. centers perpendicular to the framing. The trade-off in extra labor and material is minimal, the strapping makes a bigger target for screws than the edge of joists, and it reduces nail-head pops and cracking associated with the drying process of new framing lumber. Strapping is also easy to shim if the joists are uneven in an old house, allowing you to level out a ceiling. Electricians like it because it makes it easy to run cable without drilling through joists. And strapping allows you to easily maintain the 12-in.-o.c. recommendation for installing MR drywall in a ceiling, whether the ceiling joists are 16 in. o.c. or 24 in. o.c.

I've hung a fair amount of ceiling drywall using my head as a support, but simple 2x4 T-supports cut slightly longer than the height of the room work better. So do helpers. Remember to plug gaps around any openings in the ceiling with either Durabond, which fills in large gaps very well without cracking out of the joint, or caulk.

Chapter 12

INSTALLING FIXTURES AND COMPONENTS

TOILETS AND BIDETS

CABINETS,
COUNTERTOPS,
AND SINKS

FAUCETS

After the major bathing fixtures have been installed and the flooring and walls are finished, it's time to install the rest of the major components of the bathroom. If the rough-ins have been done correctly and drain and supply lines are all in the right locations, then this part of the job should go smoothly, marking the beginning of the end of this particular bathroom project. But if mistakes have been made during rough-in, now is the time they show up, and the headaches begin.

TOILETS AND BIDETS

Toilets are by far the easiest bathroom fixture to install. One-piece toilets are a little awkward to handle because of their weight and size, but they don't require much assembly beyond mounting the toilet seat. Nowadays, two-piece toilets often have factory-installed tank bolts and tank gaskets, which makes assembly pretty simple. And two-piece toilets are easier to handle than one-piece toilets, especially if you mount the bowl first before completely assembling the rest of the toilet. After the bowl is installed and any necessary assembly of the toilet completed, all that is left is to connect the cold-water supply. This is again pretty easy because the angle stop and the threaded fill valve on the tank are so accessible.

Bidets, on the other hand, aren't quite so straightforward. For one thing, the location of drain and supply connections are far more variable on a bidet than on a regular toilet, so that the rough-in has to be done to match the manufacturer's schematic. For some bidets, the drain connection is similar to that of a shower pan; for others, the connection is almost identical to that of a sink. Bidets also require both a hot- and cold-supply connection, like on a sink, and the valve might be located either on the bidet itself or on the wall behind it (see the drawing on p. 48). For these reasons, it's important to refer specifically to the manufacturer's literature when installing a bidet.

Seating the flange

The first step in any toilet installation is to secure the toilet flange to the closet bend, which was hopefully roughed-in in the right location, and to check that it is adequately supported with framing and secured in place with strapping or stabilizers (galvanized for cast iron, plastic for plastic pipe). The closet-bend pipe stub should be cut flush with the finish floor, making sure that there is room around the perimeter to insert the flange. In some cases, you'll have to chip away tile with a cold chisel or cut out flooring with a reciprocating saw to make sure the flange fits.

Cutting the pipe flush is pretty easy if the drain system is plastic, but it's a little harder if it is cast iron. An internal pipe cutter can easily trim the cast-iron stub to length if it is long, but a right-angle grinder is more likely to be in your collection of tools and will accomplish the same task. Just score around the outside of the pipe until there is a shallow groove, then use a wrench to break off the excess pipe stub. Use the grinder to clean up the edge.

After the pipe is cut flush to the floor, the flange can be attached to the closet bend, with the bolt slots parallel to the back wall. Plastic flanges are simply cemented in place to the plastic drain

pipe, then screwed to the floor. Be sure to use galvanized screws to secure the flange to the floor, and predrill tile with big enough holes so that it won't crack as the screws pass into the subfloor. If you are installing a cast-iron system, an instant-set flange is a two-piece clamping alternative to a leaded flange. Though more expensive than a regular flange, its neoprene gasket makes a tight seal between the metal collar and drainpipe that is as effective as a conventional oakum and poured lead connection but is much easier to install.

Setting the bowl

Closet bolts attach the toilet bowl to the flange and come in standard (2¼-in.) and long (3½-in.) lengths. They should be of solid brass, and any other nuts or washers used to make this connection should also be of either brass, chrome-plated brass, or stainless steel. Don't use

A wax ring ensures a leak-proof seal between the flange and the toilet bowl. When setting the bowl, apply even pressure and gently rock it back and forth until it is flush against the floor.

cheaper plated-steel hardware, which will quickly corrode in this environment and eventually make the toilet impossible to remove. Once the closet bolts are in place, the toilet is ready to be set.

A wax-and-plastic gasket, or wax ring, is used to make a leak-proof seal between the flange and the toilet (see the photo on p. 185). Some manufacturer's instructions will direct you to place the wax ring onto the toilet, but putting it directly on the flange makes it easier to set the bowl. Once the bowl is in position again, with the closet bolts situated in their openings, make sure that it is square to the surrounding walls. Gently rock the toilet back and forth while applying downward pressure until the toilet bowl is close to flat on the finish floor. Then put on the washers and nuts (again, don't use plated steel, the type that often comes with wax-ring kits) and tighten them slowly and carefully, alternating a few turns a side, until the bowl is securely fastened down. Don't overtighten the nuts, though; porcelain is brittle and will crack.

Mounting the tank

If the toilet is a close-coupled two-piece unit, the tank will have to be installed onto the bowl. Some plumbers I've worked with prefer to premount the tank before setting the bowl because it is a little easier to make the connections at the back of the toilet before it is set in place. But the toilet can be awkward and heavy to handle this way, so others prefer to install the tank after the bowl is fastened to the flange. In either case, check to be sure that the large flush-valve nut on the bottom of the tank has been tightened at the factory. In some cases, the large tank-to-bowl gasket will be pre-installed and conceal the nut, but the nut won't be tight enough to prevent leaking, so you'll have to check this before actually assembling the tank to the bowl.

Two-piece toilets need to be assembled, but take care to make connections tight enough to prevent leaking but not so tight that they crack the bowl or tank. Pipe dope helps gaskets seat properly and prevent leakage.

Different toilets have slightly different assembly sequences and hardware, but in general either two or three flat-headed bolts fasten the tank to the bowl. Don't be afraid to use plumber's putty underneath the bolt heads or pipe dope on gaskets when assembling the toilet, whether or not this is in the installation instructions (see the photo above). Tighten the nuts slowly, alternating turns at each nut and taking care not to twist the rubber washers under the bolt head. Usually it's best to hold the bolts still with a screwdriver while tightening the nut from underneath with a wrench.

Connecting the water supply

A major cause of fill-valve failure in a toilet is debris and sediment. In new construction, there is still a lot of debris in the water-supply line that hasn't yet been flushed out when it comes time to hook up the toilet. So it makes sense to give the system a flush into an empty mud bucket before hooking up the water supply. And if you empty the filled bucket into the toilet bowl, you can check for leaks in the wax seal.

The angle stop is a compression-fit valve that fits over the supply stub. A closet supply tube makes the connection between the angle stop and the tank's threaded fill-valve supply, but usually the location of the angle stop is not directly aligned with the fill-valve supply. This means that the supply tube will have to make some curves as it connects point A to point B. However, there are braided stainless-steel supply tubes specifically made for toilets that make this connection easily (see the drawing at right). Braided supply tubes shouldn't be used in houses with high water pressure, and in some areas they may not be allowed by code. But they are very easy to install, especially in retrofit applications where extreme changes in direction are necessary.

Chrome-plated brass tubing makes the most reliable closet supply connection and can be used for houses with high water pressure, though it is more difficult to get a good fit and more time-consuming to install than braided tubing (see the photo on p. 188). There are tubing benders available that make curving the pipe easier, but bending can also be done by hand in most cases, though you'll need to be careful not to kink the tubing. Chromed-brass supply tubing is available with either a flat head (see the drawing at right) or an acorn head (see the drawing on p. 194). The flat-head type has a plastic sealing pad that sits against the bottom edge of the fill-valve supply. A flat connection is vital for a leak-free installation, and flat-head tubing works better if the other parts of the connection are brass. The acorn head looks like it sounds and actually extends up into the fill-valve supply so that an absolutely perfect connection isn't necessary for a leak-free installation.

Teflon tape should be wrapped around the male threads of the fill-valve supply before connecting the supply tubing. After the water is hooked up, check for leaks at the angle stop and at all the plumbing connections. Also, check the

Toilet-Supply Connection

Chromed-brass supply tubing makes an attractive and durable connection between the angle stop and a toilet's fill-valve supply. Flexible stainless-steel braided supplies are an easily installed alternative for systems with water pressure under 80 PSI.

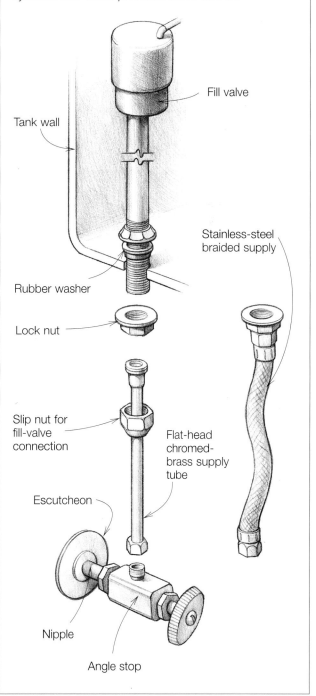

Fill valve

Tank wall

Stainless-steel braided supply

Rubber washer

Lock nut

Slip nut for fill-valve connection

Flat-head chromed-brass supply tube

Escutcheon

Nipple

Angle stop

The water-supply connection between the angle stop and the toilet fill valve can be easily made with braided stainless-steel tubing, while bendable chromed-brass tubing is a good choice for water-supply systems with high pressure.

tank bolts to make sure that they aren't dripping water on the floor, and flush the toilet a number of times to make sure that everything is kosher. Now the closet bolts can be trimmed to size with a hack saw, and the closet bolt caps can be filled with plumber's putty and pressed into place on the bolts. In some areas, code will require that the base of the toilet be sealed to the floor with caulk. I don't like to use caulk where I don't need to, though, and sealing up this area will conceal the fact that there is a leak if one occurs around the wax ring, while not actually preventing any damage (though it can help keep dirt from accumulating here and prevent bugs from moving in under the toilet).

CABINETS, COUNTERTOPS, AND SINKS

There's more to installing a bathroom sink than simply hooking it up to the DWV and water-supply system. In many cases, a fair amount of cabinetry needs to be installed (and perhaps even built) first, which also means that a countertop will be needed as well. In other cases, the sink will be a self-contained freestanding or wall-mounted unit, but even then it will probably require some brackets to hold it in place.

Installing vanity base cabinets and bathroom cabinetry

Compared to installing a run of kitchen cabinets, installing a few bathroom cabinets is a breeze. Like with any cabinet installation, you'll first need to check the condition of the floor and walls to see if they're plumb, level, square, and straight, and verify the exact location of the cabinetry. While I usually draw a kitchen-cabinet layout on the floor and wall, that isn't usually necessary with bathroom cabinets.

If the floor is out of level, then the cabinetry will have to be either shimmed to level or scribed to the floor. While shimming is faster and easier, especially for long runs of cabinets, it leaves a gap at the base that needs to be covered with some type of molding. For the few cabinets that usually are installed in the bathroom, scribing leaves a cleaner look. To scribe, I'll run a width of masking tape around the perimeter of the cabinet base, temporarily shim the cabinet (or cabinets) to level, set my scriber to the distance that the cabinetry extends above a reference level line on the back wall, and scribe the cabinetry at floor level.

Don't be tempted to try to pull a cabinet snug to an out-of-plumb or crooked back wall; it will just rack the cabinet, making the doors appear to be warped. Instead, run masking tape along the back edge of the cabinet and scribe to that wall too. Some cabinets also need to be scribed to fit a sidewall, either on the face frame itself or with the use of a filler strip. There are a number of ways to cut to scribe lines, but I've had good success using a belt sander fitted with a coarse-grit belt.

If there are multiple cabinets, they need to be attached together; usually I do this first before attaching them to the wall. I usually remove the hinges and drill countersunk holes through the stiles (in face-frame cabinetry) at hinge locations so that the screws will be concealed. Don't use drywall screws; they'll snap off. No. 8 wood screws are stronger and allow adjacent cabinet stiles to be pulled tightly together. Once the cabinetry has been scribed and fitted together, it can be attached to the wall.

Installing a countertop

Most bathroom countertop installations aren't complicated because there are rarely corners to turn—runs are generally straight—and because the countertops are generally small. The simplest installations simply involve fastening down the countertop to the cabinetry, usually with drywall screws driven up through the cabinet corner blocking into the underside of the countertop. Most short vanity countertops don't need scribing to the back wall, but if they do, a belt sander works well for this purpose. It efficiently removes material slowly enough for good control, and leaves a smooth edge on different types of countertop materials.

Countertops occasionally need to be scribed to fit sidewalls as well. Probably the trickiest fit to make is a recessed countertop that fits between two sidewalls. I've tried measuring and eyeballing the fit (with mixed results), but the most accurate way to do this is with a template (see the photo above). Cardboard is cheap and usually readily available, although other sheet-type materials can work just as well as long as the exact length and outline of the opening can be transferred accurately to the countertop.

Bathroom countertops and cabinetry should be scribed to fit closely to bathroom floors and walls. Here a countertop template (used to transfer measurements to the actual countertop) is being scribed to the back wall.

Of course, a tile countertop is built on-site, so its installation is different than prebuilt countertops. While there may be occasion to install a mortar-bed substrate for a tile countertop, it's faster and easier to use ½-in. backer board laminated with epoxy thinset to a ¾-in. AC plywood substrate. Joints in the backer board should be taped with fiberglass mesh tape and adhesive forced through the tape and into the joint, which effectively edge-glues the backer board together. If the countertop will have a tile front edge, the edge of the backer board should also be taped and thinset adhesive forced into the joint between the backer board and the plywood (see the photo p. 190).

Layout and setting a tile countertop is pretty straightforward and follows the procedures discussed in Chapter 10 (pp. 168-172). I try to choose tile and countertop sizes that minimize cutting if I can because countertop tiles are so visible. Availability of trim tile also influences selection and layout. Working at countertop height is a real pleasure compared to laying floor tile, but be sure to protect cabinet fronts and finished surfaces from stray globs of

Backer board over ¾-in. AC plywood makes a good substrate for tile countertops. Joints should be reinforced with fiberglass mesh tape and filled with thinset adhesive before actually setting the tile.

adhesive and grout. To finish up, I like to use a 100%-solids epoxy grout because I like its ability to withstand stains and mildew.

Installing a self-rimming sink

Self-rimming sinks are easy to install; they simply rest on the countertop and don't require careful fitting and trimming. Still, cutting a big hole in the middle of a countertop is not a job for the timid, and putting the hole in the wrong place will ruin your day. Most new sinks come with templates to make the job easier, but even with a template you'll have to pay attention to clearances in the front and back of the sink. I've found that sometimes the template can be shifted forward slightly, which leaves a little more room for the water-supply hookups when the sink is in place. If there isn't a template, it's possible to make one with cardboard, or if there is an old countertop that used the same sink, you can transfer the cutout to the new countertop.

Position the template on the countertop so that the cutout is properly located (you don't want part of the sink to be contacting a curved surface, such as you would find on the front of a post-formed countertop). When the positioning looks correct, tape the template down so it won't move but also so it will allow you to place masking tape underneath the cutout outline. While not absolutely necessary, masking tape makes it easier to see the outline on some types of countertops and can help prevent chipping as the cut is made.

I normally use a jigsaw with a high-quality blade appropriate for cutting plastic laminate to make the cutout, first drilling a pilot hole inside the cutout line. (Masking tape on the saw base helps protect the laminate from the saw's rough surface. See the left photo on the facing page.) I've seen routers used to make this cut, though bigger routers (and some jigsaws) can't usually make the cut near the backsplash because of the width of their base. The cutout should be supported as you make the cut so that it doesn't fall away near the end and chip the laminate. A good way to do this is by hot-melt gluing or by screwing a couple of support strips to the underside of the countertop across the opening after the cut has been started. Some sinks will also have protrusions in the casting for the sink overflow that may require a notch in the cutout so that the sink sits flat in the opening.

If there are openings for the faucet in the sink, now is the time to install it before setting the sink onto the countertop. Before setting the sink down, roll out a continuous snake of plumber's putty around the opening (see the right photo on the facing page), then press the sink down into place. Putty will squish out from the opening until the sink is down tight against the countertop. Some plumbers use adhesive caulk instead here, but if the sink needs to be removed later it will be hard to do without damaging the bowl or the countertop. After the sink is connected to the plumbing and drain lines and the plumber's putty has been trimmed away, a small bead of silicone caulk around the perimeter, between the sink and the countertop, will ensure a watertight installation.

Installing other types of sinks

Rimless sinks depend on a stainless-steel mounting rim to hold the sink bowl in place, flush with the countertop surface. After making the countertop cutout (using a template or the mounting rim's central partition) as a guide, lay a continuous ¼-in.-diameter snake of plumber's putty on the inside of the rim partition and set the bowl in place. Punch-outs in the rim that hold the sink temporarily in place can be pushed out with a screwdriver. Apply another snake of putty on the outside of the rim before setting the whole assembly in place in the cutout. Rim clips spaced equally around the perimeter of the sink pull the rim down against the countertop and snug the sink up against the rim. These are available in different sizes to fit different countertop and sink thicknesses.

Undermount sinks function better than rimless sinks because water can be swept off the countertop and into the bowl, without the rim of the sink getting in the way. Some countertops have premounted bolts or female threads cast into the underside of the countertop to which are fastened clips that hold the sink bowl in place. A bead of silicone caulk between the upper rim of the bowl and the underside of the countertop helps hold things in place and keeps water from seeping into the joint. Often now, both the sink and the countertop will be made of the same solid-surface material and can be glued almost seamlessly together.

Wall-mount sinks work well in small bathrooms and are more accessible for wheelchair users. They are supported by metal hangers that are attached to the wall, so blocking needs to be added during the framing stage. It's a good idea to premount both the faucet and the hot- and cold-water supply tubes on these sinks before installation because there isn't usually a lot of room to maneuver once they are in place. The

A template is used to mark the sink cutout on a countertop. Masking tape (seen on the saw base to protect the countertop from scratches) can also be used on the laminate to make the line easier to see and to help prevent the laminate from chipping.

The sink should be set in plumber's putty rather than adhesive caulk so that it can be easily removed later if necessary. A bead of silicone caulk seals the joint between the sink and the countertop after the sink is in place.

Undermount Sink Installation

Undermount sink

Often used with natural stone or tile countertops, undermount sinks are held in place with clips and mounting bolts. Solid-surface undermount sinks can be glued directly to a solid-surface countertop, eliminating the hardware and seams of a regular undermount installation.

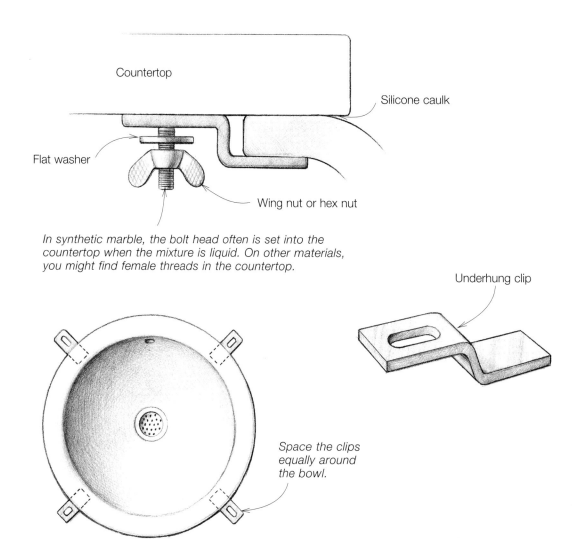

Countertop

Silicone caulk

Flat washer

Wing nut or hex nut

In synthetic marble, the bolt head often is set into the countertop when the mixture is liquid. On other materials, you might find female threads in the countertop.

Underhung clip

Space the clips equally around the bowl.

supply tubes can be left long, and then cut to length once the sink is in place.

Pedestal-sink sizes and styles vary widely, and their installation requirements vary from manufacturer to manufacturer. In some cases the sinks are supplied with mounting brackets that connect the sink basin to the base, while other sinks and bases connect directly to the wall. Also, drain and supply rough-in specifications vary from sink to sink, and installation will be difficult if the rough-in specs haven't been closely followed. Since the supply and drain connections are exposed, care should be taken while completing the final plumbing hookup.

FAUCETS

In many cases, the best time to install a faucet is before the sink is installed. If the faucet will be mounted directly on the countertop, not having the sink already in place can make it easier to tighten the faucet down and make the supply connections. Sometimes, in fact, it's next to impossible to reach up underneath and behind a sink to make faucet connections when it is already mounted in a vanity. In some situations—for example, a tiled mudded-in sink—it's better to hold off mounting the faucet until the sink and countertop are in place. Otherwise, the faucet will get in the way, making it harder to set the tile and more likely that adhesive or grout will damage the faucet. When the faucet is installed depends on the type of sink.

Assembling the faucet

Regardless of when the faucet gets mounted, cavities on the underside of a center-set faucet body should be packed with plumber's putty first (see the photo above). And try to make sure that washers and lock-mounting nuts that connect the faucet body to the sink are brass or stainless steel; plated-steel hardware quickly corrodes, making future removal close to impossible. After the faucet body has been hand-tightened, be sure to check that it is

Before setting a faucet in place, cavities should be packed with plumber's putty to keep moisture out.

centered on the drain opening before snugging nuts down with a wrench.

Because they are all in one piece, center-set faucets install more easily than wide-spread faucets. Made up of separate spout and valve components that need attaching to the sink, wide-spread faucets also require a manifold to bring water from the valves to the spout, which means a few more connections to make. The spout gets installed first, with some plumber's putty spread at the base of the spout and on the flat washer that attaches the spout to the sink or countertop. Again, align the spout with the drain opening before snugging up the lock-mounting nut.

The spout tee goes on next, and depending on the design of the faucet it will have either a top and bottom opening (through which the lift rod will pass) or a single top opening (if the lift rod is external). Teflon tape should be wrapped around male threads and pipe dope applied to female threads before making connections.

Supply Tubing Options

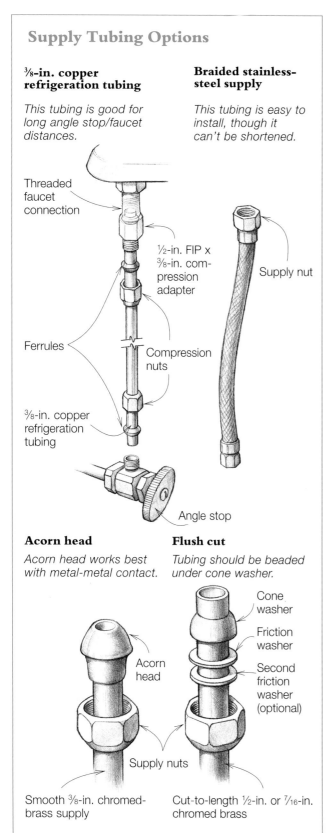

⅜-in. copper refrigeration tubing

This tubing is good for long angle stop/faucet distances.

Braided stainless-steel supply

This tubing is easy to install, though it can't be shortened.

Threaded faucet connection

½-in. FIP x ⅜-in. compression adapter

Supply nut

Ferrules

Compression nuts

⅜-in. copper refrigeration tubing

Angle stop

Acorn head

Acorn head works best with metal-metal contact.

Flush cut

Tubing should be beaded under cone washer.

Cone washer

Friction washer

Second friction washer (optional)

Acorn head

Supply nuts

Smooth ⅜-in. chromed-brass supply

Cut-to-length ½-in. or ⁷⁄₁₆-in. chromed brass

The valves can then be installed, with the manifold connections pointing either toward or away from the spout depending on how far apart the valves are, the length of the manifold tubing, and how well it loops as it makes the connection from valve to spout tee. Most manifold tubing is made of plastic now instead of brass or bendable copper tube, so it's easier to make this connection, but you'll need to avoid kinking the tubing. After everything is connected, the mounting nuts can be tightened, the escutcheons filled with plumber's putty and threaded down over the valves, and the handles attached.

Installing hot- and cold-water supplies

Supply connections for a sink faucet can be made either with braided stainless-steel supply tubes or chromed brass tubing. Plastic supply tubing is also available but should be avoided because plastic-to-metal connections aren't very reliable. Another option is ⅜-in. coiled copper refrigeration tubing, but it requires a ½-in. x ⅜-in. compression adapter at the faucet connection (see the drawing at left).

Braided stainless-steel tubing is by far the easiest to install, and unless it will be exposed (like with a pedestal or wall-hung sink) or the system has high water pressure (above 60 psi), it's my choice for most faucet supplies. The tubing comes in various lengths and has integral nuts on either end, so the tubing can't be cut. But the connection is quite painless for a plumbing procedure, requiring no cuts and only a few turns with an adjustable wrench (and perhaps a basin wrench for the faucet connection).

Chromed-brass supply tubing is generally ⅜ in. in diameter, though larger ⁷⁄₁₆-in.- or ½-in.- diameter sizes might be used in older houses or when water pressure is low. Acorn-head supply tubing makes the most reliable faucet connection, though old tubing that has previously been used with another faucet should probably be discarded since the acorn head will

Pop-Up Waste Assembly

Before the sink can be connected to the DWV system, the pop-up waste assembly needs to be installed. The drain's seat flange should be set in plumber's putty to keep the sink from leaking, and using pipe dope on female threads is always a good policy.

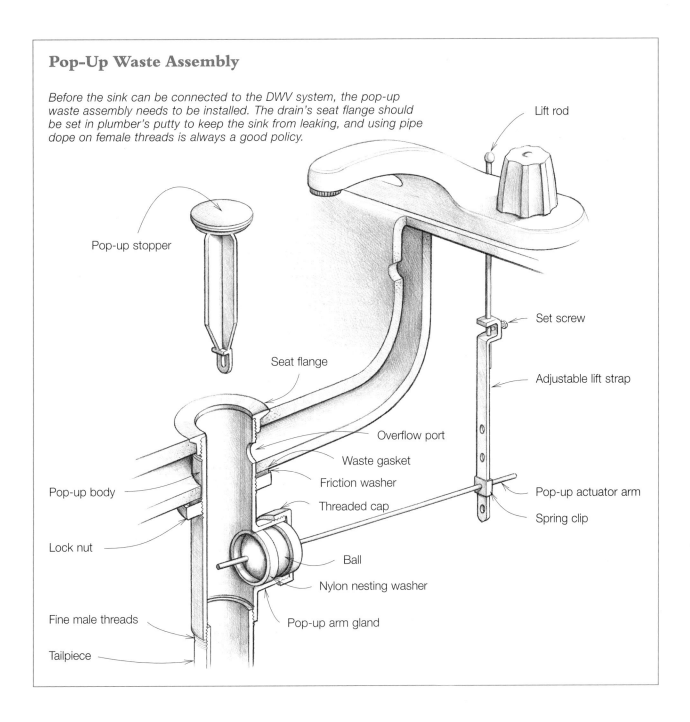

Lift rod

Pop-up stopper

Seat flange

Set screw

Adjustable lift strap

Overflow port

Waste gasket

Friction washer

Threaded cap

Pop-up body

Pop-up actuator arm

Spring clip

Lock nut

Ball

Nylon nesting washer

Fine male threads

Pop-up arm gland

Tailpiece

have been compressed by the old faucet and will probably leak. Some supply tubes (particularly older ones) are flush-cut and require a rubber cone washer at the faucet connection. This type of tubing is a little trickier to make leak free, especially if you don't have a beading tool to make the required bead in the tubing.

Installing pop-up wastes and traps

After the sink and faucet are installed, it's time to install the pop-up waste assembly and connect everything to the DWV system (see the drawing above). Though there are plastic pop-up waste assemblies, the better ones are made of brass and come in a number of designs. They are

Trap Connections

While tubular-brass traps look better and in some cases are required by code, plastic traps (either of ABS or PVC) can be built of larger diameter 2-in. pipe and therefore have better drainage, and their cemented joints are less likely to slip or leak.

Tubular-brass trap connections

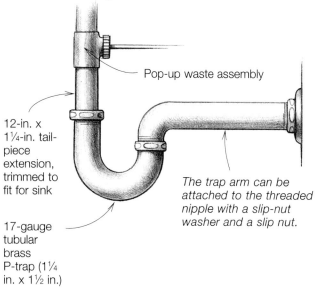

Pop-up waste assembly

12-in. x 1¼-in. tail-piece extension, trimmed to fit for sink

17-gauge tubular brass P-trap (1¼ in. x 1½ in.)

The trap arm can be attached to the threaded nipple with a slip-nut washer and a slip nut.

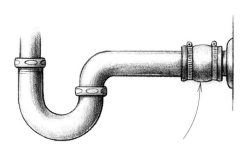

The trap arm can be attached with mission coupling, either 2-in. or 1½-in. copper, plastic, or steel to 1½-in. bath waste.

ABS/PVC trap connections

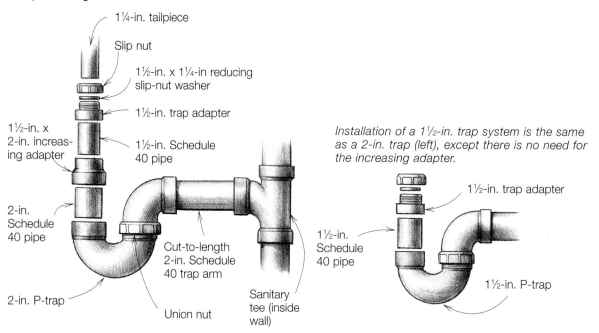

1¼-in. tailpiece

Slip nut

1½-in. x 1¼-in reducing slip-nut washer

1½-in. trap adapter

1½-in. x 2-in. increasing adapter

1½-in. Schedule 40 pipe

2-in. Schedule 40 pipe

2-in. P-trap

Cut-to-length 2-in. Schedule 40 trap arm

Union nut

Sanitary tee (inside wall)

Installation of a 1½-in. trap system is the same as a 2-in. trap (left), except there is no need for the increasing adapter.

1½-in. trap adapter

1½-in. Schedule 40 pipe

1½-in. P-trap

usually included with the faucet, though often you have the option of substituting a different pop-up. A snake of plumber's putty should be wrapped around the seat flange before setting it in place in the drain opening. Also, another snake of putty should be placed on top of the beveled gasket that makes contact with the underside of the sink before tightening everything. Pipe dope should be used on the female threads of the pop-up body where the tailpiece screws into it. After the pop-up body is in place, the arm and lift strap can be assembled.

The trap connects the 1¼-in. tailpiece from the sink to the sanitary tee of the DWV system, which is typically 1½ in. or 2 in. in diameter. Traps are made of either plastic or brass and consist of a bewildering array of parts to make this seemingly simple connection (see the drawing on the facing page). I have a box full of slip nuts, increasing adapters, P-traps in various sizes, and union nuts, yet it always seems that I don't have the specific part that I need whenever I have to hook up one of these Rube Goldberg-like contraptions.

Plastic traps depend on cemented joints and a union nut, which connect the P-trap to the trap arm. Avoid the thin-wall plastic traps and stick with Schedule 40 ABS or PVC pipe, which are more rigid and less likely to flex and fail. The trick in fitting plastic systems is getting the trap riser and trap arm lengths correct, so some dry assembly will be necessary to check alignment before cementing the parts together. While a 1½-in. trap meets code and doesn't require a reducer, a 2-in. trap is less likely to clog up.

Tubular-brass traps look more elegant than plastic and should be used in exposed locations. Connections are made with slip nuts and slip-nut washers, and getting the trap arm and trap riser lengths right is also tricky. Often an extension is needed on the factory tailpiece to reach the P-trap. While an extension with a

Whether made of plastic or of tubular brass, sink traps require careful fitting to ensure a watertight connection that also looks good.

belled opening that slides up over the existing tailpiece is available, I think that threaded extensions between 6 in. and 12 in. long make a more secure connection. After all, they aren't called "slip joints" for nothing.

Any faucet should be flushed out after it has been installed to rid the supply lines of sediment. Unscrew the aerator first, turn the water flow on, and let it run for a few minutes before adjusting temperature or volume. This helps particles to flush out before they have a chance to grind against valving surfaces.

Chapter 13

FINISHING UP

TUB AND SHOWER GLASS DOORS

WALLS, CEILINGS, AND TRIMWORK

THE FINAL INSPECTION

Bathrooms can be quirky places and full of finicky details, so normal finishing sequences that work in other parts of the house might be turned topsy-turvy here. For example, I usually like to paint walls as late in the construction process as I can to keep them from being marred. In a bathroom, though, walls typically get painted before the toilet is installed in order to ensure that the area behind the tank gets painted. So the steps in finishing up a bathroom that are presented in this chapter aren't necessarily done in a particular order. That will be dictated by the requirements of the job and the availability of specialty contractors.

TUB AND SHOWER GLASS DOORS

Tub and shower doors range from simple premanufactured sliders to elaborate custom-built frameless units. Most builders I know rely on local glass fabricators to supply and install anything that requires custom glass fabrication. Working with tempered glass and the special hinges that these systems use is fussy work, and experienced glass shops have the equipment and expertise to make the process go smoothly. And if a panel turns out to be too small or too large because the opening has been measured incorrectly, it's nice to know that someone else is responsible for the error, which will be an expensive one.

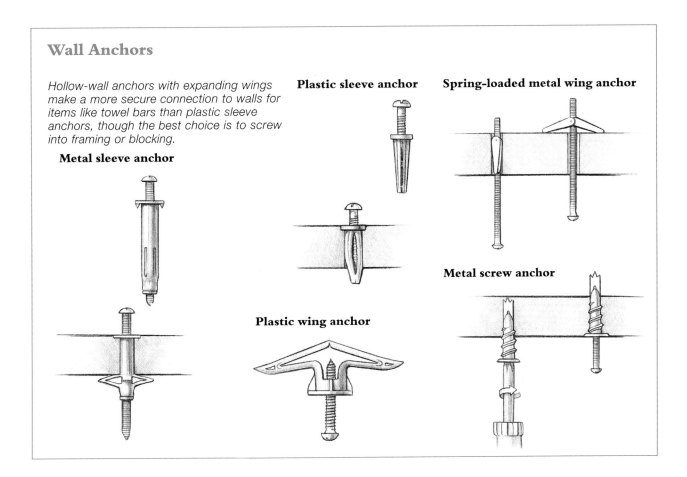

Wall Anchors

Hollow-wall anchors with expanding wings make a more secure connection to walls for items like towel bars than plastic sleeve anchors, though the best choice is to screw into framing or blocking.

Metal sleeve anchor

Plastic sleeve anchor

Spring-loaded metal wing anchor

Metal screw anchor

Plastic wing anchor

Simple premanufactured units aren't difficult to install though, and most kits come with good installation instructions. Hopefully the tub rim and sidewalls are level and plumb, but just to be sure check them with a level. Most enclosures can accommodate a fair degree (about ¼ in. or so in 6 ft.) of deviation simply by adjusting the panel rollers, but anything more than that might make a glass enclosure impractical. In such a case, a shower curtain supported by a screw-in or compression-fit shower rod might be a better choice. Hinged doors generally have even less leeway than sliding doors to accommodate crooked walls. And even if sliding doors will function properly in an out-of-plumb or out-of-level installation, they'll look odd because the panel door edges won't be parallel with the enclosure jambs.

Another variable hidden within the wall structure is the presence or absence of suitable blocking or studs in which to anchor the enclosure frame. If there isn't anything solid, wall anchors can be used, but try to steer clear of plastic anchors, which never seem to hold very well for very long. My choice for fastening objects like tub-enclosure frames, towel bars, and surface-mounted toilet-paper holders securely to walls in the absence of blocking or studs is corrosion-resistant hollow-wall anchors that have expanding wings that grip against the back of the wall when the anchor is tightened. These are available in different sizes to fit different wall thicknesses, making them suitable for use with tile, drywall, and other wall materials (see the drawing above).

Judicious use of caulk when installing a tub or shower enclosure will prevent leaks and protect framing from water damage.

When cutting the metal track, jambs, and header bar that comprise the basic frame of the enclosure, be sure to measure carefully and cut cleanly and squarely with a good hacksaw guided by a miter box. Also, note the presence of curves at the corners, and take the time to file or grind the corners of the track and jambs to shape. While caulk can fill in the gaps, it won't hide a poor fit. Also, cutting metal parts about $\frac{1}{16}$ in. short will ensure that they fit without being forced into place, and filing the cuts smooth helps keep the walls from being scratched during installation.

Because I don't like the look of a lot of caulk all over the place, I try to minimize its use and conceal it if possible. For example, I'll try to apply caulk to the underside of a tub or shower track before setting it in place, if I can, rather than gooping it up afterward. The same is true of enclosure jambs. If you pre-position the parts first, while they are still dry, and then mark

their position with a pencil line, you can apply masking tape just outside of the line. Then, when the track and jambs are set in place, the excess caulk that squeezes out can be smoothed over onto the tape and easily removed. This also leaves a straight bead. Of course, there is some caulking that must be done after the enclosure is in place. For this, I use as small a bead as possible, apply it sparingly, then carefully tool the joint (see the photo above). (For more about caulk, see the sidebar on p. 202.)

If the tub or shower enclosure is ceramic tile, don't try to take a shortcut and mount screws in grout lines without drilling holes. Most likely, the tile will crack because the screws will be bigger than the joint between the tiles, and it will also be hard to seal the hole against moisture. Also, don't tighten screws too aggressively in tile because doing so can crack the tile. After I've drilled appropriate holes with a carbide-tipped masonry bit, I'll squirt silicone caulk in before inserting the screws to help waterproof the holes.

WALLS, CEILINGS, AND TRIMWORK

Whether the final bathroom wall and ceiling finish will be paint or wallpaper, the key to a good finish is preparation. After the drywall has been taped and sanded (and any surface texture applied), prime the walls and ceilings. Wallpaper requires both a primer and sizing (a paste that prepares the wall for glue) before application. Some primers are specifically formulated to be used under wallpaper, such as Shieldz, eliminating the need for sizing and protecting drywall's paper face from damage when the wallpaper is eventually removed. For paint finishes I use a low-perm primer.

In some cases, ceilings that have been finished with a sound-deadening texture don't technically need priming and painting, but they should be finished anyway to enhance their ability to retard water vapor. Because the ceiling is out of the way and not subject to the dings and scratches that walls are, I usually try to finish-coat the ceiling immediately after I've primed it.

Find and fix flaws

Right after the walls and ceiling are primed is a good time to look for flaws in the finish. Make an inspection of the room, circling with a pencil areas that need fixing, then come back later to fill in with a fast-drying vinyl spackling compound like DAP or with Durabond (if there are some larger flaws).

Most drywall flaws are small and easily patched with a single application of compound. You'll find flaws at taped seams and near metal corner beads, like the wall of a tub surround. Deeper dings will need a couple of layers of spackling compound, and bubbles in tape should be cut out with a sharp utility knife and patched (see the photo above). After flaws have been patched

Use a sharp utility knife to completely cut out bubbles in drywall tape, then patch with a fast-setting joint compound. (Photo by the author.)

and sanded or sponged smooth, they should be spot-primed so the patch won't telegraph through the finish paint.

Prepare woodwork

I usually prime wood trim with an alkyd-based primer called Underbody (from Benjamin Moore & Co.) after I've spot-primed knots and discolorations with B-I-N primer/sealer (from William Zinsser & Co., Inc.). Underbody is admittedly more fussy to work with than some other wood primers because it dries slowly (though there is a faster-drying latex version) and should really be sanded out before a top coat is added. When possible, I try to prime wood trim and sometimes even give it its first top coat before installing it. This allows me to efficiently sand it smooth and ease the edges before priming, to back- and edge-prime the trim, and to sand out the Underbody while working at a comfortable height. As the trim is cut to fit, I spot-prime the end cuts with B-I-N. Back-, edge-, and end-priming will keep woodwork from absorbing moisture and keep it more stable so gaps don't open up and wider

Caulks and Sealants

Most folks don't shop for caulks and sealants like they do for bathroom fixtures, but considering the job that caulks are expected to do and their high visibility, it might not be a bad idea. The problem is, there are an awful lot of caulks and sealants on the market, so choosing among them is difficult. Caulks basically do two jobs in the bathroom: seal against moisture intrusion and provide a pleasing joint between fixtures and wall finish materials. For the most part, careful detailing will minimize the reliance upon caulk for both functions, but there are still instances when it is necessary.

Types of caulk
While there are about a dozen types of caulks available for residential use, caulks for use in bathrooms fall into three basic categories: latex, acrylic latex (sometimes with silicone), and silicone.

Latex caulks are easy to apply and easy to clean up because they're water based and hold paint well. I like to use them when painting with latex paint because they are cheap and fill cracks and holes easily, and can be painted over almost immediately. However, they aren't very water resistant or flexible, so they're a poor choice for general-purpose applications in the bathroom.

Acrylic latex caulks are more flexible than regular latex and are usually available in a fungicide-treated version for bathroom use. The fungicide gradually leaches out of the caulk over the course of about 5 to 15 years, helping to prevent mildew growth for that period of time. These caulks are a bit more expensive than plain latex caulk, but they are paintable and work well as a general-purpose caulk, which makes them worth the extra money. There are also siliconized versions of acrylic latex caulks, but the percentage of silicone is so low (typically less than 2%) that the caulk's performance is not appreciably altered. Most caulks that are tinted to match stock colors of different manufacturers fall into this category.

Silicone caulks in tub-and-tile versions that contain a fungicide are available, and though they cost considerably more than acrylic latex caulks, their durability and flexibility make them good performers in the bathroom environment. They do have some drawbacks, however, including the fact that they are difficult to work with: They set up fast, need a well-cleaned substrate to stick to, and are hard to form into a smooth bead. Silicone caulks aren't generally paintable either (even the so-called "paintable" ones), though the clear and white formulations cover most situations that you'll encounter in the bathroom. I've also noticed that some silicone caulks tend to get dirty easily, and when they do get dirty they are hard to get clean again.

Working with caulk
An open tube of caulk is a bit like Pandora's box, and it's hard to keep the mischief contained in it from spreading everywhere once it's opened. Part of the problem is that caulking is often approached as almost an afterthought. But a few simple steps will make caulking less of an annoyance and improve its appearance and performance.

1. **Prepare the surface.** Silicone caulk especially doesn't adhere well to dirty or contaminated surfaces, whether they are new or old. Old caulk should be removed from tubs and sinks, and all surfaces should be thoroughly cleaned of old soap film and dirt before recaulking. In severe cases, this may mean cleaning with a detergent, which should then be cleaned off with a water-soluble solvent, such as isopropanol, and allowed to dry. Rubbing alcohol also works well on soap film.

2. Prepare the caulk. Caulk should be worked at around room temperature, so cold tubes should be warmed up before using them. Different-size joints require different-size tip openings, but in general the smaller the tip opening the better. Many caulking guns have an integral nipper for cutting off the tip, but a sharp utility knife or shears do a better job because they are more accurate and leave a cleaner cut. A 45° angle cut allows the tip to be held against the joint without scraping out caulk, but a straight cut works well too, depending on the type and size of joint being caulked.

3. Tool the joint. I've pushed caulk in front of the tip, and I've pulled caulk; in some cases, you don't have a choice. In either case, the idea is to avoid leaving voids and to inject enough caulk into the joint. Outlining the joint with masking tape makes it easier to clean afterward and guarantees straight joint lines. Immediately after the caulk is applied, it will need to be tooled, which will help improve adhesion, remove air pockets, and smooth the joint surface. Special caulking finishers, plastic spoons, and even tongue depressors work better than fingertips for tooling the caulk and leave a smoother and more

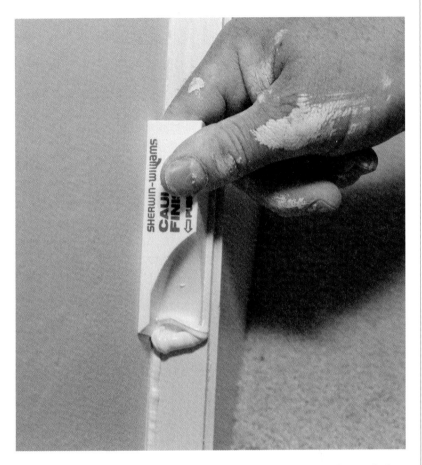

After the caulk has been applied to the joint, it needs to be tooled to remove air pockets. Special caulking finishers work better than fingers to smooth the joint and remove excess caulk.

professional-looking finish (see the photo above). And having a couple of rags handy to wipe up excess caulk from hands and tools will help to keep it under control.

4. Clean up. If you've used masking tape to outline the joints, be sure to remove it before the caulk begins to skin over. Most caulks indicate on their labels the appropriate solvent for cleanup.

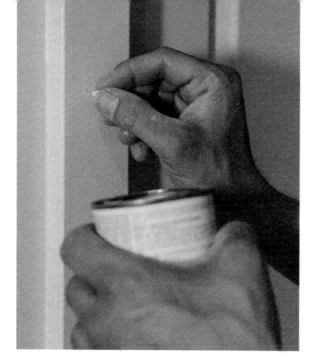

Nail holes in woodwork should be filled with putty before finish coating.

to the touch in a matter of minutes and several recoats can be done the same day—makes waterborne finishes my choice. Another advantage of waterborne urethanes is that they can be used to edge- and back-prime shortly before installation because they dry so quickly.

Nail holes need to be filled in, but don't make the mistake of filling them before the finish has been applied. The oils contained in some wood putties can slightly stain the area immediately surrounding the nail hole. Another reason to wait is that most finishes change the color of the wood, so color matching will be more accurate later. Though I've used colored pencils, I don't like them as much as colored putty because the colors can be intermixed for a better color match.

boards won't cup. Often trim will need to be sanded in place after it's installed, in which case the sanded area will need repriming.

Nail holes in woodwork can be filled with a number of different products, like latex caulk, Elmer's Carpenter's Wood Filler (from Borden Corp.), and DAP '33' glazing compound, a putty used for sealing glass to sash (see the photo above). I like to use DAP '33' because it is quick and clean to use, doesn't require a knife to apply it, doesn't need sanding out, and can be immediately painted with an alkyd or latex paint. Gaps and joints in trimwork should be filled in with caulk after priming.

Naturally finished woodwork requires a more conscientious approach on the part of the builder because paints and caulks can't be used to hide flaws. I think that waterborne urethanes offer the best combination of protection, ease of use, environmental responsibility, and quality of finish for exposed wood trim. Oil-based urethanes are arguably more durable, but the trade-off in workability—waterborne finishes dry

Plug leaks
After the cosmetic blemishes have been fixed, make sure that any remaining gaps around electrical boxes, recessed lights, ventilation fans, plumbing, and other penetrations through the walls or ceiling have been filled. For the most part, a good acrylic latex caulk or silicone caulk can be used to seal up these leaks, though you might want to use either an expanding or non-expanding foam to fill larger gaps.

Apply finish
After all the prep work, painting or wallpapering might seem anticlimactic, and hopefully it will be. I generally use a standard-size 9-in. roller to apply wall paint and a 2½-in. angled sash brush for trimwork. I've also successfully used the foam painting pads with short nylon bristles for cutting in around trimwork, though many other painters use masking tape to make it easier to cut in. While the theory of masking tape is good, in practice (at least for me) it has tended to allow leaks underneath and lift off fresh paint when being removed, though I understand that these problems have a lot to do with the age and quality of the tape being used.

Different painters also have different preferences for how they paint a room. Most paint the walls first, then the trim; others will first do the trim (often with spray equipment), let other tradespeople finish up their work, then return to paint the walls when the danger of damage to painted surfaces has mainly passed. Some painters rely on spraying equipment, partly because of the smooth, even finish it leaves on trimwork, while others paint everything with a brush. In short, there is no absolute right or wrong way to paint a room.

I always assume that a room needs three coats of paint: one prime coat and two finish coats. A good-quality roller cover helps make rolling the paint on easier, but I haven't found that even top-quality lamb's wool covers eliminate the need for a second finish coat. I try to roll the paint on methodically, usually working from right to left and from the wet edge of the paint. Rolling slowly helps to reduce paint splatter, and I frequently renew the paint on the roller. Running the roller lightly over a freshly painted section before moving on to the next will help to even out the texture of the paint and eliminate roller marks. I roll as close to the ceiling and adjacent walls where I've already cut in as I can to minimize the texture variation between roller and brush.

Touch-up is a touchy problem. If there are dings or scuffs that need repainting, my experience is that the entire wall needs repainting. Some scuffs will clean off, especially if the paint is a higher-sheen washable paint (which should be used in a bathroom anyway). You can try to fill in a ding, but make the touch-up area as small as possible by using a small brush and not trying to feather out the edges, which usually makes the repair more noticeable. In most cases, the touched-up area ends up looking almost as obtrusive as the original ding.

Most pros rely on a steady hand and a quality brush to paint trimwork, but painter's-quality masking tape or nylon-bristled foam painting pads can also help.

THE FINAL INSPECTION

After the walls have been painted or papered, and the finishing touches—like towel bars and knobs—have been installed, then the job of a builder is virtually done. Now is the time to look everything over again to be sure that it works. Check under the sink for leaks; chances are, there will be a few nuts that need tightening, especially around compression fittings. The trap and drain should also be checked, particularly if it is chromed brass. I also check all the electrical functions, including the GFCI circuit, and make sure cabinet drawers and doors work smoothly. The final act is to flush the toilet several times, letting it fill completely between flushes, to be sure that the fill valve is working properly. While you are waiting, check the toilet again for leaks around the tank bolts and water supply.

Before shutting off the lights, take a last look around for missing caulk or dings in the paint. When you are satisfied that everything is in order, you can take your leave. By the way, don't forget to close the toilet lid before you go.

APPENDIX: NKBA GUIDELINES FOR BATHROOM PLANNING

The National Kitchen & Bath Association first adopted planning guidelines for bathroom construction in 1992. Its original *27 Guidelines for Bathroom Planning* was expanded in 1995 to include new industry research and an increasing awareness of the special needs of the disabled. The most recent version consists of 41 planning guidelines and reflects the increasing influence of universal design criteria in bathroom planning, making bathrooms more accessible to more people throughout their lives. The following is a summary of their most recent design guidelines. For further information, write or call the NKBA (see Resources on p. 209).

ENTRIES, WALKWAYS, AND CLEAR FLOOR SPACES

1. Doorways should be at least 32 in. wide when possible. While a narrower clearance may sometimes be necessary, it may result in an entrance that is not fully usable by all people. Walkways should be a minimum of 36 in. wide.

2. There should be clear floor space equal to the width of the door on the push side and greater than the width of the door on the pull side to allow for opening, closing, and passing through the door.

3. There should be a 30-in. by 48-in. clear floor space in front of the sink. This rectangular space can be measured either horizontally or vertically. If there is a knee space under the sink, up to 19 in. of the 48-in. dimension can extend under the sink.

4. The minimum space in front of the toilet should be 4 ft. by 4 ft., and at least 16 in. of that space should extend to either side of the centerline of the fixture. This space can be reduced to 30 in. by 48 in. with the understanding that the reduced dimension may limit access by some people.

5. The same clearances for a toilet apply to a bidet.

6. The clear floor space in front of a tub should be 60 in. wide (the length of the tub) by 30 in. deep for a parallel approach or 48 in. deep for a perpendicular approach. Up to 12 in. of the 60-in. dimension can extend under the sink if there is access to knee space there.

7. The space in front of a shower should be 36 in. deep by the width of the shower plus 12 in. However, if the shower is more than 60 in. wide, the space may be the width of the shower.

8. The clear floor spaces required by each fixture can overlap.

9. There should be space planned for turning 180° with a mobility aid. A minimum diameter of 60 in. is needed for 360° turns, or for a minimum T-turn space, 36 in. by 36 in. by 60 in. is required. A smaller 30-in. by 60-in. space can be substituted if necessary, but it won't allow for full use by all users.

10. A minimum clear floor space of 30 in. by 48 in. is required beyond the door swing in a bath.

SINKS

11. Vanity height should fit the size of the users. If more than one is installed, one may be 30 in. to 34 in. high, while the other may be 34 in. to 42 in. high.

12. The sink should provide adequate knee space, with a recommended width of 30 in. and a minimum of 27 in. above the floor at the front edge.

13. The bottom edge of the mirror over the sink should be no more than 40 in. above the floor (or 48 in. above the floor if it is tilted downward).

14. There should be a minimum clearance of 15 in. between the centerline of the sink and any sidewall.

15. The minimum clearance between double bowls in a sink is 30 in. from centerline to centerline, but in any case the space must be wide enough to allow for proper installation.

SHOWERS AND BATHTUBS

16. The recommended usable interior dimension for a shower is 34 in. by 34 in.; the minimum is 32 in. by 32 in., although the smaller dimension may make the shower unusable for some people.

17. Showers should include a bench or seat between 17 in. and 19 in. above the floor and at least 15 in. deep. Provisions should be made during construction for the future placement of an attached shower seat by reinforcing the walls.

18. Showers that are 60 in. deep should have at least a 32-in.-wide door opening. A 42-in.-deep shower should have a wider 36-in. entry to allow for turning and maneuvering.

19. Shower doors should open into the bathroom, not into the shower.

20. There shouldn't be steps in the tub or shower area, and safety rails should be installed.

21. Showerheads should be equipped with a pressure balance/temperature regulator or a temperature-limiting device.

22. Shower controls should be located between 38 in. and 48 in. above the floor, but instead of being centered they should be offset toward the room above any grab bars and should be accessible from both inside and outside the fixture. A handheld shower can be used in place of or in addition to a fixed shower, and should be no higher than 48 in. above the floor in its lowest position. Tub controls should also be accessible from inside and outside the fixture and offset towards the room. They should be located between the rim of the tub and 33 in. above the floor, below any grab bars. If separate hot and cold controls are used in a tub (not permissible in a shower), the hot control is always on the left as viewed from inside the tub.

TOILETS AND BIDETS

23. The distance from the centerline of a toilet or bidet to any other object (except grab bars) should be at least 16 in. The total clearance (from wall to wall) can be reduced to 30 in. if required, but that may limit use by some people. These clearances should also be maintained when a toilet and bidet are planned next to one another.

24. Toilet-paper holders should be installed within reach of a person seated on the toilet, ideally slightly in front of the edge of the bowl and 26 in. above the floor.

25. Enclosed toilets should have a minimum area of 36 in. by 66 in., with a swing-out or pocket door.

GRAB BARS, STORAGE, AND FLOORING

26. Walls should be reinforced during construction to receive grab bars that can bear a 300-lb. load. Grab bars should also be installed as needed in the bath, shower, and toilet areas. These bars should be between 1¼ in. to 1½ in. in diameter (if the cross section isn't round, the width at the largest point shouldn't exceed 2 in.). They should also extend 1½ in. from the wall, have a slip-resistant surface, and be installed between 33 in. and 36 in. above the floor. Towel bars are not adequate substitutes for grab bars. The recommended width for grab bars in bath and shower areas is at least 24 in. on control walls and back walls, and at least 12 in. on head walls. A second grab bar can be installed on the back wall the same width as the bar above it and 9 in. above the tub deck. Shower stalls should have grab bars on each wall (optional on the bench wall) and be no less than the width of the wall they are attached to, less 9 in.

A grab bar at least 42 in. wide should be located on the sidewall nearest the toilet starting not more than 12 in. from the back wall. An optional 24-in.-wide grab bar may be located on the back wall.

27. Storage for bathroom supplies should be provided within 15 in. to 48 in. above the floor.

28. Storage for soap, towels, and other personal hygiene items should be available to a person seated on the bidet or toilet but shouldn't interfere with use of the fixture. It should be 15 in. to 48 in. above the floor.

29. In the tub/shower area, storage for soap and other items should also be provided within the 15 in. to 48 in. range.

30. All flooring should be slip resistant.

CONTROLS AND MECHANICAL SYSTEMS

31. Exposed pipes and mechanicals should be covered by a protective panel.

32. Controls, dispensers, outlets, and operating mechanisms should be 15 in. to 48 in. off the floor and operable with a closed fist.

33. All mechanical, electrical, and plumbing systems should have access panels.

34. Mechanical ventilation to the outside equaling a minimum of 8 air changes per hour should be provided. The formula is Cubic Space (LxWxH) x 8 (changes per hour) ÷ 60 minutes = minimum cubic feet per minute (CFM).

35. Ground-fault circuit interrupters (GFCI) must be specified on all receptacles, lights, and switches. All fixtures above tub/shower units must be moisture-rated.

36. In addition to a primary heat source, auxiliary heating may be planned in the bathroom.

37. No fixture should be within reach of a person seated or standing in the tub or shower area. Every functional area should be well illuminated by appropriate task lighting, night lights, and general lighting. The vanity should include both overhead and eye-level side-lighting locations.

38. If possible, include a window or skylight equal in area to at least 10% of the floor area.

39. Controls, handles, and door and drawer pulls should be operable with one hand, require only minimal strength for operation, and not require tight grasping, pinching, or twisting of the wrist.

40. Countertop edges should be eased to eliminate sharp edges, and corners should be clipped or radiused.

41. Any glass in enclosures, partitions, or within 18 in. of the floor should be laminated glass with a plastic interlayer, tempered glass, or approved safety plastic.

Reprinted with permission of The National Kitchen & Bath Association, 687 Willow Grove Street, Hackettstown, NJ 07840; (800) 843-6522.

RESOURCES

Manufacturers and Associations

American Aldes Ventilation Corp.
4537 Northgate Court
Sarasota, FL 34234-2124
(800) 255-7749

American Lighting Association (ALA)
World Trade Center Suite 10046
PO Box 420288
Dallas, TX 75342-0288
(800) 605-4448

American Olean Tile Co.
1000 Cannon Ave.
PO Box 271
Lansdale, PA 19466
(215) 855-1111

American Standard Inc.
One Centennial Ave.
PO Box 6820
Piscataway, NJ 08855-6820
(908) 980-3132

Anti-Hydro International, Inc.
45 River Rd.
Flemington, NJ 08822
(800) 777-1773

APA-The Engineered Wood Association
PO Box 11700
Tacoma, WA 98411-0700
(253) 565-6600
(253) 620-7400 (product help desk)
help@apawood.org
http://www.apawood.org

Avonite, Inc.
1945 Highway 304
Belen, NM 87002
(800) 428-6648

Bemis Manufacturing Co.
300 Mill St.
PO Box 901
Sheboygan Falls, WI 53085-0901
(800) 558-7651
corp@bemismfg.com
http://www.bemismfg.com

Benjamin Moore & Co.
51 Chestnut Ridge Rd.
Montvale, NJ 07645-1862
(201) 573-6620

Blue Heron Enterprises, Inc.
842 E. Douglas Ave.
Bellingham, WA 98226
(800) 803-1284

Borden Corp.
180 E. Broad St.
Columbus, OH 43215
(614) 225-4000

Broan Manufacturing Co., Inc.
926 W. State St.
Hartford, WI 53027
(800) 445-6057

Building Officials and Code Administrators International, Inc. (BOCA International)
4051 W. Flossmoor Rd.
Country Club Hills, IL 60478-5795
(708) 799-2300

CareMate Inc.
4175 Guardian St.
Simi Valley, CA 93063
(800) 339-6350

Compotite Corp.
355 Glendale Blvd.
Los Angeles, CA 90026
(800) 221-1056

Crane Plumbing
1235 Hartrey Ave.
Evanston, IL 60202
(847) 864-9777

Dallas Specialty & Manufacturing Company
1161 Ruggles Dr.
Grand Prairie, TX 75050
(800) 222-5644

DAP Inc.
PO Box 277
Dayton, OH 45401
(800) 543-3840

Delta Faucet Corp.
A Division of Masco Corp. of Indiana
55 E. 111th St.
PO Box 40980
Indianapolis, IN 46280
(800) 345-3358
www.deltafaucet.com

DuPont Corian
Barley Mill Plaza
PO Box 80012
Wilmington, DE 19880-0012
(800) 426-7426

Easy Heat Inc.
31977 U.S. 20 East
New Carlisle, IN 46552
(219) 654-3144
www.easyheat.com

Eljer Industries, Inc.
17120 Dallas Pkwy.
Dallas, TX 75248
(214) 407-2600

Fantech Inc.
1712 Northgate Boulevard
Sarasota, FL 34234
(800) 747-1762

Feeny Manufacturing Co.
PO Box 191
Muncie, IN 47308
(800) 899-6535
(765) 288-0851

Formica Corp.
10155 Reading Rd.
Cincinnati, OH 45241-4805
(800) 367-6422
(513) 786-3400

Georgia Pacific
133 Peachtree St. NE
Atlanta, GA 30303
(404) 652-4000

Gerber Plumbing Fixtures Corp.
4600 Touhy Ave.
Chicago, IL 60646
(847) 675-6570

Glashaus, Inc.
    450 Congress Pkwy., Suite E
    Crystal Lake, IL 60014
    (815) 356-8440
    (Weck Glass Blocks)

Grohe America, Inc.
    241 Covington Dr.
    Bloomingdale, IL 60108
    (630) 582-7711

HEWI, Inc.
    2851 Old Tree Dr.
    Lancaster, PA 17603
    (717) 293-1313

Home Ventilating Institute (HVI)
    Division of Air Movement and
        Control Association (AMCA), Inc.
    30 West University Dr.
    Arlington Heights, IL 60004-1893
    (847) 394-0150

International Paper—Decorative
Products Division
    8339 Telegraph Rd.
    Odenton, MD 21113-1397
    (800) 638-4380
    (Nevamar)

Jacuzzi Whirlpool Bath
    2121 N. California Blvd.
    Suite 475
    Walnut Creek, CA 94596
    (800) 678-6889

James Hardie Building Products
    10901 Elm Ave.
    Fontana, CA 92337
    (800) 426-4051

Jammin' Johns
    2920 Frankfort Ave.
    Louisville, KY 40206
    (800) 565-6467

Kitchen Cabinet Manufacturers
Association (KCMA)
    1899 Preston White Dr.
    Reston, VA 20191-5435
    (703) 264-1690

Kohler Co.
    444 Highland Dr.
    Kohler, WI 53044
    (920) 457-4441

KWC Faucets, Inc.
    1555 Oakbrook Dr. #110
    Norcross, GA 30093
    (770) 248-1600

Lasco Bathware
    3255 East Miraloma Ave.
    Anaheim, CA 92806
    (800) 877-0464
    www.lascobathware.com

Laticrete International, Inc.
    1 Laticrete Park North
    Bethany, CT 06524
    (800) 243-4788
    webmaster@laticrete.com
    http://www.laticrete.com

Mansfield Plumbing
Products, Inc.
    150 First St.
    Perrysville, OH 44864
    (419) 938-5211

Moen, Inc.
    PO Box 8022
    North Olmsted, OH 44070-8022
    (216) 962-2000

Myson, Inc.
    49 Hercules Dr.
    Colchester, VT 05446
    (800) 698-9690

National Fire Protection
Association
    1 Batterymarch Park
    Quincy, MA 02269-9101
    (617) 770-3000

National Kitchen and Bath
Association (NKBA)
    687 Willow Grove St.
    Hackettstown, NJ 07840
    (800) 843-6522
    http://www.nkba.org

The Noble Co.
    Box 350
    614 Monroe St.
    Grand Haven, MI 49417
    (616) 842-7844

Nutone Inc.
    Madison & Red Bank Rds.
    Cincinnati, OH 45227
    (513) 527-5100

Omega Cabinets
    1205 Peters Dr.
    Waterloo, IA 50703
    (319) 235-5700

Orbit Manufacturing Co.
    1507 W. Park Ave.
    Perkasie, PA 18944
    (215) 257-0727

OSI Sealants, Inc.
    7405 Production Drive
    Mentor, OH 44060
    (800) 624-7767

Otto Bock Orthopedic Industry,
Inc.
    3000 Xenium Lane North
    Minneapolis, MN 55441
    (800) 328-4058

Peerless Pottery Inc.
    PO Box 145
    Rockport, IN 47635-0145
    (800) 457-5785

Pittsburgh Corning Corp.
    800 Presque Isle Dr.
    Pittsburgh, PA 15239-2799
    (800) 992-5769

Porcelain Enamel
Institute, Inc.
    PO Box 158541
    4004 Hillsboro Pike
    Suite 224B
    Nashville, TN 37215
    (615) 385-5357

Porcher, Ltd.
    6615 W. Boston St.
    Chandler, AZ 85226
    (800) 359-3261

Precision Plumbing
Products, Inc.
    Division of C. H. Perrott, Inc.
    Airport Business Center
    7021 NE 79th Court
    Portland, OR 97218
    (503) 256-4010
    (Tempera automatic pressure com-
        pensating valve)

Price Pfister, Inc.
    13500 Paxton St.
    Pacoima, CA 91331
    (800) 732-8238

Runtal North America, Inc.
  187 Neck Rd.
  PO Box 8278
  Ward Hill, MA 01835
  (800) 526-2621

Sign of the Crab, Ltd.
  3756 Omec Circle
  Rancho Cordova, CA 95742
  (800) 843-2722

Sloan Valve Co.
  10500 Seymour Ave.
  Franklin Park, IL 60131
  (847) 671-4300

Southern Building Code Congress
  International, Inc. (SBCCI)
  900 Montclair Rd.
  Birmingham, AL 35213-1206
  (205) 591-1853

St. Thomas Creations
  1022 W. 24th St.
  Suite 125
  National City, CA 91950-6302
  (619) 474-9490

Sto-Cote Products, Inc.
  Drawer 310
  Richmond, IL 60071
  (815) 675-2358
  (Tu-Tuff vapor barrier)

Swan Corp.
  One City Centre, Suite 2300
  St. Louis, MO 63101
  (314) 231-8148

Symmons Industries, Inc.
  31 Brooks Dr.
  Braintree, MA 02184
  (617) 848-2250

Tile Council of America (TCA)
  100 Clemson Research Blvd.
  Anderson, SC 29625
  (864) 646-8453

Tile-Redi
  2570 N. Powerline Rd. #504
  Pompano Beach, FL 33069
  (888) 445-8453

Toto Kiki U.S.A.
  1155 Southern Rd.
  Morrow, GA 30260
  (800) 938-1541

Tubular Skylight, Inc.
  5704 Clark Rd.
  Sarasota, FL 34233
  (941) 927-8823

USG Corp.
  125 S. Franklin St.
  Chicago, IL 60606
  (800) 874-4968
  USG4YOU@usgcorp.com
  www.usgcorp.com

Walney Ltd.
  108 W. Walnut St.
  North Wales, PA 19454
  (800) 650-1484

William Zinsser & Co., Inc.
  173 Belmont Dr.
  Somerset, NJ 08875
  732-469-4367

Wilsonart International, Inc.
  2400 Wilson Pl.
  PO Box 6110
  Temple, TX 76503-6110
  (800) 433-3222
  (817) 778-2711

Wirsbo Co.
  5925 148th St. West
  Apple Valley, MN 55124
  (800) 321-4739

Zoeller Pump Co.
  3649 Cane Run Rd.
  Lousiville, KY 40211
  (800) 928-7867
  (502) 778-2731
  (Qwik Jon)

Publications

International Plumbing
  Code (IPC)
    published by:
    Building Officials and Code
      Administrators International, Inc.
      (BOCA International),
    4051 W. Flossmoor Rd.
    Country Club Hills, IL 60478-5795
    (708) 799-2300

    International Conference of
      Building Officials (ICBO),
    5360 Workman Mill Rd.
    Whittier, CA 90601-2298
    310-699-0541; (800) 284-4406

    Southern Building Code Congress
      International, Inc. (SBCCI)
    900 Montclair Rd.
    Birmingham, AL 35213-1206
    (205) 591-1853

Uniform Building
  Code (UBC)
    published by the International
      Conference of Building Officials
      (ICBO)
    5360 Workman Mill Rd.
    Whittier, CA 90601-2298
    310-699-0541; (800) 284-4406

Uniform Plumbing
  Code (UPC)
    published by the International
      Association of Plumbing and
      Mechanical Officials
    20001 Walnut Drive South
    Walnut, CA 91789-2824
    (909) 595-8449.

Web sites

  www.arcat.com
  www.bathweb.com
  www.build.com
  www.ebuild.com (Environmental
    Building News)
  www.faucet.com (Faucet Outlet)
  www.hhinst.com (The Healthy
    House Institute)
  www.ipr.com (Interpro)
  www.theplumber.com

INDEX

BOOK PUBLISHER: Jim Childs

ACQUISITIONS EDITOR: Julie Trelstad

ASSISTANT EDITOR: Karen Liljedahl

EDITOR: Jennifer Renjilian

LAYOUT ARTISTS: Tom Lawton, Rosalie Vaccaro

PHOTOGRAPHER, EXCEPT WHERE NOTED: Carolyn Bates

ILLUSTRATOR: Robert La Pointe

INDEXER: Harriet Hodges

TYPEFACE: Stone Serif

PAPER: 70-lb. Utopia Two Matte

PRINTER: R. R. Donnelley, Willard, Ohio